Lo de Mora

Order this book online at www.trafford.com
or email orders@trafford.com

Most Trafford titles are also available at major online book retailers.

Print information available on the last page.

ISBN: 978-1-4120-6905-2 (sc)

Trafford rev. 10/29/2021

www.trafford.com
North America & international
toll-free: 844-688-6899 (USA & Canada)
fax: 812 355 4082

TABLE OF CONTENTS

PREFACE

History has always intrigued this author. He realized, since very young, that without history, man keeps reinventing the wheel. Man must learn from his experience to build the future.

In search for a true story of Mora, the author has not found a satisfying one. He has read many available stories of it written by many others before him, yet his curiosity to know more about his beautiful valley, he has done many interviews with citizens who have lived during his lifetime.

The opinions or "FACTS" listed in these reports are those of the many persons who have contributed the information. The author has added his own experiences as well. He is aware that, his opinion not always matches the opinion of his peers since everyone is different and sees things in a different light. The author's intention of these reports is more to record all the information he has gathered and pass it on to whoever is interested and hopefully will add from where he left off.

He tried to mention as many names of the citizens so that if there are any relatives, friends or whatever, they may recognize them. Some may not like what is said about the person they knew.

Truth many times hurts. He, fully aware of this fact, tries to write it as it is. He expresses his sympathy for those who construe his work as an insult to their antecedents, for this is not the intention that these reports were written.

For over forty years, this author has been getting information from whatever source(s) available. Most of the information has been from people who claimed to know the facts. To collate it has been the hardest chore.

The author's desire is for the reader to enjoy his works and to imagine what his predecessors went through, what they experienced, lived, loved and died for.

The information gathered here is from different office records yet most was orally transmitted. The author fortified these facts by getting a second and in many cases, a third opinion. Instead of a bibliography he acknowledged the many persons who were kind enough to affirm or deny in few cases, the facts or information presented to them. In some cases, the information was passed from great grandparents to grandparents and on down to the present generation.

The reader will notice that the author has written these reports in a very unorthodox way. His intention is to pass his knowledge of this valley to our posterity. There may be much redundancy. Yet he feels that repetition is necessary to put the points across. You will notice the author includes as many names of persons who crossed his path. The reason is to document those people who were in existence at the time and who contributed to it

1

DEDICATION AND ACKNOWLEDGMENT

These book is dedicated to my beloved family, Benjamin, my father, Rosaura, my mother, Genevieve, my wife, my children: Grace, Judy, Richard, Jeanie, Paul, John, Carmela and Brian, and my four grandchildren, Paul Jr., Allegra, Angelica and Elisa and my great granddaughter Aaliyah.

I would like to thank and forever be grateful to the many who have made these reports possible.

To my Dad, Ben, who kept a daily Diary and was my inspiration to attend college, to my mom, who told me stories and was the one who instilled the love of reading in me. To my wife for always supporting me in my ambition and her patience in putting up with my arrogance. To my children for their understanding and patience for the time I robbed from them instead of sharing those moments I should have spent with them when they were growing up. To my friend and fellow worker, Levi Madrid and his wife Laura. To the John Hanosh family, the Frank L. Trambley as well as the Pete Trambley family, to my cousins and very close friends, Willie Lucero and his wife, Stella, and Zack Montoya and his Wife Eloisa, to the priests from Father Juan B. Perez on to the present priest, Father Tri, to all the sisters Of Loretto who were my teachers during High School specially Sister Frances Alois, as well as all my grade school teachers especially Ophelia Florence and Mrs. Peter Baca, to Mr. and Mrs. Amadeo J. Padilla, Tony and Mary Padilla, Pedrito and wife Maximianita Trujillo, Benino Casados, Agapito Montoya, Steve and Martina Sanchez, Phillip N. and Emma Sanchez, Luis and Susie Martinez, Matias A. Martinez and his wife, Tillie, Andres Quintana, Jose (Police) Garcia, Alfredo Roybal and wife, Novela, Frank Lucero, Juan and Isabelita Herrera, Antonio Herrera, Feleciano Herrera, O.B. and Eloyda Gonzales, Dona Tonita (Chana) Romero, Maximiliano Lucero, Arturo J. and Sofia Romero, Arturo and Dolores Medina, Martin Medina his wife and family, Anastacio Trujillo, Rafael Trujillo, Decederio Gallegos, Frank Martinez Sr. Fidel Valdez Sr. Onofre Quintana, Don Quintana, Pablo Quintana, Leandro Muniz, Juan and Eloisa Maes, Floyd Maes, Arturo Maes Sr., Mr.& Mrs. Elfido Sandoval, Manuel (Mil-dollars) Martinez, Manuel Padilla Sr. Amadeo Aragon, Joe A. Martinez, Agnes V. Martinez, Richard Branch, Melaquias (Mimi) Chavez, Leo and Mela Rimbert, Gilbert and Magdalena Ortega, Bobby Ortega, Fermin and Mary Pacheco, Matias Zamora Sr. and Matias Zamora Jr. Isaac and Juanita Castillo, Vidal Castillo, Casimiro Paiz, Leonore Manchego, Nick A. Martinez, Horacio T. and Celia Martinez, Candelario Lucero, Ricardo Pino, Arturo Pino, Ulick Strong, Florentino Sanchez, Mike Montoya, Dona Genoveva Casados, Juan Casados, Tomas (Tio) Casados, Jacob, Leo and David Madrid, Luis Zamora, Stevan Zamora, Aurora and Bill Ledoux, Erminia and Lawrence Rudolph, Viola and Benjie Bustos Sr., Barbara and Frank McNeff, Adelina and Dino Fuggiti, Lila and Margarito Maes, Juan Mora, Victorino Mora, Alejandro Mora, Arturo Mora, Juan B. and Elena Olguin, Dona Erlinda Gutierrez, Mr. and Mrs., Frank Gauna, Bill and Bell Gauna, Chano, and Louie Gauna, Max E. Martinez, Max Martinez Jr., George (Canello) Maes, Facundo and Juanita Martinez, Juan Bernal, Flavio P. Vigil, Napoleon Sanchez, Feliberto Sanchez, Sam Romo, Patsy Sanchez, Max Valdez, Albert N. Valdez, Eligio Lujan, Eliza Quintanilla, Simon Maes, Juliette Sanchez Van Sicklen, Phillip C.U. and Vangie Sanchez, Jose F.(Pancho Ganchete, el Pelon) Martinez, Mr.& Mrs. Reme

Casados, J.V. Casados, Isidoro Campos, Benjamin Vigil, Maria Tafoya, Bernie Arellano, Arthur R. Romero, Mr. & Mrs Harold Dineen, Glen Hunt, Paul and Consuelo Montano, Steve and Stella Archuleta, Charles Padilla who created the cover for this book. Charles' secretary, Debra, Eddie and Vangie Herrera, Ben and Marcelina Bustos, Mrs. Jack McQuitty and the many of those I have failed to mention.

All of them contributed and/or verified much of the information written here. The only regret I have is that I could not published these reports during the life time of many persons mentioned here.

I need to acknowledge The New Mexico Highlands University for being instrumental in expanding my knowledge, which has made it possible to do this kind of work. Specially, I would like to recognize Dr. Lynn Perrigo whom I have admired as a historian. I would like to recognize Dr. Minor Major and Dr. Welch all from Highlands University.

Many of the stories and facts, I have written pertain to the people living in the valley at the time these works took place. Many of the facts are still true today such as the characteristics or behavior of the people today.

The Authors family
Front row from left to right Erminia Rudolph, Benjamin Alcon De Buck Rosaura, and
Aurora LeDoux
Back row from left to right Lila Maes, Barbara McNeff, M.B. , Viola Bustos, Adeline Fuggitti.

MORA BEFORE MANKIND CAME

Then God said "Let the waters below the heavens be gathered into one place and let the dry land appear" and so it was. 1:9 Genesis

Mora was a lake millions of years ago. The proof is the sediment that exists in this valley.

It was a lake extending from La Cordillera to la Presa and maybe down to La Cueva. What is known through hear say, studies and conjecturing is that by the time the first humans passed through this valley, it was more of a swamp. A river flowed through the swamp. By the time Mora became populated, it had dried to the point where many springs existed. Some still exist.

This valley was and is surrounded by mountains. The Sangre de Cristo Mountains form a complicated wall which made it difficult for the first people to enter through it. The entrances are few and were a big challenge to all who came here first. The West break lies at a steep and arduous pass where three small tributaries canyons of the eastward flowing river come near the Tres Ritos Canyon.

The lake was a big one when it covered a length of more than 3 miles more or less from the present site of Mora where two mountains meet and must have been the lowest point for water to flow on down.

As the lake filled up and Mother Nature did her thing, the water ate itself a gateway to drain the vast lake. The lake became a meadow where wild life was abundant and this is about the time the first humans visited it. How long it took for this to happen is not known.

There was another natural dam five miles or so from la Presa. This is situated where La Cueva now is.

This is the most logical pass from the East into the valley.

By the time history was first documented in this area, the valley contained a river which was named the Mora River. It was and is still fed by two main tributaries, namely, the Agua Negra River which has its beginning at Chacon and the other coming from El Rio de la Casa, Southwest of Mora. These two tributaries meet at Cleveland, known as San Antonio when the first Spanish settlers settled here. Cleveland is a small hamlet three miles west of Mora.

The Mora River was a sinuous one which had many sharp bends and also many beaver dams. The waters were pure and crystal clear. The route of the river has changed and is not so snake like as it was then.

The vegetation was plentiful and if there ever were any dinosaurs, no one knows for up to this time no remains have been found. If any anthropologists have studied this site, nothing has been shared. Some geologists have checked the formation of the valley and have found fossils of small animals.

In the early 1800 s, no trees existed in the mountains surrounding the valley. As late as the 1920 s, only a few pine trees existed on the mountains North of Mora and then only at the foot of those mountains.

The formation of the valley is known because many wells have been dug. There is a formation of a dark clay followed by a gravel level, sand level and a rock formation showing that rolling stones settled in the valley long before it was covered with dirt and sludge.

Mora was a heaven for wild life since berries and grass were in abundance, not to mention fresh water.

Mora, New Mexico

This top picture is the earliest picture available
It shows the valley as it looked when the first white men visited the valley around 1880
The bottom picture shows the valley from a picture taken in 1990

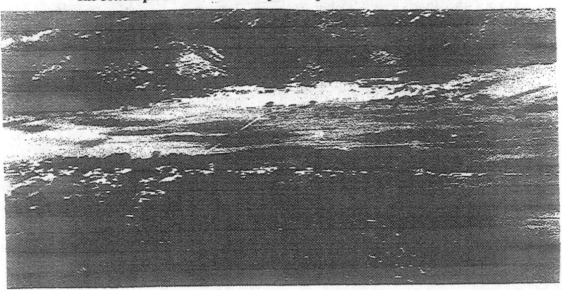

THE FIRST HUMANS IN THE VALLEY

The first humans to have used the valley as a hunting, fishing or gathering grounds were the Indians.

Who these Indians were, remains an unsolved problem. If any Indians documented their occupation of this fertile valley, documents are not to be found. If there are any in existence they may be in some other forms that have not been found or if they have been found, they have not been interpreted and documented.

Indians who used this valley as was documented by the white persons much later were the Picuris, Comanches, Utes, Apaches, and Jicarillas among others.

Mulberries and other kinds of berries grew in abundance so it is known that some tribes gathered berries as well as roots and other edibles.

The fertile land produced grass so many types of wildlife such as deer, elk, bear, beaver, musk rats and others thrived in the valley. Indians came to fish, hunt and to gather berries. No signs of Indian built homes are in evidence. It is believed that most of the tribes who passed through the valley were nomads. They camped here until they got tired or the animals were scared off and so they moved on. There was no shortage of water so they stayed here for a long time.

Pueblo Indians lived in their land and did not move on. The Picuris were this type of people so they visited this valley often. The Indians had no mode of transportation except their own two feet. They had no written documents except carvings on rocks and in some caves. There were no written documents that could prove they owned the land. Wire was not invented so there were no fences. Any part of the valley could be used at their discretion. The many springs and rivers could be used as their bathtubs. The trees provided Protection from wild animals and the elements of time. To them, living in such a free and unpolluted environment was the life. This did not mean that they had it easy and were free from any suffering. There were other tribes, wild animals and the torments of the weather that were unfriendly to them.

Some caves exist to this day north of the valley across of where the American Legion Rodeo Grounds are situated. North west from these caves is a valley known as the Comanche. In the 1940's and early 1950's, some children visited those caves and played there. They found arrowheads and shards of pottery and even some pottery.

Among the boys who played and knew these places well are Arcenio and Max Gutierrez and Jerry Gonzales, as related to this author by them.

How long the Indians inhabited those caves is a mystery as of yet.

Indians going back to their Pueblo

No documents to prove who were the very first Europeans to visit the valley have been found. There are many claims as to who did come first. Probably, the first Europeans who passed through this valley were trappers.

The Spaniards were the first to document their visits and so it is that we start what we believe is the history as seen and written.

How Mora got its name is not an easy problem to solve. One story goes that Mora means mulberry and in Mexico the term is applied to the shrub or tree of capulincillo variety. They also apply the word to mean any wild cherry or berry. Berries were in abundance in the valley and surrounding mountains. Was Mora named after the berry that abounded in the vicinity?

Another theory is that it might have been named Mora after some outstanding leader by the surname of Mora for there were and are Spaniards known by that surname. No one by that name is recorded in the original Mora Land Grant, yet it is possible that someone passed by without him being recognized. There were individuals such as Mora Pineda and Garcia de la Mora who came to New Mexico after the re conquest of 1692. People of this name were living on the frontier of Mora County at the end of the 18th century.

Another theory is that the name itself means procrastinate.
Mora, being such beautiful, calm peaceful valley (aside of some human elements) that in summer, a traveler feels like delaying the trip one more day.

Another theory is that in 1822, a fellow by the name of Mora came to survey the place and so Mora was named for him.

Still, another theory and probably the most popular is that a
Frenchman, identified by some persons as Ceran St. Vrain, found a dead man on the banks of the river and called it the "L'Eau de mort" which means the water of the dead. Records show it as Lo de Mora and some people say it is a contraction of Spanish El Ojo de Mora which means the (water) spring of Mora.

Which version or theory is the true one is not known for sure because records were destroyed when the burning of Mora took place in 1847. Maybe there were never any records in this subject.

Dear reader, I leave it up to you to believe which theory you feel more comfortable or believe which makes more sense to you. All the mentioned theories are pertinent.

Some incidents that occurred in the valley in the very early days of this valley that some of the old folks have told the author are: In 1696, Don Diego De Vargas followed a Picuris band into the valley as they fled to the plains after an unsuccessful rebellion against Spanish authority.

Other interesting incidents are included here.

In 1715, Don Juan Paez Hurtado launched a campaign against the Apaches traveling down the Mora Valley.

In 1778, Don Bernardo de Miera y Pacheco mapped the Mora Valley in his "Plano Geografico de los Discubremientos".

By 1818, Settlers were requesting a priest.

In 1820, Fray Juan Bruno Gonzales of Picuris made a confessional tour to San Antonio de lo de Mora where all settlers were Catholic. These people petitioned him to send a secular priest to them. Seventy five signed petition to the vicario in Santa Fe. There were 300 residents in the valley.

On December 26, 1821, Merijilda Vigil transferred her title to land in exchange for land Buenaventura Duran had in Taos. Who granted that title is unknown.

Top picture is the valley view from Southeast of town. Both Pictures taken 1993. Bottom picture is the West side of town showing the La Jicarita Mountains snow covered to the right of the Picture.

1492 Jews were expelled from Spain.

16th century the Black Legend

1692 The re conquest of New Mexico

1715 Don Diego De Vargas followed a Picuris band into the Mora Valley as they fled to the plains after an unsuccessful rebellion against Spanish authority.

1754 Governor Velez Cachupin mentioned a raid entering the Rio Grande Valley and passing through Mora Valley.

1778 Don Bernardo de Miera y Pacheco noted the valley "Rio de Mora" and mapped Mora Valley in his Plano Geografico de los Discubrimientos"

1818 Settlers requested a priest.

1820 Fray Juan Bruno Gonzales of Picuris made a tour to San
Antonio de lo de Mora where all were Christians who petitioned him to send them secular or regular priest.

1821 Opening of Santa Fe Trail

1835 The Mora Land Grant

1836 George H. Buck was born in Maine (this author's great-grandad)

1839 Father Jean Baptiste Lamy came to U.S. from France.

1843 Col. Charles Warfield declared Mora land for Texas

1845 There were 489 persons in 115 households in Lo de Mora

1846 Col. Stephen W. Kearney left from Kansas. August 15. He camped at Las Vegas. August 18. He took New Mexico Territory without firing a shot. The American flag was raised.

1847 Mora revolt. The town was destroyed by U.S. troops from Las Vegas.

1850 New Mexico was organized as a territory. A contract to supply flour to several forts was awarded to Ceran St.Vrain. 1851 Protestant denomination was being introduced to the territory.
Jean Baptiste Lamy was assigned as priest in the Southwest He was the first U.S. priest in New Mexico.
Fort Union was established.

1852 Loretto Sisters started academy in Santa Fe
Jean Baptiste Lamy was appointed Bishop of Santa Fe.

1854 William Pelkan was appointed by congress as a surveyor general for New Mexico Territory.

1856 Small Pox epidemic claimed over 100 victims. Apaches made raid and took women. livestock and children to sell in slavery

1858 Apaches staged another raid similar to the one of 1856.

1859 Territorial legislature divided Taos into two counties—Taos and Mora.

1860 There were 236 household heads in Mora.
Joseph Rouelle from Illinois built a hotel. later known as the Walton Hotel still later. The Butler Hotel as it was known in the 1940's)
John Bickell, an Englishman built a saloon.

Dr. Kane, an Army surgeon, said to have been the first to perform the first major surgical operation in the territory.

There were 5,566 people in the county when it became a county.

The Christian Brothers founded the Christian Brothers School.

Two story adobe building was built as the first courthouse.

Second floor was used as courthouse. Lower floor was the jail.

1861 St. Gertrudis Church was fixed with board and wood shingle pitched roof and belfry.

1862 Pepe's hall was where Trambley's residence and store now stand.

Sisters of Loretto arrived at Mora.

Manuel Alcon de Buck was born 5/18 (Author's grandfather)

1864 Post Office was established.

1865 Sisters of Loretto opened up St. Mary's College for girls in Mora.

1867 The population was 800. It included Spanish, Mexican, Irish German, Syrian and French.

Brother Germanus was transferred to St. Michaels in Santa Fe.

1869 Colfax County was carved out of Mora County.

1870 Christian Brothers school had 47 boarding boys and 3 teachers

There were 8,056 people in the county.

1871 Christian Brothers School became a boarding school for boys.

1875 Jean Lamy was appointed Archbishop of the New Mexico Territory.

1880 People started to use barb wire to fence their property.

1881 Presbyterian Church opened its Mission School in Mora.

There were 9,751 people in Mora County.

1884 Mail came in three times a week. The population was 700.

Boys school closed and the Sisters of Loretto became coed.

1886 The surrender of Geronimo.

The Apaches and other tribes after this, gave no more trouble.

Benjamin Alcon de Buck son of Manuel and Seferina Gonzales and father of this author was born January 17.

1888 Ideas de Mora was published December 16. The convent burned down for the first time.

Rosaura Montoya mother of this author was born to Francisco Montoya and Jesusita Apodaca Montoya on October 5.

1889 Bids for new court house were let out. $45,370 was the bid.

1890 November 13. The County Commission accepted the new building. It was built by Italian contractors Damacio and Pelinni.

Mora County ranked first in money spent for land, fences and building Improvements. There were 10,618 people in the county.

1891 Charles U. Strong was County clerk.

1891 Mosquito, a local news paper was published.

Governor Bradford Prince urged legislature of New Mexico to pass a law for public school system in the territory. Territorial Legislature created a board of education and required the Governor to appoint a Superintendent of Public Instruction. First Superintendent of Public Instruction was Amado Chavez.

1893 John Dougherty was shot to death by La gavia de Silva.

1895 Presbyterian School closed. It was moved to Albuquerque which became Menaul.

1900 There were 10,304 people in Mora County.

1903 Territorial business directory lists 5 general merchandise stores in Mora although
dependent in larger mercantile warehouses in Las Vegas for supplies and credit.
Sisters' convent was rebuilt and available as a residence.

1904 The great flood at Mora.

1906 Carson Forest became Carson National Forest.
George Henry Buck, great grandfather of this author, died.

1907 El Eco Del Norte founded by Enrique Sosa Sr. It was published every Friday at Mora.
The county asked for money to build road.
County Commission attorney asked Governor Curry for territorial money to build
a permanent road to Mora.

1910 Only 60,000 acres of the original Mora Grant held by settlers with legal titles were
privately owned.
El Mensajero published and was owned by Benedicto Sandoval. Diego Chacon was
editor. It lasted until 1925.
There were 26 counties in New Mexico

1912 New Mexico became the 47th State in the Union.
Sisters of Loretto celebrated their 50th anniversary.
July- Jack Johnson came to Mora. He was heavy weight champion and was to
defend his title at Las Vegas, New Mexico against Jim Flynn from Colorado.
Mora had a village band.
Superintendent of Mora County Schools, Manuel Madrid invited Governor McDonald
to attend the Sisters 50th anniversary.

1913 A contract was given to J.J. Fuss to construct and install an electric light and water
works that would serve the most densely settled part of the county extending 3
miles on either side of Mora.
Benjamin Alcon married Rosaura Montoya (Author's parents)

1914 County Commission contracted with local business men to
install 6 miles of telephone lines in and around the village.

1917 First World War declared.

1918 First World War ended.

1919 April 19, The Mora Trust and Savings Bank of New Mexico was worth $68,238.37 J.
Andrew Myers, clerk.

1920 El Eco Del Norte was sold to Felipe Chacon.

1921 Harding County was carved out of Mora and Union Counties.

1922 The two story public school building was built near the Catholic Church.

1926 This author was born.

1928 Phillip N. Sanchez visited Farwell, Texas and got Dr. J.J. Johnson to come to Mora.

1930 El Sol de Mora was published by Anastacio Trujillo.

1932 Franklin D. Roosevelt elected president of the United States.
Welfare and the ruination of the working person begins.

1933 September, Monday 25 Governor Arthur Salegeman died at Albuquerque. He was
      buried September 28.
      Thursday April 6, Sister Doloritas was buried.
1934 August 17 Tito Melendez's boiler exploded. Five or six were hurt and Thomas
      Williams was killed. The boiler ran his saw mill.
      The brick jail house was razed.
      Petition to build new court house was made February 7.
      Election for court house was held September 7, 787 yes votes 285 no votes.
      Estevan H. Biembaum died.
      There were many swamps. Much of the land was planted with corn, wheat, barley,
      peas, and oats.
1935 Saturday and Sunday October 19 and 20 El Centenario
      celebration took place. Mass was celebrated in front of the court house.
1936 January 6, Kahn Hotel's roof burned down.
      May 17, Trambleys Hall, Garage and Leandro Bustos home
      burned down during a church sponsored activity. ($50,000 loss)
      High School graduation held May 19. Among graduates were Viola Alcon and
      Stevan Zamora. Dance held at Sosa's Hall and another at the old courthouse.
1937 County Commission saw a need to enlarge and improve facilities. A bond issue for
      $25,000 passed.
1938 The W.P.A. built a new school house by the old two story building at El Rancito. It
      was Pueblo style.
      Dr. J. J. Johnson moved to Las Vegas. His wife died at this time.
      February 7- petitions in special meeting to build new court
      house.
1939 Pueblo Revival style court house was built by W.P.A.
1940 Coronado's Cuarto Centennial was celebrated.
      Population was 1129.
1941 World War II U.S.A joined war when Japanese bombed Pearl Harbor.
1942 Sister Convent burned down the second time.
1943 Dr. Husted was doctor in Mora.
1945 Second World War came to an end after bombing Japan with two atomic bombs.
      (Hiroshima and Nagasaki)
1946 July Julia K. Strong died.
      Sunday October 6, convent building burned down for the third time.
      The St. Gertrudis Credit Union was formed.
      R.E.A. Electrical Cooperative took over the electric franchise from Karavas.
      The Catholic Veterans of America was to be organized.
1947 Dr. Crane was the town's doctor.
      May 20, Los Socios de La Union Catolica started to rebuild the convent.
1948 The Mora Public School which was built by the W.P.A burned down
      The American Legion organized. (Post #114)
1949 Present school was built.
1951 Agua Negra telephone was bought by Levi Madrid. It had hand crank telephones.

1958 The School system tried for first time to become an Independent district under the leadership of Amadeo Aragon, the then County School Superintendent but it failed.

1960 The Hippie movement promiscuity and return to nature.
      The old court house burned down.

1961 The Mora County Schools became the Mora Independent Schools on January 1. under the newly elected County Superintendent Manuel B. Alcon. Board members of first Independent Schools were Frank L. Trambley, Julia Espinoza, Marcelino Torres, Feleciano Herrera, and Miquelita Pacheco.

1963 Dr. Marion Morse from Mora Valley Clinic climbed a 9,000 feet peak on horseback to treat survivors of A.F.B. wreckage.

1968 The State Road # 3 going through town was paved and raised 3 feet.   State Road was changed to State Road # 518.
      The St. Gertrudes Church burned down (July).

1970 Yuppie Movement. Hippies join the working class.

1971 Benjamin Alcon de Buck died December 25.

1978 Town Meeting was held at Court house. The purpose was to better the community and the environment.

1980 Gays start to come out of the closet. A new illness comes into being (AIDS) Promiscuity at its peak. Abortion becomes a problem.

1981 The Mora County Star was published at Mora by L. Starer. It did not last long.

1984 Rosaura M. Alcon died February 24.

1988 Fish Hatchery was proposed.
      Mora in a state of bankruptcy.

1990 Gays and Lesbians fight for equal rights. Little Paul Pacheco Jr. died May 26.

1991 Opposition to fish hatchery.
      Fish Hatchery was scrubbed. A research center was proposed.
      Jeanie Alcon married John P. Abeyta.

1992 Levi Madrid died March 13, at the age of 96 years 5 months and 7 days.
      Angelica Marie Abeyta was born June 10.

1993 Gays and Lesbians march in front of the White House to fight for their equal rights. President Clinton learns that to promise is a different animal from keeping promises. The first 100 day tenure in office proves a hardship to him and he changes his mind in many things.
      O.B. Gonzales died March 29.
      Mora County Commission names a Mora Incorporating committee. Among those named three accepted, namely, Manuel B. Alcon, William Romero and Richard Olivas.
      Petitions were gathered—182 of them.
      Election is set for January 4, 1994.

1994 Election for incorporating Mora is defeated 49 for to 157 against. Opposed to incorporating were Decky Trambley, William Gandert, Jacobo Pacheco, Phillip C.U. Sanchez, Flosha Sanchez, Andres Pacheco, Moise Medina, Ernest E. Martinez, Damian Pacheco, Barney Martinez, Justin Valdez.

1995 Robert Richard Alcon married Carmela Romo August 12.

1995 Robert Richard Alcon married Carmela Romo August 12.
1996 Elisa Janelle Abeyta was born July 12.

       The above information was gathered from too many sources and from the author's and others point of view. To document each item as its source would take too much time and space and the idea of this works is to give information as to the author's knowledge.

The author feels his works is not an act of faith so whatever you want to believe or if you do not, feel free to look up your own sources as he has done.

Top picture Mora Valley in 1847-Battle of Mora
Bottom picture Mora Valley around 1927

MORA COUNTY POPULATION
1820-2000

1820 300 residents and all of them of Spanish decent.

1821 First pack animals came down the Santa Fe trail.

1835 Grantees were from the Rio Grande Village of Alcalde, Velarde and Embudo. 67 were from the western slop, villages of Santa Barbara, Chamisal and Trampas.
The Mora Grant was given to 76 settlers.

1843 An estaimated 200 wagons made the crossing some used it as a cut off to go to Taos.
Texas sent a contingent of soldiers under Col. Charles A. Garfield to take additional land from Mexico. A pitch battle in Mora took place.

1845 489 persons in 115 household resided in the valley.

1847 U.S army occupied New Mexico.

1856 smallpox took over a hundred lives.

1860 5,566 included the hamlets of Carmen, Ledoux, Chacon and Guadalupita.
This year, Mora County was carved out of Taos County.

1870 8,056 people resided in the county.

1880 9,751 people resided in the county.

1890 10,618 was the population of the county.

1900 10,304 was the population of the county.

1910 12,611 was the population of the county.

1920 13,915 was the population of the county.

1930 10,322 was the population of the county.

1940 10,981 was the population of the county. Up to this time, farming and ranching were the main occupations. The flour mills were doing much business.

1950 8,720 population had diminished. Many went into the armed services, while many went to work in the factories in California and other points in the western coast.

1960 6,028 was the population in the county.

1970 4,673 was the population in the county. Some Hippies included.

1980 4,205 was the population. Some Hippies and yippies included.

1990 4,206 was the population.

2000 4,861 was the population in 1999 as per Secretary Of State.

THE EL ALTO DEL TALCO VILLAGE

El Alto del Talco was probably founded before or at the time El Lo de Mora was settled. This would be before the 1835 date when Mora's History, according to the old folks remembered or were told, was settled.

El Alto is situated by the mountain where the first road was made, coming from Las Vegas. (South of the village of Mora)

That road came through the small village and led into the village of St. Gertrudes, now known as Mora.

The hamlet was in the form of a fortress with buildings all around and the chapel in the middle. This was the custom since it was the only way to protect themselves and their livestock from marauding Indians. (Chapel was more of a prayer house or an honorario).

Among the first families who settled at El Alto were the Muniz, Medina and Maes families. Representatives of these three families built an honorario or place to worship God before the St. Gertrudes parish was established. This honorario was to become the chapel of Santiago which is still that- The Santiago Chapel.

At the time, it was a meeting place to praise God since none of them were ordained priests. A morada was also established. After some rebuilding and remodeling, there stands the morada where the penitentes would have their Holy Week services and people would take them food.

They had Calvarios (Big Crosses) at a higher elevation than the morada. This morada stood at the foot of the mountains.

The chapel which today exists, has been rebuilt at least once. Records of the first one do not exist or if they do, this author does not have that information.

What we do know is that in 1942, the chapel was in dire need of fixing. Don Facundo Valdez and Don Juan Maes were the mayordomos and they asked the people around the community for help. By 1946, the church was finished. This is the present building. According to those who helped in the rebuilding, it used to face the East. Now, it faces the North.

Today, services are held at the chapel once a year. That is, on the 25th of July which is the day of Santiago (ST. James) who is the patron of the workers (laborers). Once in a while the chapel is opened for a velorio or any other activities the members see fit to have.

The last velorio this author remembers attending in this site was when Dona Mercedes died. Before that they had velorios for the saints. This custom died when Dona Mercedes left this green earth.

The most active people in this chapel are the Valdez and Maes family and only one Medina descendant remains. There are some Muniz, among them are Samuel and Dorothy. Some have served as mayordomos. Valdez family are mostly the Facundo's and Fidel's progeny.

The Medina family has moved out of the county. They still own land surrounding the chapel.

Of the Maes family still active is Jenny Maes.

Others who have served as Mayordomos are Genevieve H. and Manuel B. Alcon, Carolina Olivas, Lucas and Marcella Valdez Mr.& Mrs. Facundo Valdez Jr., Sam Muniz, his sisters, Facundo Valdez, his wife, Andy Valdez and wife and others.

After the second World War, a very active person named Lucas Valdez has, faithfully rung the procession bell, with out missing a year.

The El Alto Del Talco Chapel picture taken 1993.Top picture is view from West side. Bottom picture is the chapel from the North side. 1990

THE MORA LAND GRANT

Governor Albino Perez granted 827,621 acres of land known as the Mora Land Grant or la Merced de Mora on September 28, 1835.

Judge Manuel Sanchez of the District Court of San Jose de las Trampas conveyed the grant on October 20, 1835 with the boundaries of said grant to be - East bounded by the Aguajo de la Llegua. West by the Estillero, North by Rio de Ocate and South by the mouth of the Sapello.

The Mora Grant is numbered thirty-two on the list of grants reported to the Secretary of the Interior by the Surveyor General of New Mexico, and through him to Congress.

The order of the Governor making the grant is not on file in the office of the Surveyor General of New Mexico, where it should be found, and as will appear from the report of Surveyor General Pelham, hereinafter, was probably burned in the town of Mora when that town was destroyed by the United State troops in 1847. The earliest paper relating to the grant is a report of Manuel Antonio Sanchez, constitutional justice, dated October 20, 1835, reciting the juridical possession of the grant given to him, which he says was in compliance with the Superior decree of Don Albino Perez, political chief of the Territory, dated September 28, 1835.

Congress confirmed the grant on June 21,1860. On March 3, 1879, Congress approved "An Act to Confirm Certain Private Land Claims in the Territory of New Mexico,". The land was given and granted to the following settlers:

Jose Tapia, Carmen Arce, Juan Lorenzo Aliso, Juan Antonio Garcia, Carlos Rinto, Mateo Ringinel, Manuel Suhazo, Geronimo Martin, Francisco Sandobal, Francisco Lore, Francisco Conen, Jose Mestas, Ramon Archuleta, Antonio Aba Trujillo, Juan de Jesus Cruz, Maria Dolores Romero, Faustin Mestas, Maria Dolores Sanchez, Jose Miguel Pacheco, Yldefonso Pacheco, Manuel Sanches, Juan Trujillo, Felipe Carbajal, Jose Maria Garcia, Miguel Garcia, Gabriel Lujan, Manuel Arguello, Ygnacio Gonzales, Jose Guadalupe Ortega, Felipe Arguello, Manuel Gregorio Martin, Juan Cristobal Trujillo, Tomas Encarnacion Garcia, Carlos Salazar, Francisco Arguello, Francisco Sena, Jose Ygnacio Madrid, Miguel Paez, Manuel Paez, Miguel Mascarenas, Cecilio Montano, Cruz Medina, Bernardo Martin, Miguel Arguello, Ramon Amado, Pedro Aragon, Esteban Valdez, Manuel Sanches, Juan Ignacio Sanches, Francisco Sarracino, Albino Chacon, Damacio Chacon, Teodocio Quintana, Jose Garcia, Rafael Paez, Nepomoceno Gurule, Jose Vigil, Nestor Armijo, Andres Ornelas, Mateo Montoya, Juan de la Cruz Trujillo, Juan de Jesus Lujan, Francisco Trujillo, Andres Trujillo, Juan Andres Archuleta, Ramon Abreu, Jesus Maria Alarid, Vicente Sanchez, Mateo Sandobal, Juan Lopez, Pedro Chacon, Miguel Antonio Mascarenas, Antonio Arguello, Jose Silva, Juan Jose Vigil and Miguel Olguin.

Exempted from this grant were twenty five square Leagues of land of John Scolly and others. Another stipulation was that the United States reserved to itself the building and improvements situated on the Fort Union Military and Timber Reservation as was established in 1820 300 residents and all of them of Spanish decent. In 1821 First pack animals came down the Santa Fe Trail. In1835 Grantees were from the Rio Grande Village of Alcalde. Velarde, And Embudo. 67 were from the western slope villages of Santa Barbara, Chamisal and Tramps at that time.

Another stipulation was that the Confirmation by Congress on June 21, 1860 shall only be construed as quit claims or relinquishments on the part of the United States, and shall not affect the adverse rights of any other person or persons.

Top picture shows the mountains South of Mora.
Bottom picture is the Hermits Peak in the distance!

LIFE IN THE ST. GERTRUDE'S VALLEY

In the early days of American History, their dress was very simple and made out of either fur, hide and later wool and cotton were woven. By the time, these people came to America, they were wearing woven clothing. Some still wore animal skins or furs.

Underwear was not known. No one had thought about this thing and besides, there were no sophisticated restrooms, so going around without underwear was a very convenient thing to do. Women wore big, loose skirts that saved them from many embarrassments for they carried their own private tepee. They would sit down on their haunches any time mother nature called. As for the men, they did not even need to find a fitting tree.

They were very hard workers. They worked from dawn to dusk, the sun being their only light. They would get up as soon as El Lucero (Morning Star) came out. They would get some cold water and wash their face with it. It needs to be remembered that at this time there were no running water, sinks, nor hot water heaters available. They had to do with what was available, such as the river, stream or a crude vase. To conserve water, which was not at premium price, but it was too cold or to far to fetch it, they would wash their face and hands with a cupful of it.

Their meals were what they had harvested for there were no Furrs, Supersaves, Smiths or Albertsons groceries stores. People were self sustaining.

By the time the Americans took New Mexico, After 1848 There were mills to make flour, sugar refineries, and other things that made life more bearable. Some cereals they ate were cornmeal, wheat in different forms, as well as other corn products and garden crops. Candy was unknown with the exception of peloncillo which was a pyramid shaped made of brown sugar. By the 1900 s, kids would make caramelo, sugar heated until it melted. Many burns were suffered by kids who experimented with this candy when they were anxious to taste it and it was still hot. It would stick to the finger and God knows what suffering of this kind of burn is.

The emphasis during these people's life is WORK. The vast majority of the men, women, and children were kept busy at the farm, ranch or wherever they were. Every one carried his or her own load. Welfare or Relief was not known until the early 1930 s so there were no programs to depend on. He who did not work was incompetent for one or more reasons. His or her family would take care of him. One needs to remember that at this time the money as we know it now was very scarce and few families had some. Most of the buying took place as a barter, the exchanging one thing for another.

Up to the 1920 s, the houses had dirt floors, flat roofs, and no glass windows. To the modern generation, this is like it never happened. But to mention a few of the conveniences they had and we do not agree those were conveniences, there were outhouses known as toilets. A hole on the ground which produced water was known as a well and was also used as a cooler for milk, watermelons and other things that needed to be kept cool. The only way water was heated was in a tub or a calenton (A tank built in wood stoves) The Environmental People were not born yet. And if they had tried to interfere with this people, they would have not lasted long.

The inconvenience to bathe a big family on Saturday night was a nightmare to the poor mother who may have had seven or more kids to wash. Many were the mothers who had to use the same water to bathe as many kids as the water could stand. Most of the time, the second child had to be bathe in cold water just as the next in line had to. Cleanliness had a different connotation. A bath once a week was desirable but to some, it was not a rule.

Ice cream came much later as did the candy bars and other goodies.

Because of biases against the Hispanic, and the pay was always less when they went to work as laborers, the girls looked forward to marrying an Anglo and many of them did. They were looking for security for their children and an Anglo name would provide this security. Hispanic women are the most beautiful women and had little trouble in catching an Anglo to marry. Those who were not beautiful by nature knew how to dress and behave beautifully. Many girls had children and gave them Anglo names. Sometimes they divorced their husbands. The children had already earned the Anglo name.

During the 1920 s and even before then, talks about improving the county were many and one thought was building a dam at different places on the sinuous Mora River. Mora had been an agricultural center after the days of the trappers and hunters were over. The dams would serve during dry years. The people who were afraid of the dams breaking and inundating the valleys below were in the minority if not the ones who spoke the loudest and the dams were never built. Too many citizens were biased and if they did not have anything to do with the work even though it was for the benefit of the whole community, they were opposed. This has been the problem for many years and it still exists. Politics has been one of the Mora's prides. This is what has kept Mora from becoming a progressive town. Politicians, since the early 1900 s and even before, have controlled the people by keeping them ignorant and poor.

In the 1930's when welfare came to being, the ones who were active would control the programs and the rules and regulations were the ones they set that would rule the game. One cannot blame one political party or the other because most of the time the barons of both parties worked in cahoots.

During the 1940 s, a proposition to straighten the sinuous Mora River was proposed and part of the river was straightened up to the then Steve Sanchez property. He had the foresight of the little dams made by beavers, fishing holes, and swimming holes for the kids and so he was against the project.

During World War II, many people from the village went to California, other states or to the Armed Forces. They worked at the shipbuilding factories as well as in the airplane factories and other types of work. The housewife position began its downfall and the family as was known before, changed. Divorces became a common thing and later cohabitation took over. Partying and eating at restaurants, cafes and drive inns became a custom. Many of the boys who went to California would visit their old hunting grounds and came to show off their Zoot suits. With their Zoot suits, they brought a different vocabulary and so the vernacular took a change to the better or worse depending on how one would look at it. New inventions and many conveniences came into being and there was no way to go back to the good ole days.

Right after the Second World War, many projects were initiated that have made the Valley a better place to live, as examples, the Mora-San Miguel Electric Cooperative. The La Jicarita Telephone. The city water system and the sewer system. Needless to say that even with opposition the people in favor still went ahead and got these projects going.

After 1946. The G.I.'s returned as did the factory workers. Many moved out or remained where they worked. Agriculture in Mora waned and it was easier to go buy at the store than to grow vegetables. Those who returned, came with new ideas and not only had the humans changed but so did the weather. It used to rain for days at a time and the season was warm. The seasons became colder than usual. There were many crop failures and the blossoms in trees froze. People became more dependent upon the federal government and the stores.

Schools also changed. They became municipals, independent districts and were consolidated. The school became an entertainment center instead of a learning center. Discipline turned to be child abuse in many cases.

The hippy movement became a way of life and many children lost not only their virginity but became drug addicts and lawless. Most of these Hippies were well educated and well off but they were looking for a slower life and were also demonstrating against the establishment. They sought freedoms that they believed they did not have at home. They found out that money was not everything. Their freedom was to do whatever they pleased and promiscuity came to be prevalent.

The year 1970, saw a change from the Hippies to the Yuppies. These people kept some characteristics of the hippies but they believed in work. They opened their Doctor's offices or became professional. Co-habiting instead or marriage was the vogue.

In the 1970 s, a research program sponsored by the New Mexico State University was proposed. There was opposition to the drilling of a 2,000 feet well. The Research center took place but the well was never dug. If it was dug, the community did not know about it.

After the election of 1970, the idea of me first and the county last, took place.

Also, during this time many town meetings were held to better the county and to help the environment. One such meeting took place on February 9, 1978 where 27 participants took part. The following were present: Lazaro(Larry) Garcia, Joseph Maestas, Arturo Martinez, Juan Hernandez, Ivan Roper, George DeHerrera, Lydia Abeyta, Jess M. Garcia, Orlando Arellano, Secundino Aragon, Manuel B. Alcon. Eusebio Arellano, H.K. Pete Beck, Randy G. Martinez, George B. Martinez, Frank Lujan Jr., Johnny Martinez, Samuel G. Martinez, Scott Hartung, Ida L. Martinez, Rosita Romero, Jose T. Barela, Eloisa DeHerrera, Andres D. Maes, Jack Roper Sr. Veronica Medina, and Marion Emerson.

The issues discussed were: Water rights, -wells gone dry, -new industry,- other counties take away water, -N.M.S.U Research center, -Environmental controls, -Need of bilingual doctor and dentist, -Funeral Home for the community, -More concern for human needs, -less politics,-resolve the issue of more or less involvement in religion, and Priest understanding local needs.

Talk about incorporating the village has been brought out many times but as of yet nothing has happened to bring this about.

Around this time, the water and sewer associations were merged.

During this time, Suing, workmen's compensation, drugs, alcohol, sex, cohabiting and food stamps became the vogue. Promiscuity was prevalent.

In the 1980 s, Mora was in the verge of going bankrupt and talk of merging the county with neighboring counties were discussed. The County commissioners, Lillian Sanchez, Abelino Espinoza and Matt Maestas won the election and they straightened things out a bit.

The Gay movement took momentum and came out of the closet. Up to now, they had been hiding and were ashamed to admit that they ailed this unnatural phenomena.

During the 1980 s, Jacob Alcon, a former citizen of the county and a resident of Albuquerque was named by the governor to the Wild Life Commission and he bought the idea of a fish hatchery being ideal for the county. The state Representative, Bill Richardson and Senator Dominici took the issue to Congress and obtained a substantial amount of money to build it, but again the biases showed their ugly head and no fish hatchery was built. Instead a research office was proposed. Many are the ones who criticize and no matter who does things, some one will be against them.

By the 1990 s, Murders, rapers and other criminals, as well as the Gay movement had taken over. Their rights were in the forefront with the help of criminal lawyers and judges, and these became the justice of the country. Juries were afraid or for other reasons found them not guilty. The games played by courts and the lawyers were that the witness answer questions with a yes or no and no explanation was permitted and the way the criminal was caught was the way justice was handed out no matter if the criminal was caught red-handed. If he was found guilty, he was taken to prison and he had more rights as to the comforts of home. Besides, if he was found guilty, he was given two life times or more plus a few more years, as their sentence. How a person got more than one life is a thing, a regular person does not comprehend.

Criminal rights had preference over their victims. They had the right, at least that is the opinion of many people, to kill, rape, maim or whatever and could become violent because they were insane at the time. No matter what the penalty was, they could be paroled and many were. Many of them were freed and returned to commit more crimes. Prisons became overcrowded and the judges had the excuse that there were no more places to commit these criminals so they were set free. Judges had to be elected and so had to find votes. The prestige of the office meant more to them than justice so they would cater to the criminal whom they feared and about this time, it seemed that there were more bad guys than good.

Justice has many faces. "Justice for who?" is the problem. Semantics has taken many changes. Do we remember when square meant a straight honest person. Gay meant a happy person, bad meant evil.

Other changes such as the wagon pulling the horse, running into the house to use the rest room, not everything that goes up comes down, women are equal as men, and many other reversals have been made.

In 1994, for the third time a group of people tried to incorporate the valley. The County Commissioners were Henry Sanchez, Jacob Regensberg, and Joseph Pacheco. They appointed a committee of a few members to carry the incorporation forward. Of all the appointees, only three had the guts to volunteer. Richard Olivas, William Romero and Manuel B. Alcon took over. They failed to approach the politicians of the two parties and so because they had no say so they were against the proposition. These men followed the rules to incorporate and got over 180 petitions signed. With the exception of two who signed were enthused to allow the citizens to vote yes or no for the incorporation. Some refused to sign the petitions.

Some who had tried to incorporate before were now against it.

Top picture is the St. Gertrudes Catholic Church   in the early 1900's
Bottom picture is the main street in the 1920's

THE 1904 MORA FLOOD

Thursday, September 29, 1904, the valley of Mora had been blessed with a steady rain. Not a heavy rain but a steady one which would continue for days with little interruption at all.

It had rained every day the previous week and by the 29th of September, the river was overflowed to the point where there was a little stream of water flowing down the Mora street.

At first, people thought little about the rain since steady rains were very usual and good for the crops. Men went about their business praising God for the blessed rain. This was their custom.

Late in the evening of that date, the run off in Main Street begin to worry even the strongest and faithful people. They now begin to pray that the rains would go away.

We need to remember that most of the houses at this time had thatched roofs with mud as the top covering. The floors were also dirt floors. It is hard to imagine the wet floors and furniture, although the furniture was home made and only the very essential pieces existed. People were very poor but proud. Some people tried to cover the roof with other materials that were available but the roof still leaked.

The stream became wilder and faster and by nightfall it had become a river. In the river flowed logs, dead animals, parts of buildings, pig sties, chicken coops, bridges and more.

There was nothing people could do to prevent this catastrophe but to observe and pray. Neighbors woke up the neighbors who had much faith and had gone to sleep.

The only thing they figured was the safest to save their hides was the court house which at that time was where the new court house and fire department now stands. This court house was completed in 1889.(As of 2000 A.D. the fire department building has been moved to La Cordillera).

People from La Cordillera or upper town where my mother-in-law's family lived, packed a few belongings and marched to the court house which was a mile away.

Folks from Mora proper were occupying the place as well.

At this time the fall term of the District Court was in session and the two local hotels, namely the Waltons and the Khan Hotels were filled to capacity so many jurors had to rely on the good people in town for a place to stay.

The school children had been dismissed from school early. To them, it was a holiday and they ran and splashed in the water puddles. They could care less that it rained.

As the flood grew so did the roaring of the river. You who have never experienced a flood will never be able to imagine how frightful this noise is, specially when you know your life is at stake.

All through the night and onto the wee hours of the morning, this exodus took place. Kids slept but their parents, Catholic and Protestant alike, prayed and got together which was unusual for there was a strong prejudice amongst them. The fact is that the raging flood did more damage to the streets which at that time were not paved

There are as many different stories as there were people and most of their accounts are similar.

One that Levi Madrid recounts is the one about a juror whose name he recalls as Pedro Cordova who had been appointed as a juror.

Mr. Cordova had been sleeping in a rented room by the Sister's convent when the flood reached that house, someone woke him up and he dressed in a hurry. He had laid his best suit on top of the bed covers and had set his shoes under the bed. When he got up half asleep because the owner had banged on the door and told him to get up and save himself, he jumped out of bed and splashed water all over. The water was eight to ten inches deep. He felt all around for his shoes and the pressure to get out was great so he took his suit and dressed up and followed the crowd to the court house.

The next day he fooled many people for he had on the fancy suit with cut away frock coat, which was the style. His pants were rolled up above his ankle. He was bare footed but in good spirit.

When people ventured to the streets there were ruts instead of the street and deep holes here and there where trees had been uprooted.

The bridge on the Guadalupita road was gone so there was no way to cross the river at this stage.

My Mother-in-law recounted that all they could carry was the clothing they were wearing.

The Mora Flood of 1904
by Levi Madrid

JACK JOHNSON TO LAS VEGAS TO FIGHT JIM FLYNN
WORLD BOXING CHAMPIONSHIP
1912

1912 was the year and July was the month the fight would take place in Las Vegas New Mexico.

Johnson and some of his promoters came to Mora and had a hearty meal at the Butler Hotel. (At this time, the hotel was known as the Walton Hotel. A Mr. Walton was owner and manager of said hotel).

The Mora Band played during the meal. Some of the band players were, Levi Madrid, Henry Sosa, Marcelino and Fernando Pacheco, Juan Antonio Gutierrez, Leo Maes, Placido Romero "El Charita", Arturo Rimbert and Casimero Trujillo and Timoteo Sena who was the leader. All together, there were forty members in this band. They played during the meal and after the meal Johnson complemented them telling them that this was the best band he had ever listened to and gave them a $20 tip.

Mr. Enriques Sosa had a photography shop and made quite a bit of money selling pictures of Johnson, to his followers and any other fan who dared pose with him.

Johnson was a black man and the whites wanted to see his competition win. He had many whites following him and among them some white girls whose parents did not approve of that friendship. At this time Black was a bad word in the vernacular. Prejudice was at its height. It was impossible for a white to approve the friendship between a black and a white much less between male and female.

After the fight, Mr. Sosa kept on making money with his negatives which at this time were printed in glass. He sold a copy to one of the girl's brother for $5 and the boy thought it was the only negative left, so he gladly paid the $5 and left. The first rock he encountered, he used as a tool to break the negative to pieces. But Mr. Sosa, a good businessman, had kept copies of them. The idea of getting rid of the negatives was to save embarrassment to the girls families.

The story of Jack Johnson may be better explained by reading a story by Richard Paul who at the time was the Optic sports editor. July 27, 1979 is the date of this article yet bias against blacks was predominant sixty seven years after the fight took place.

Right hand picture is the Butler Hotel 1912
Left hand picture is the Butler Hotel 1890's

RELIGION IN ST. GERTRUDES VALLEY

When Mora became populated, the majority of the people were Hispanic and Catholic. They gathered in private houses to pray on Sunday and at other times.

Among the Catholics were some Jews who claimed to be Catholic because of the late 1400 Inquisition in Spain, they had gone underground so as to survive. Privately, they observed their Jewish customs such as abstaining from eating pork and other of their unique beliefs.

In 1818, the citizens were asking for a priest. A priest(Father Cadel) came from Picuris to take care of the spiritual needs of the Mora people.

After the Americans took New Mexico in 1847, the Protestants came in and people were more openly in practicing their religion but many of their children, knowing the Catholic religion since birth were so acculturated to the Catholic religion that they remained Catholic. Many of the ex Jewish children wondered why the customs at home were different but remained ignorant of the fact that their predecessors were Jews.

By 1852, Father Jean Baptiste Lamy had come to New Mexico and in 1852, he had been appointed Bishop of Santa Fe. He had met Reverend Munnecon, a French priest, and had assigned him priest of the St. Gertrudes' parish. He had arrived recently from France and the Indians and Penitentes did not make him feel comfortable. Bishop Lamy did not agree with the Penitentes' method of worship. Bishop Lamy was making changes and had moved Rev. Stephen Avel, another French Priest, to serve the Mora Parish.

On August 3, 1858, Rev. Avel drank poisoned wine and died soon after. Some people claimed that because he disliked the rituals of the penitentes or to please the Bishop, he had disapproved the membership of the penitentes in the church. This people had poisoned the wine. Others claim that Father Munnecon felt uncomfortable with the change that he had poisoned the wine. Today it still is a mystery as to who did it. It was said that a woman who had some knowledge about the poisoning had warned Father Avel about the wine being poisoned but he had already consecrated the wine and had to drink it. Father Avel was buried in New Mexico four years after he came with Bishop Lamy's caravan in November 1854.

Whoever was to blame, he pardoned them from his death bed.

Father Damozo Talarid succeeded Rev. Avel, then Padre J.B. Salpointe took over. At this time the parish covered 200 miles from North to South, from Pueblo, Colorado on down to New Mexico. He used the Raton Pass through Wooton's toll gate to get to his Colorado Missions.

While in Mora, the roof of the church needed repairs, so his first project was to rebuild the church. This was around 1861.

The Mora people have always been helpful and ready to help anyone in need especially in church matters. They cooperated and soon the church was back in use.

Later on, a frame tower and a new vestry were added.

During this time, people were very superstitious and believed in the mal ojo–a curse that may be given a child because it is beautiful or for any other reason. They believed in witches who were also called mal-hechiceras (wrong doers) and had the power to become anything from black cats to owls.

Hispanics were very emotional and as easy as they could love they could hate so many were the violent fights that occurred. Many were because of politics, love, cows or whatever riled the person.

Father Salpointe saw them as barbarians who needed to be educated. When he saw how the penitentes inflicted self-punishment or heard the witch stories, he decided that the answer was education. At this time there were very few children who could afford going to school. Parents needed manpower in their fields and had the children work from dawn to dusk. There were few commodities and less money but they were all self-supporting.

Bishop Lamy had invited the Sisters of Loretto to come to New Mexico Territory in 1852. In 1862, a contingent of sisters arrived at Mora. They opened the St. Mary's College School for Girls in 1865.

Sister Mary Borgia Ward, Sister Cecilia Ribera and Sister Agnes Martinez of the community of the Sisters of Loretto, came to Mora April 4, 1864. Sister Ann Joseph Mattingly and Sister Isabel Martinez came to help start but were not part of the community assigned to teach in Mora. Fifty girls enrolled that first year.

The following year, Sister Vicente Gonzales and Sister Escolastica Zamora were added to the staff. Kitchen served as laundry and refectory (Dining room). The dormitory became a classroom by day. Diet for year was bread and beans. Cleaned wheat served as coffee after a good toasting. Salt was used whenever available. Teachers had no well so they went from house to house begging for water.

After several years of precarious existence, the sisters were asked to take over the school as a public school for girls at the salary of $25 per month.

In 1860, The Christian Brothers School had opened its doors in Mora. They had forty seven boarding boys. By 1870, three teachers took care of them. This school was located where Stevan Archuleta's property at El Ranchito now stands. The campus was surrounded by an adobe wall and there are the ruins of some of the houses still standing on the Northwest side of the property (1999).

Brother Dometian was its first director. He resigned when Father Salpointe was named Bishop of Arizona.

Brother Geramius replaced Brother Dometian on April 6, 1866. Brother Juniamus replaced him and he stayed there for four years. Brother Dometian returned later but lack of finances forced him to resign.

In 1875, Bishop Lamy was appointed Archbishop of the New Mexico Territory.

In 1884, the Boys Christian school closed its doors forever and the students were transferred to the Sisters of Loretto School which, then became co-ed.

The convent burned down on December 16, 1888. Padre Antonio Fourchegu, then pastor, procured the old Brothers' College building as a temporary residence until the new convent could be built.

On February 14, 1888, Archbishop Lamy died. The brotherhood of Penitentes known as La Sociadad De Nuestro Padre Jesus kept on worshiping in their own unique way and has survived up to the present which shows the Hispanics strong will to retain their culture.

A contingency of Presbyterian settlers had established a church at Chacon or El Rito as it was known then. Most of the old settlers were faithful Catholics and they saw Protestants as an enemy.

By 1881, there were enough Presbyterians to start a boarding school. Such a school was established that year. This campus was the usual Fort-like campus of the time. The site was where the Levi Madrid's property now stands. They had barns, kitchen, a well, an horno, classrooms and bedrooms. The well and horno stood inside the patio formed by the surrounding buildings. The barn stood South of the campus.

Although it was a Presbyterian school, they welcome any and all students that would wish to enroll. They could use converts.

It must be noted that after 1846, when New Mexico became a territory of the United States, the Anglo or gringos which included the non-Hispanic and Indian ethnic groups, came with a different religion. Their Democracy was a world different from what the Hispanics and Indians were used to.

By 1895, the school closed its doors and was transferred to Albuquerque and is now known as Menaul School.

Many Catholics as well as non-Catholics attended the Menaul School throughout the years. Some also attended the Allison-James which was another Protestant school in Santa Fe. My Mother and Rosaura Romero's mother among others attended this school. Some returned to teach at Mora and surrounding towns later. (Some Menaul graduates were Flavio P. Vigil, Ignacio Maestas, Ofene Garcia, Fermin Pacheco, Abel Vasquez, Amadeo Aragon among others).

After 1900, there were the Presbyterian and the Catholic churches in the valley of Mora. Much later other sects came and went. In the 1960 s, the Hippie contingency showed its face and changed many kids' attitudes.

Today there are the St. Gertrudes Catholic Church, The Presbyterian Church, The Assembly of God Church among others in the valley.

The stories of these churches in themselves could cover volumes.

The following priests have had residence or visited and administered the sacraments at one time or another. Some may have been deacons and had not been ordained at that time when they appeared in the St Gertrude's register.

Father John Tourangeau, the present priest,(1990) was kind enough to let this author browse through the Baptismal records from 1900 to the present, so the record of those priests who had residence or visited the St. Gertrudis Parish since 1900 was available.

The idea of this write-up is to give information of what priests and when they were in the parish. Some names have been guessed as far as the spelling is concerned since the signatures are not too clear and the records are written in long hand in most cases.

Father J.C. Balland (Claude) was in the parish in 1900. He was the parish priest until 1916. He returned on December 3, 1918 to marry his brother Peter to Martha. Then again in 1931 to baptize his nephew, Peter Jr.

Rev. J. Collins' name appears in '1910. Rev. Maurice Olier's name appears as early as 1911 and on through 1932. He also served in Wagon Mound.

30

Rev. Jean R. Alanis 1912. Rev. N. Tudaire, 1915, Rev. Antonio F.Peres, 1919.

Rev. Guglio Gremand or maybe Jules Gremand. It may well be that Guglio and Jules is one and the same. 1911. Rev Bernard Fajanelli in Feb and April 1920. Rev. Maximo Mayeuz 1921, Rev. Jos. Assemuler 1925-1926, Rev. J. Francis Mitchell 1927-1933, Rev. Juan T. Sanchez 1932 and again 1939, Rev. Robert Hammond 1932-1934, Rev. Leo Oelmann 1934, Rev. John Dold 1935, Rev. George De Vloo 1934, Rev. Juan B. Peris 1934-1942,(This priest, the author knew well because he served him as altar boy, driver and deacon)Rev. James McNiff 1936-1938, Rev. Jose Ma. Osca 1936, Father Angelico Chavez, 1937(Native son of Mora)Rev. Anthony H. Vorst 1938, Rev. Max Mayeaux 1938-1939, Rev. Roman Altemeras 1939, Rev Hissaua 1939, Rev. Napoleron Missonae 1939, Rev. Leon Missonae 1939, Rev. Silviano Pratat 1940, Rev. Rafael Perez Vargas 1940, Rev. George Boenninghausen 1940-1941, Rev. Miguel Castura 1942, Rev. Amejena 1944, Rev. Francisco Rodrigez 1944, Simon Trujillo 1945. In 1948, the Dixon Case removed the Sisters of Loretto from teaching in the Public Schools. Rev. Henry J. Rael 1953, about this time the St. Gertrude's Catholic School was opened and a Gym and classrooms were built. Rev. John S. McHugh 1954, Rev. J. Moynihen 1954-1957, Rev. Frank Montoya , my first cousin, Baptized my son, Robert R. Alcon 1957), Rev. James Flanagan 1958-1961, Rev. Osidro Bonilla 1960, Rev. Fidelio Buck 1960, Rev. Ramon Jimenez 1961, Rev. John J. Moran 1962-1964, Rev. Raymond V. Dunn 1962, Rev. William Morrison 1962, Rev. Walter Plimmer 1963, Rev. Questa 1961, Rev. Daniel Higgins 1961, Rev. John Crew 1962, Rev. Raymond V. Duran 1962, Rev. Frank Cunningham 1962, Rev. Edward Kimm 1962, Rev. Augustine Calderon 1963, Rev. Lucian C. Hereoien 1963, Rev. Manuel Campos 1963, Rev. Dennis McKarlin 1963, About this time the St. Gertrude's Catholic School was closed. Rev. Augustine T. Gurule 1964, Rev. Walter R. Washilla 1964, Rev. Jesus De Alba 1964, Rev. Anthony Carron 1964, Rev. H. Ruelas 1965, Rev. Mariano Santos 1965-1966, Rev. Charlie Julian 1965, Rev. Joseph Delmore 1965, Rev. Rafael Herrera 1966, Rev. Vincent Maddalena 1966, Rev. Leonard L. Bayer 1966-1976, Rev. Clive C. Lynn 1976-1982, Rev. Sabine Griego 1978, Rev. Michael O'Brien 1982-1985, Rev. Vidal Martinez 1984, Rev. Gregory W. Tipton 1985, Rev. Joseph Theisen 1988, Rev. Polm Faudie 1988, Rev. Walter Cassidy 1989 (Father Cassidy was retired and was assistant to Father John ever since. Father Cassidy is a great artist and sculpturer and also a native son of Mora was very well liked), Rev. John Tourangeau 1989-1992. Father John, as he was known by those who loved and respected him was so loved by the congregation.

The parish was at one of its lowest morale when Father John arrived. He, truly was God's messenger for he had the patience of Job and treated everyone as his brother and sister. He was as emotional as any Hispanic could ever hope to be although he was not Hispanic. For those who had a hard time pronouncing his name he said his name was Gallegos. He was very humorous. His door was opened at all times and no one was ever refused help when he or she approached him.

The sad day came when, in the latter part of April, he was advised he was to be transferred to Clovis. Petitions, letters and telephone calls were sent asking Archbishop Sanchez to consider lending him until he would finish all the unfinished projects he had started. These petitions, letters, etc. fell on deaf ears.

May 30, Father John offered his last mass as priest of the parish. He gave his sermon praising the bishop, and the in-coming priest and asked everyone to welcome Father Tim Martinez as they had Welcome him back in 1989. There were no dried eyes including his, during and after mass. Even the bravest men could not hold their tears.

He advised people to keep on going and continue the good work. He said he would come and visit whenever he could.

Never had the valley acted to this degree whenever transfers were made. All the congregation wished him well and hoped that he may be reassigned to Mora again.

This never happened because Father John left the priesthood soon after.

Father Tim was reassigned to Ranchos De Taos and Father Tri was assigned to this parish in 1990. Here he stayed until 2003 when he was reassigned to a parish in Santa Fe. Father Tri was very well liked and was missed by the parishioners and specially by the children who loved him dearly.

January 14, 1993, was another day of sadness for Mora. The beloved Priest Michael O'Brien died in Albuquerque. His rosary was recited at Taos on the 15th of that month and he was buried at the Santo Nino Cemetery about five miles Southwest of Mora where he had asked to be buried. He suffered and died of cancer.

Fr. Walter Cassidy,

Father Walter Cassidy Top picture is when he was ordained Bottom Picture was taken a short time before his death.

This is a picture of the first rectory of the St. Gertrudes Catholic Church up to 1950 s. When Rev. Linn demolished it.

EDUCATION IN THE VALLEY OF ST. GERTRUDES

The information in this chapter was acquired from different sources, word of mouth of various persons, works of different people and mostly from records made available to this author from the court house and the Mora Independent Schools superintendent's records, the Catholic Church records, many themes of various authors, as well as from literature gathered by the author as he attended different meetings.

By the time the white man came to this valley, the Indians indoctrinated their children at home and out in the field since their only need was to survive. The men trained their boys to hunt, trap, and to bear pain and hardships. The women took care of the girls and taught them to cook, care of their home, things about girls and how to plant and reap. Their education was very simple and each family would teach their young ones according to their traditions.

When the trappers arrived, the Indians observed them and learned a few tricks from them. They became more sophisticated in dressing themselves, riding horses, and many other aspects of life. The white man also learned things from them since they were more acquainted and adapted to the environment .

By 1846 the culture made an adjustment. The American culture brought ideas of democracy. Democracy in the United States was instituted for the benefit of the middle class, Protestant, well-educated, businessmen. Spaniards or Hispanics were believers in church, penance, and hard work. They had very little respect for education as serious business. Their goal was hard work, penance and their ultimate goal was to go to Heaven. It needs to be stressed that not all of the people involved were the way they are pictured in this history. What is meant is that there were exceptions to the rule but those who were the voices that were heard fit the written words expressed in this works.

Discipline was much different than what it is called today. Anyone who misbehaved was punished severely and woe be to the poor student who misbehaved. The parents were very strict disciplinarians. They would be horsewhipped, slapped, kicked or paddled. This discipline was also permitted to the school teachers. If the child was punished in school, his or her parents were notified and when they went home in the evening, they would get it worse there. There was the woodshed that was dreaded when the parent took the kid by the ear, by the hand, or however.

According to some old timers, the first school in the St. Gertrudis valley was built around 1847. The probable site is by the river behind the residence of the Phillip N. Sanchez. Around that year was when the American culture was introduced to the citizens of this valley.

Teachers took care of their own problems sometimes referring the big ones to the parent. Switches and a visit to the woodshed was practiced by parents. Rest assured, the culprits who had sense enough and went through such an ordeal, would behave nicely while they remembered. Most of the children had enough sense to imprint the experience in their mind so that it lasted in there for the rest of their life. This kind of philosophy was used until the late 1950 s and even into the 1960 s.

According to Juliette Sanchez, the first public school was started in 1854 under the supervision of the Sisters of Loretto, who, rapidly, and successfully established and accredited the school. The site of this convent was by the Catholic Church.

Around 1862, The Sisters of Loretto were asked by the Archbishop Lamy to move to New Mexico and educate the natives of Northern New Mexico. That is, to his way of thinking since he believed the people were in dire need of being civilized. He did not condone the penitentes, much less their way of worshiping their God.

In 1865, the sisters were ready to start the St. Mary's College for girls. Later on it became a boarding school.

Sometime around the 1860 s, according to Don Frank Lucero, the Christian Brothers established a boys school. This school was situated in what today is the Steve Archuleta residence. Remains of those buildings are still in evidence. They had erected an adobe wall around the campus. Some of the walls were in evidenced in the year 1940. (Frank Lucero's older brother, Agustin attended)

This school lasted until 1884. The problems of continuing them were many . The students were transferred to the Sisters of Loretto which then became coed.

By 1881, There were enough Presbyterians to start a school of their own, since the sisters were teaching the children a catechism that the Presbyterian elders did not approve.

This campus was situated just East of the present Courthouse. They had built buildings around the campus with two openings. One on the West side and one on the East side. The Westside is still an alley. This was a self sustaining school. On the South side, they had fields where the students and staff grew their produce. They had an Indian Oven, A well and outhouses in their enclosure.

The kitchen stood in the Southern side of the campus. It was a long building built of adobes. It had a long table with a slit in the middle that served as a drain for dish water. The water flowed out and into a hole on the East side of the building. On the Western side of the campus was a two story as well as on part of the Northern side of the campus. There were trees on the Northern side which faced the Main Road.

Mora had a population of 700 at this time.

The school was closed in 1895 and transferred to Albuquerque where it became the Menaul School. Some of the students got their education there. To name a few; Fermin Pacheco Sr., Ignacio Maestas, Flavio P. Vigil, Harry Sandoval and others.

The convent burned down in 1882. There is some disagreement on this date. Some say it was December 16, 1888. The school kept on as usual in different houses. The convent was a two story building where the sisters resided in the top story while the lower story was used as classrooms. The subjects taught were the 3 R's and religion (4Rs) The term of school was six months or depending when the children were sent. This was after all the crops were gathered.

In 1891, Governor Bradford Prince asked the legislature to pass a law for a Public School System. It was passed and a Public School System Board of Education was created. A Superintendent of Public Instruction was named. He was Amado Chavez. The way to choose this superintendent was different from how he is chosen today.

The school building in Mora proper was by the river behind the Phillip N. Sanchez's residence. Some of the students who attended this school in the latter parts of the 1900's were Levi and Ben Madrid, Cora Walton (an Indian adopted by Mr. and Mrs. Walton, Emma, Annie and Margaret Strong Felipe, Manuel and Stevan Sanchez, Joe Fuss, Maggie Allan among others.

As far as is known the first County Superintendent was Rafael Romero who served until 1909. He was followed by Blas Sanchez who served from 1910 to 1911. The following Superintendent was a Presbyterian Minister by the name of Manuel Madrid who served from 1912 to 1916. Mr. Madrid was Levi's dad.

Dr. Hoag was school doctor. Some teachers named in 1912 and 1913 were: J.J. Romero, Roman A. Valdez, Bersabe Romero. Benjamin Gandert, Sebastian Esquibel, and David Lucero at Guadalupita, Bessie E. Tipton, B.B. Douglas and Amanda Wasson at Shoemaker. District #4, Eugenio Romero, and Blas Gallegos At La Cueva Estefanita Arguello was janitor at the salary of $2 per month. Merenciana R. De Korte rented her house for a school building at $4 per month., Agustin Vigil Y Valdez, and Albino Maes, District #6, David Cruz and Dionicio Pacheco at Golondrinas at Pedro Padilla's house, Elauterio Baca, Mrs. Harriet Martinez and T.A. Martinez at Ocate Cordillera, Mrs. Soledad P. Sanchez and Roberto Cruz at Lucero, Alice D. Kier, A.L. Willson, and Shirley B. Beck at Watrous.

In 1912, some teachers mentioned, who were teaching at Mora District #1 were Sister J Frances, Reyes Romero and Sister Doloritas. In the early 1900's, the convent was rebuilt and school was being taught by the sisters since they were the only ones who were able to teach because of their qualifications. This changed later on in the early 1920's when the eighth grade graduates were allowed to teach. Among these teachers were Emma Strong Sanchez, and Josefita Olivas Baca.

By 1912, the people accepted the Protestants as equals and Manuel Madrid was elected Mora County School Superintendent. This was the year that New Mexico was accepted into the Union as the 47th state. The Sisters of Loretto also celebrated their 50th Anniversary and Governor McDonald was asked to attend this anniversary.

Teacher's top salary was $50 a month.

Minutes of the Board of Education show an act that on March 13, 1917 created-an act entitled-an act creating County Boards of Education.

Members of that board were Mrs. Frank A. Roy elected for 4 years, Mrs. Rose C. Cassidy Secretary, for 4 years, Mr. Jesus L. A Abreau elected for 2 years, J. Frank Curns, Vice President, elected for 2 years, and Mr. Milnor Rudolph elected, County Superintendent who served up to 1918. In the year 1917, the teachers' salary was increased to $65. monthly.

The school districts that composed the Mora County schools in 1917 were: #1 Mora, #2 Cleveland, (town, El Valle and Vallecitos), #3 Guadalupita (town and upper), #4 Shoemaker, #5 La Cueva, Buena Vista and Cebollita, #6 San Jose (LeDoux), #7 Golondrinas and Loma Parda, #8 Ocate, #9 Holman, #10 Lucero, #11 Watrous and Valmora, #12 Wagon Mound, #13 Levy, #14 Armenta, #15 Llano Coyote included Rainsville, #16 Rito or El Pozo, #17 Abuelo, #18 North Carmen, #19 Tiptonville, # 20 Mesteno near Roy (Velasquez), #21 Naranjos, #22 Los Cocas, #23 Turquillo and Canada del Carro, #24 Solano, Lopez, #25 Las

Colonias, #26 Los Borregos, #27 Gascon, #28 Canon Agua Negra, #29 Monte Aplanado, #30 South Carmen, #31 Los Hueros,#32 Optimo, #33 Roy, Escondido, #34 Halls Peak, Aurora, #35 Nolan, #36 Mills #37 Los Manueles, #38 Ojo Feliz and Corral Apache, #39 Mofre (Murphy), #40 Monte Vista, #41 Armonia, #42 El Alto, Chupaderos, #43 El Oro, #44 Ocate Junction, #45 La Gallina (Abbott) #46 El Rito, #s 47, 48,49, 50, 51, 52, 53, 54, 56, 60, and 61 also existed, however the names of this school districts were not available. At one time there were 62 school in the county. Each hamlet had its own one or more room schools.

Board members were Frank A. Roy, Rose Cassidy, Jesus L. Abreau, and J. Frank Curns. District #56 was separated from district 32.

Second grade teachers were asking for a uniform salary of $65, but for-the never fails -reason, that there was a lack of funding, they were refused.

Some teachers approved in 1917, their salaries as well as the district, are as follows: Elizabeth Epps, District #60 at $60 a month, Charlotte McAffee #20, at $65, Miss Willie L. Day #46, at $60, Mrs. Alice Upton #24, at $65, Miss Floripa Chavez #14, at $50, C.J. Pendergraft #20, at $75, W.A. James #42, at $65, Jennie Jardee #12, at $65, Ida May Stevens #41, at $70, Miss Alice Jackson #20 at $65, Lura Cunningham #40 at $60, Miss V. Martin #50 at $65, Mr. D.C. Clark #43 at $65, Miss Minnie L. Allan #35, at $60, Mrs R.D. Reed #24 at $75, and Mr. Abenicio Alcon #54 at $50.(My Uncle)

Jose de Garcia Cruz was contracted to transport children of school age on the northern part of the district to school house, not to exceed 20 children at a cost of $160.

In 1918, Districts #20 and #36 were consolidated about this time as were El Queso, La Cueva with Buena Vista.

District 53 was consolidated with district #1.

Consolidation fever was running strong about this time. Districts 6, 18, 30, and 52 tried to consolidate but failed. Other consolidations did take place.

Alfredo Lucero was Superintendent from 1919 to 1920.

In 1920, the county was cut smaller and ceded part of its land to Harding County.

In the year 1919, according to "El Eco Del Norte" published by Enrique Sosa Sr., the eighth grade graduates were: David Madrid, Jose Joaquin Lopez, Manuel Santos Melendez, Mary Albina Abeyta, Mary Elenore Gonzales, Rumaldo Gonzales, Grace Sabina Madrid, Agustina Valdez, Maclovia Pacheco, Ursula Casados, Celina Maes, and Juan A. Rodarte. Alfredo Lucero was County Superintendent and J. V. Conway was assistant Superintendent of Public Instructions. Felipe Chacon, Editor of the El Eco Del Norte was the main speaker of this event. He spoke in English and urged the students to continue their educational career.

This year, 1919. The Mora County School Board turned over the schools that covered the village to the Board of Education of the Incorporated Village of Wagon Mound. Wagon Mound is the only incorporated town in the county up to the present(1999)

Grace Ogden, the first lady in this county was elected Superintendent of Mora County Schools in 1921 an served up to 1922.

The highest grade taught in the Mora Schools was the eighth grade.

In 1922, a two story school building was built in church property next to what was part of the old Christian Brothers School for Boys campus. A fifty foot deep well was dug, and there were trees planted. This is the first school attended by this author in 1933.

Juan Pacheco was elected in 1923 as Superintendent of Mora County Schools and served until 1924.

Cosme Garcia was elected Superintendent in 1925 and served until 1926.

Mrs. Antonia A. Sanchez was the second woman to hold the position of Mora County School superintendent and served from 1927 to 1928. The highest grade taught in the Mora High School was the ninth grade. In 1928 they upped it to tenth grade and in 1929 to the eleventh grade.

Levi Madrid who was Manuel Madrid's son served from 1929 to 1932. He followed his father's footsteps who had broken the record of serving more than one term. Alfonso Sandoval served two months in 1931.

In 1930, there were 46 school districts, namely: District 1 Mora, 2 Cleveland, 3 Upper Guadalupita, 4 Shoemaker, 5 Buena Vista, 6 Ledoux, 7 Golondrinas, 8 Ocate, 9 Holman, 10 Lucero, 11 Watrous, 13 Los Febres, 14 Armenta, 15 Rainsville, 18 El Pozo, 17 El Abuelo, 18 North Carmen, 19 Tiptonville, 20 Velasquez, 21 Naranjos, 27 Cocas, 23 Turquillo, 24 Lopez, 25 Las Colonias, 26 Los Borregos, 27 Gascon, 28 Agua Negra Canyon, 29 Monte Aplanado, 30 South Carmen, 31 Los Hueros, 32 Optimo, 33 Escondida, 34 Aurora, 35 Levy, 36 Guadalupita, 37 Los Manueles, 38 Ojo Feliz, 39 Murphey, 40 Monte Vista, 41 Armonia, 42 El Alto, 43 El Oro, 44 Ocate Junction 45 Las Gallinas, and 46 El Rito.

In 1930s, the campus of the elementary school was divided by a lumber fence. There was a deep well where the students used a rope and a bucket to get their drinking water. There were two outhouses, each on either side of the fence. The Western side was for the boys and the Eastern side was for the girls. Later on the fence was removed.

Healthy rules were, if known, not used. The children drank out of the same bucket, sat in the commodes over the urine wet seats and most never wiped their fannies after using the toilet. Washing their hands after using the outhouse was out of the question. There being no such rules and if there had been any, they never were obeyed.

In the girls' side, there was a culvert like used as a fire escape from the second floor.

The 1930 graduating class of Mora High School was the first twelve year to graduate from the Mora high School. The students in this class were Tito Trammel, Alberto Martinez, Magadelena Lujan, Maria Tafoya, Manuelita Esquibel, Adela Branch, Katherine Trambley. Their sponsor and teacher was Sister Mathias. Levi Madrid was the County School Superintendent at this time.

Matias Zamora was County Superintendent from 1933 to 1934. His Assistant was Benjamin Alcon. School teachers recommended for the 1934-35 school year and their districts are as follows: District #1 Sister Ann Thomas, Sister Mary Ida, Sister M. Mathias, Sister M. Malachy, Sister Mary Ann, and Sister M. Beredina, also, Mary P. Cassidy, Ofelia Florence, Amalia Sanchez,Celia C. Madrid, Mrs Peter T. Baca, District #2, Celia Cassidy, Albert N. Valdez, and Rosemary C. Quinn (town), Ben Medina and Ninfa S. Maes (El Valle),

Jesse M. Martinez (Vallecitos), District 3, Max R. Valdez, and Carlos R. Valdez, District #4 Mable Irene Myers and Cencionita Montoya, District #5 David A. Madrid, Anastacio Trujillo (Buena Vista) and Isabel T. Mora (Cebollita), District #6 Rafael Trujillo and Agatha T. Aragon, District #7 Frances Medina (Golondrinas) and Juan R. Bernal (Loma Parda), District #8, Celia Martinez, District #9 Mrs. Eusebio Arellano, Annie Gandert (Holman)and Flavio P. Vigil (La Sierra),District #10 Luis Montoya, District 11 Mrs. Bye Hill Lister (Principal) Mrs. Ernest Tipton, Lucille M. Reynolds, Opal Brimmage White, District #13 Luis D. Ortega, District #14 Eloida Sandoval, District #15 Alfonso Duran and Virginia L. Medina (South) Claudio Duran (North) and Maclovia Warder (La Jara) District #16 Mrs. Alex Martinez, District #17 Eloy Romero, District # 18 Ernesto Herrera and Arturo Martinez, District #19 Eduardo Allen, District #20 Mrs. Thelma A. Byrnie, District #21 Glave Blattman, District #22 Luciano Martinez, District #23 Frank J. C. DeBaca (Turquillo) and Alberto Romero (Canada), District #24 Albert LeDoux, District #15 Juan A. Pacheco, District #26 Amalia Arellano, District #27 Mary Martinez, District #28 Mary Sanchez and Melaquias Gonzales, District #29 Facundo Martinez and Ignacio Maestas, District #30 Amadeo Aragon and Esther Aragon, District #31 M. A. Lucero, District #32 Zacarias Montoya, District #33 Antonio I. Valdez, District #34 Timoteo Romero, District #36 Clorinda M. Sandoval and Josephine Regensberg (Town) Louis Zamora (La Mesa), District #37 Sofia Mondragon, District #38 Eusebio Vasquez and Margarito Duran, District #39 Dolores Trujillo, District #41 Charlotte O. Bucher and Demecia Arguello, District #42 Marie J. Romo and Magdalena Lujan(El Alto) and Corina C. De Baca (Chupaderos), District #43 Demetrio Quintana, District #44 Mrs. Leila Blattman, District #45 Elaisa Fernandez and District #46 Placido B. Ortega. Truck drivers were Albert Zimmerman, J.V. Wengert, Cayetano Medina, Alejandro Arellano and Frutoso Aragon for the Wagon Mound route.

What needs to be explained here is that if the superintendent was of the opposite party or did not agree with the people who controlled the board, he worked with his hands tied. Most of the time he was allowed to compromise with the board and got some of his preference in.

The graduates of the Class of 1933 were: Nora Barnum, Lourdes Lujan, Mary Salazar, Corina Valdez, Rosa Martinez, Laura Gonzales, Cornelia Abeyta, Delfinia Salazar, Pablita Martinez, Juliette Sanchez, Angelina Trujillo, Felicitas Quintana, Angelina Archuleta, Jose Medina, Aurelio Maes, Joe E. Gandert, Nappy Sanchez, Louis Balland, Demesio Valdez, Bartolo Valdez, Pablo Martinez, and Thimothy Romero.

Class moto was "Building for Eternity" Class Colors Pink and White and Class Flower Pink Carnations. Graduation exercises held Friday Evening May 19, 1933 at seven o'clock at the Court House.

To give the reader a chance to compare how the teachers were moved from one school to another every time a new superintendent took over a list of those hired who had not voted "right", the author has provided a list of those teachers hired for the term 1935-36. All Sisters and Sencionita Montoya, Mrs. Peter B. Baca, Amalia Sanchez, Ofelia Florence and Corina C. De Baca for District #1, District #2 Rosemary C. Quinn, and Celia Cassidy (Town) Celia Madrid, Fernandita Bernal and Cleo Vigil (Town) and Ninfa S. Maes (Vallecitos) District #3 Josephine Regensberg and Alice Rivera, District #4 Mrs. Emily B. Raybon and Dorris Petterson, District #5 Margarito A. Lucero, and Martinez and

Aragon(Sebollita),District #6 Rafael Trujillo and David Madrid, District #7 Luis Zamora (Golondrinas) and Abel Vasquez, (Loma Parda) District #8 Elaisa Fernandez, District #9 Flavio P. Vigil, Mary Sanchez (Holman) and Ben Medina (Sierra), District #10 Luis R. Montoya, District #11 Abran Fernandez, Principal, Margarita Medina and Mrs. Ernest Tipton and Mrs. Mary Faver (Valmora), District #13 Isabel T. Mora, District #14 Eloida Sandoval, District #15 Isabel Lucero (North), Dionicio Maes and Ramitos Montoya (South) and Juan Sanchez (La Jara) District #16 Eloy Romero, District #17 Zacarias Montoya, District #18 Agatha T. Aragon and Dometila M. Sandoval, District #19 Nancy Wallace, District #20 Antonio I. Valdez, District #21 Glave Blattman, District #22 Max R. Valdez (Town) and Sofia Lucero (Sisneros), District #23 Antonio Sisneros (Turquillo) and Manuel Maes, (Canada Del Carro), District #24 Demecia Arguello, District #25 Juan A. Pacheco, District #26 Eusebio Vasquez, District #27 Mary A. Martinez, District #28 Virginia Espinoza and Mary Pacheco District #29 Ignacio Maestas and Juan R. Bernal, District #30 Amadeo Aragon and Secundino Aragon, District #31 Jose D. Lucero, District #32 Manuelita Sandoval, District #33 Charlotte O. Bucher, District #34 Timoteo Romero, District #35 Lelia Blattman (Principal) Lottie Dillard and Aurora Garcia, District #36 Tito Trammel, Doloritas T. Lucero and Annie Fresquez, District #37 Zacarias Montoya, District #38 Trinidad Lopez, Mrs Canuto Melendez (OjoFeliz)and Mrs. Santos Melendez(Corral De Los Apaches), District #39 Facundo Martinez, District #40 Alberto LeDoux, District #41 Clara Holbrook and Emma Doris Myers, District #42 Magdalena Lujan Principal and Lily Jaramillo (Alto) and Alberto Lopez (Chupaderos), District #43 Rebecca Romero, District #44 Rae Price, District #45 Sofia Mondragon, District #46 Luis D. Ortega.

According to Facundo Martinez, teachers who taught during this time (and according to various others who asked not to use their names,) most of their tenure had to wait for their pay (miserable as it was) sometimes up to six months to get paid. They would depend on some board member who had a store to get their credit and then they had to sell their checks for half of what they were worth.

They also stated that if one or a member of his/her family did not vote right, the teacher, either lost the job or was sent far away from home. The transportation was by foot, horseback, buggy and horse or for those more fortunate, an automobile. The sufferings of these poor souls will never be realized. Politics was a way of living and if the teacher gambled on the wrong candidate, the punishment was forthcoming and needless to say, their salary was, either reduced or paid to the big guys running the party or they had to leave the country and get a job elsewhere. Their favorite punishment place was La Armenta which was the farthest school the Mora people could be sent.

Mrs. Phillip N. Sanchez (Emma Strong) was the Superintendent from 1935 to 1936.

There were four school bus routes namely, Evaristo Trujillo who was paid $40, Juan D. Herrera $35, Alejandro Arellano $141, J.V. Wengert $75, Albert Zimmerman $75, and Daniel Medina $50.

The pay for teachers was for first grade teachers $90, and $70 for teachers holding an elementary certificate, the school day was from 9:00 A.M. to 4:00 P.M. and in 1935 school started first week of September. Dr. J.J. Johnson was the school doctor.

Father John B. Peris exchanged a certain tract of land so as to straighten the boundary line between the school and church properties.

The graduating class of 1936 included Stevan Zamora, Viola Alcon, Eugenio Abeyta, Matilde Abeyta, Alice Cassidy, Pat Romero, Leonore Maes, Leonore Valdez, Leonore Romero, Ricardo Pino, and Marie Chacon. The graduation dance was held at Sosa's Hall and at the old courthouse.

Mr. Benjamin Gandert was Superintendent from 1937 to 1938.

The school built in 1922 served until 1938 when a Pueblo Style building was erected South of the old Christian Brothers old campus and in church property. This school was built by the W.P.A., a program funded by the federal government.

Celia Martinez was the County Superintendent from 1939 to 1942. Sisters' Convent burned down in 1942 and again in 1946, both times, arson was suspected but there never was proof.

Mrs. Arturo J. Romero was County Superintendent from 1943 to 1946. This was during World War II.

Around the early 40 s, the coaches were John Cassidy, Ignacio Maestas and Flavio P. Vigil. It was Mr. Vigil who took the Mora High School Basketball team to compete at Santa Fe. Needless to say they were defeated royally. The team was named "Mavericks" by Sister Marie. The place where the team practiced was the court room in the old stone courthouse which had all broken windows and the floor was something else not to say anything about the size. The ball would go out the window and it took whoever went for it about five minutes or more to climb the stairs and fetch the ball.

The first Maverick team consisted of: Right forward and Captain, Louis Silva, left forward, Narciso Fuentes, center, Ruben Borrego, right guard Orcelio Medina and left guard, Manuel Alcon. Other members on the team included Frank C. Trambley, Richard Branch, Andres Pacheco, Ernest E. Martinez and others.

At this time the war (World War II) was going full blast and the school used to sell savings stamps for Uncle Sam. The high school was the Pueblo Style Building at El Ranchito. Woodwork shop was by the Church and the Convent. Wood work teacher was Mr. Frank Martinez.

El Moreno, the school paper was the High School's paper with the following persons in their following positions: Editor—Patsy Sanchez, Assistant Editors, Margarite Balland, Tillie Sanchez, Gilbert Maes, Catalina Romo, Manuel Alcon, Ernesto Martinez, and Pauline Maes. Circulation Alfonso Lucero, Luis Lucero, Josephine Maestas and Margaret Trujillo.

Alfonso Medina from Wagon Mound was superintendent from 1947 to 1948.

The building built by the W.P.A in 1938, burned down in 1948, and school was held in different buildings until 1949 when the new school was opened.

Benjamin Gandert came back to serve as County Superintendent in 1949 and served up to 1950 when the present site of the Mora Schools was purchased and the new buildings were erected.

In 1951 Canuto Melendez was elected Mora County School Superintendent and he served up to 1954 when he chose to go to Pecos to assume the duties of Superintendent of Schools there. Flavio P. Vigil completed Canuto's term. He served for six months.

In 1951 The Sisters of Loretto were barred from teaching at the Public Schools. They could teach if they removed their habits (uniforms). They chose to keep their habits.

In 1954, the first public school gym was built. Later on additions were made. A swimming pool was also built. A hanger for the school buses and storage was also built.

The 1954 election was as rough as any. Religion was the main issue. Party politics took a different step. Parties as had been the issue before took a back seat. Col. Salman was elected to school board and took control of the schools.

Leonore M. Valdez served from 1955 to 1956 as the Superintendent of this district.

Closed campus for High School was tried but failed miserably. A big change on administration staff and some school personnel took place. Mr. Louis Martinez was Principal.

Amadeo Aragon was elected County School Superintendent in 1957 and served up to 1960 less six months where Mrs. Luz Gandert served while the decision was made . Mr. Aragon tried to change the County System into an Independent School District.

In 1958, Mora County System District 1, 8, and 27 were consolidated into District 1. The Mora County Schools System changed to Mora Independent Schools. In 1959 The Independent District changed back to Mora County Schools by court order.

Manuel B. Alcon won the 1960 election and served as County School Superintendent for one day in 1961 after which the school system became the Mora Independent Schools and so he was appointed as Superintendent of the Mora Independent School District. He served until July 1965 when he resigned.

Politics had been a part of the school system and this person thought that it was possible to do away with it but history proved differently, he was badly mistaken. At first, he tried to convince the teachers how important they were to the schools, but they had been so brainwashed that they were second class citizens that they wanted to be driven and told what to do. The politicians would ask for donations to bear expenses for the coming elections or at least that is what they said.

In the 1960 elections, people were tired of fights and they believed that if the Independent School System would take over, the problems would be over. This was the main reason M.B. won. When he took over, there were no machines or records to go on. Mrs Luz Gandert took them home and refused to accept her loss. MBA spent many days with his assistant Levi Madrid at Santa Fe, relying on their records.

Later, the Parochial School closed and this had a big impact on the public schools. The superintendent had to rent the Parochial School Building to accommodate all the students.

The loss of the Parochial School was a great loss to the community because it also lost the Sisters of Loretto . The Hippie movement showed its face around this time and life for the children changed. Obedience to parents and older folks was at a minimum and some of their (Hippie's) ideas were adopted by the students and others. An example at hand is the smoking of marijuana, which later led to hard drugs.

Up to this time, students went to school to learn. (It must be stressed that not all the students fit this pattern) The laws were starting to change to the very liberal side. Corporal Punishment was being pushed out of the picture. With out punishment went respect for self as well as for others. Parents or teachers and others could not even talk to their children in a voice which may hurt the child. They were liable to be sued as abusing the child. Here, the child began to tell the teachers when he was not comfortable and social promotion was the name of the game.

Regardless of these changes, many students graduated and made good citizens the community became proud of.

1961 graduating class consisted of the following students: Josephine Trujillo, Ruth Gonzales, Ruby Coca, Casimiro Paiz, Felix Garcia, Ralph Chavez, Sophie Trujillo, George Montoya, Mary Lovato, Margie Martinez, Cordy Fernandez, Esther Chacon, Eddie Martinez, Noe Lovato, Tony Maes, Sammy Aragon, Idine Fresquez, Wilfred Sandoval, Oscar Cordova, Alfredo Martinez, Bennie Romero, Edmond Salazar, Roque Maes, Mary Frances Medina, Rita M. Chacon, Dixie Medina, Margarito Cordova, Max Gutierrez, Manuel Lujan, and Moises Maestas.

The Board members selected by the superintendent, were Mr. Frank L. Trambley, Mr. Feliciano Herrera, Mrs. Julia Espinoza, Mrs. Agustin Pacheco and Mr. Marcelino Torres. They were all elected the following election. Nieves Gallegos was Maintenance Head Man. Later, Jose V. Casados took over.

The list of people living in District 1 of the Mora Independent Schools as the 1964 school census showed were: *Abeyta* – Max, Alcon– Bernabe, Clyde, Eddie, Jerry, Joseph, Levi, Lupe, Manuel B., Robert R. Ronnie, Alice, April, Debra, Diane, Eloisa, Genevieve, Gloria, Grace, Judy, Idine, Jan, Margaret, Rosaura M., and Sandra. Aragon–Amadeo and Donicia, Archuleta–Steve and Frances. Arguello–Marcella, Lorraine and Ernestina. Ashe–Arthur, Patrick and Eliza. Barela– Lazaro, Benjie, Genevieve and Lillian. Barrette–Jackie, and Jamie, Blea–Manuel and Laura, Berg– Bert, John, John Paul, Kenneth Wayne, Michael, Robert, Catherine, Joann, Sandra J., Velma, Viola and Virginia. Biddle–Bobby, Borrego–Stevan, Branch– Alex, Eloy, James, Jerry, Joe, Michael, Ralph, Richard, Angela, Clorinda, Fedencia, Grace, Isabel, Mary, Ninfa, Rosalia, Bustos– Georgetta, Lorraine, Mary, Patsy, Rita and Susie. Casados– Jose, Nestor, Remie, Tomas, Anabel, Cleotilde, Crucita, and Rita, Chavez– Abran, Denis, Elmer, Frank, Phillip, Roger, Theodore, Edna, Emma, Ernestine, Jean, Phyllis, and Stella. Cordova– Eddie, Dan, Gregorio, Martin, Magdalena, Marcella, Paula, Rosie, Sebelia and Sofia, Cruz– Crecencio, DeHerrera–Felipe, Fermin, George, James, Joseph, Richard, Robert, Adelina, Eloisa, Enestine, And Theresa. Dominguez– Filadelfio, Paul, Amadita, Celia and Sandra, Duran– Manuel, Anastacia and Elenor, Eagle–Roy and Velma. Espinoza–Dan, Daniel, Gerard, Keven, Randolph, Roger, Bercy, Josephine, Lupita, Placida, Vallerie, and Vera Mae, Florence–Joe, Gallegos– Pablito, Trivinio, Trivinio Jr., Lucille, Pauline and Pauline. Gandert– Andrew, Benjamin, Ronnie, William, Donilia, Isabel, Lolita, and Mary Ida. Garcia–Gerard, Lazaro, Mike, Mike, Pat, Dolores, Jennie, Lala, Rosalia, and Theresa, Gardunio– Michael, Antonina, Pauline, and Prescilla, Gauna– Edward, Fidel, Joseph Luke, Donnie, Hazel, Jeannie, Patsy and Shirley, Gonzales– Gerome, Herman, Juan, Larry Onesimo B., Adelia, Anna Marie, Josefita, Marcella, Maria, Mary Alice, Mary Angela, Pauline, Rosana and Vicky. Guillen, Andrew, Gurule–Perfecto, Reynaldo Cruz, and Conferina, Gutierrez–David, Elias, Ernest, Filemon, Lee, Max, Diana, Doris, Jane, and Stella. Hanosh– John and Rose, Herrera–Eddie, Elaine and Vangie, Jaramillo–Reuben and Lily, Leyba– Herman, Loyd, Irish, Lucille, Mabel and Margaret,

Lopez- Dan, Eddie, Eddie Lee, Elizario, Lorenzo, Sam, Eufemia, and Margaret. Lucero-Candelario, Esequiel, Juan, Anna, Marcelina, Jane, Julia, Sarah, and Vera. Lujan- Alfredo and Emilia. Madrid-Jake, Levi and Laura. Maes- Arturo, Juan, Leandro, Adela, Eloisa and Virginia. Maestas- Damacio, David, Donaciano, Flavio, Ignacio, Jose, Jose, Leroy, Lorenzo, Moises, Paul, Valentine, Adela, Amalia, Angela, Charlotte, Clorinda, Emma, Ida, Irene, Mary Lou, Merline, Sarah, Seferina and Virginia. Manchego, Lenor and Corina. Mares-Agustine, Eddie, Jerry, Jessie, Leroy, Pete, Pete, Ruben, Magdalena, Mary, Seferina, Veronica, and Virginia. Martinez-Agustine, Albert, Albino, Alejandro, Alfred, Alfredo Jr., Aloy, Anthony, Apolonio, Arturo, Ben, Bennie, Bobby, Dan Donald, Eddie, Edward Andres, Ernest, Ernest E. , Ernest F., Facundo, Fares, Fares Jr., Felipe Frank, Frank, Gilbert, Guillermo, Guillermo Jr., Johnny, Julian, Leroy, Luis, Margarito, Marvin, Michael, Nano, Nick, Nick Jr., Oliver, Pablo, Paul, Paul, Patrocinio, Rafael, Ralph E., Roy, Roy, Steve, Ted, Tommy, Alice, Anita, Antonia, Beatrice, Catherine, Diana, Dolores, Doris, Elena, Elenore, Escolastica, Frances, Francisquita, Georgia, Geraldine, Gloria, Jean, Jennie, Jennie, Josefita, Juanita, Julia, Lorraine, Lucia, Lucy Ann, Maclovia, Martha, Margie, Maria, Mary, Matilda, Nepa L., Nora, Onofre, Orcelia, Pearl Ann, Querinita, Ramona, Reyes, Ruth Ann, Teodorita, Vangie, Virginia, Medina-Alfredo, Bences, Jose, Michael, Patrick, Adelina, Amalia, Carla, Joan, Louise, Pablita, Pearl, Melendez-Frank, Frank Jr., Joseph, Phillip, Arcelia, Connie, Louise and Ursula. Mondragon-Johnny, Mora-Juan, Manuel, Margarito and Dorothea, Montoya-Agapito, Anthony, Donald Lee, Ernesto, John F., Joseph, Alice, Barbara, Emily Jane and Gloria, Muniz-Arcenio, Carlos, David, Fred, Johnny, Rudy, Samuel, Dorothy, Eulalia, Eutimia, Josephine, Juanita, Sandra, and Susan. Olivas-Freddie, Robert, Gloria and Maggie, Olguin-Florencio, Juan, Pablo, Victorino, Anita, Clorinda, Dora, Elena and Emily, Ortega-Gilbert, Magdalena and Armida. Pacheco-Damian, Jose Lino, Jose L., Marcelino, Paul, Anne, Cathy, Consuelo, Erma Jean, Jane, Nina, and Valentina. Padilla-Andy J., Frank, Frank L., Joe, John L., Ronald, Cecilia, Dulcinea, Elizabeth, Judy Ann, Mary Jane, Noyola and Theresa. Pando-Felix, Louie, Norman, and Rosaura. Pino-Antonio, Jose, Teodosio and Perfecta. Rimbert- Leo and Mela, Rodarte-Joe, Catherine, Deluvina and Louise. Romero- Andrew, Arthur, Arturo, Celestino, Dan, Edmond, Elmer, Eli, Esequiel, Ernesto, Fred, Jerry, Johnn, Julian, Leo, Martin, Leroy Lorenzo, Manuel, Nick, Orlando, Patrick, Pete, Robert, Roberto, Rocke, Samuel, William, Consuelo, Dolores, Dora, Doris, Drucilla, Edith, Flora, Florence, Joan, Julia, Letitia, Libradita, Lucia, Manuelita, Mary, Mary, Sylvia, Virginia. Romo-Alvin, Antonio M., Dennis, Manuel, Manuel, Trivinio, Carla,Carmela, Emenencia, Frutosa, Marie and Teresina. Roybal-Orlando and Dolores. Rudolph-Dick, Diane, Doris, Dorothy, Isabel, Madeline. Salgado-Juan, Juan, Samuel, and Adelina, Sanchez-Charles, David, Gregory, Louie, Marino, Phillip, Phillip C.U., Phillip N., Albina, Emma, Evangeline, Laura, Louella, Marcella, Patricia, and Phyllis. Sandoval-Anthony, Elfido, George, George, Juan, Leroy, Levi, Lorenzo, Robert, Robert, Bernice, Bidilia, Cristella, Edwina, Elerine, Felicitas, Frances, Jesusita, Manuelita, Mary Alice, Patsy, and Pearl. Serna-Adolfo, Albert, Baby, Belarmino, Ernesto, Ernest, Roy, Arabena, Bernardita, Ginnie, Irene, Louise, Rita, and Rosita. Serrano-Josephine, Silva-Victor, Victoriano, Bertha, Leonore, Lupita and Prescilla. Spray-William, Irma T., and Kathy Jean, Sullivan-David, George, George, Anne, Mrs. John, Mary Theresa, Nicolma, Rosalee Ann, and Sharon, Tafoya-Dan and Adelina, Torres-Leroy, Rosendo, and Feloniz, Trambley-Alvin, Clarence,

Dennis, Frank C., Frank L., Frank Leon, Joseph, Praxedes, Alice, Josephine, Josephine, Rose Marie and Steffanie. Trammel-Clyde. Trujillo-Cipriano. Eddie. Emilio. Ernest. Frank. Jerry, Melaquias, Michael, Richard, Tony, Camila, Cathy. Mrs. Cipriano, Consuelo, Darline, Emilia, Emma, Geraldine, Jane, Julia, Liza, Lucia, Lucita, Refufio, Rose, and Susan. Valdez-Andrew, Max, Max Jr., Monica, Patricia, and Rosabel. Van-Sicklen, Juliette, Margaret and Patricia, Vasquez-Albino, and Seledonio. Velasquez-David, Florencio, Florencio Jr., Peter, Dora, Martha, and Mary Lou. Vigil-Arturo, Benito, Benjie, Dante, Eddie, Epifanio, Frank, Freddie, Gilbert, Jake, Jake Jr., Juan, Lloyd, Tony, Wilfred, Dora, Edna, Elaine, Ernestine, Lillian, Mary Alice, Patricia, Ruby, Susie and Stella. Weber, Frank, Jimmy, Joe, Manuel, Emily, Esperanza, Lupe, Mercy, Wood-Florence, and Jennie.

In 1965 Cirilio Maestas was appointed as the superintendent and served until 1967.

Board members during this administration were: Mrs. Fermin Pacheco, Samuel Olivas, Antonio Martinez, Marcelino Torres and Mr. Frank. L. Trambley.

Bus drivers for the year 1966-1967 were Severo Aragon, Mrs. Mauricio Duran, Dan Espinoza, Lee LeDoux, Andres J. Maes, Jose Maria Pacheco, Celia Montoya, Martin Sandoval, Rafael Montoya, Rowland Valdez, Livorio A. Vigil, Alicia Casias, Samuel Martinez, Manuel Vigil, Mrs. Tony Cisneros, John L. Vigil, Viola Sanchez, Samuel E. Maestas, Jose Samuel Martinez, Willie Chavez, Gilbert Ortega, Alfonso Alcon, Delfinio Torres, Manuel Garcia, and Rubel Medina. The feeder route drivers were Esther Gonzales, Benito Grine, Max Vigil, Florentino Fresquez, Melaquias Padilla and Julia Romero.

Personnel for the term 1966-1967 were Mora High School, Louis Martinez, Principal, Fred McClure, *Doroteo Vigil, Robert Bradshaw, Pat Romero, Horace Reid, Evangeline A. Sanchez, Consuelo Montano, Eufracio Vigil, Matias Maestas, Jr., Ignacio Maestas and Carlos Salazar. Mora Junior High School- Elias Hurtado, Principal, Luis Lucero, Max Valdez, Gene Hanosh, Amadeo Aragon, Angelina Archuleta, and Ernesto Herrera. Mora Grade School-Trinidad Lopez, Principal, Mrs. Gilbert Ortega, Mrs. Matias Martinez, Mrs. Leo Rimbert, Mrs. Manuel Velasquez, Miss Feloniz Sandoval, Mrs. Fernandita Valdez, Mrs. Tila Maes, Arturo Romero, Arturo Martinez, Mrs. Simon Lopez, Mrs. Ruben Jaramillo, Flavio Vigil. Holman Consolidated School-Nick Martinez, Principal, Virginia Chacon, Martha Romero, Secundino Aragon, Elaisa Berg, Mrs. Joe C. Trujillo, David Madrid, Mrs. Harry Nolan, and Mayo Armijo. Ocate School-Willie Lucero, Principal, Sofia Romero, Jose A. Lopez, Amalia Maes, Cora Morris, and Estella Aragon. Rainsville School-Horacio Martinez, Head Teacher and Ida Vigil. Guadalupita School-Manuel B. Alcon, Head Teacher, Juan Bernal and Mary Walk. Co-ordinator- Supervisor- Ofene Garcia. Doroteo Vigil, basketball coach, Died that year. He was the first coach of the Mora High School Basketball team to win the Basketball first state tournament trophy.

Flavio P. Vigil was appointed superintendent in 1967 and served until 1971.

Jim West was sent to take over the schools from the State department in 1971 and he stayed there until 1972.

Ernest Abreau and his assistant Margarito were appointed in 1972 and remained there until 1981 which at that time was a record of tenure in that office.

In 1981 Eufracio Vigil was appointed to the superintendents position. Around this time the High School was moved from the main building in the campus to a school building that was built as a grade school building which was South of the other buildings.

Horacio B. Martinez was appointed school superintendent in 1983 and served until 1988.

In 1962 and 1964 terms, two superintendents occupied that position, the first was Levi Madrid who ran just in case the Independent School system would resume the Mora County Schools. The other was Horacio T. Martinez. There were no schools under their jurisdiction and the salary was $1 a year.

School year 1984-85, Horacio B. Martinez was superintendent, Ruben Cordova was Assistant Superintendent, Manuel B. Alcon was High School Principal and Leonard Aragon was Elementary School Principal, Patricia Vigil was Cafeteria Manager, Lucille Alcon was Business Manager and Elauterio Trujillo (El Polia) was Plant Supervisor.

For the 1985-86 school year, the following certified personnel were hired: Dorothy Aragon, Ella Arellano, Felonis Armijo, Rosalita Benavidez, Joseph Branch, Michael Branch, Roger Chavez, Consuelo Cruz, Richard DeHerrera, Lucille Duran, Anthony Esquibel, Maria Esquibel, Ruth Fort, David Griego, Rita Griego, Nick Hernandez, Elias Hurtado, Quirinita Martinez, Samuel Martinez, Barbara Medina, Patricia Medina, Patricia G. Medina, Cecilia Montoya, Christine Montoya, Harold Nolan, Doris Olivas, Myrtelina Rael, Roma Rivera, Arthur S. Romero, Arturo Romero, Joyce Romo, Anita Roybal, Eloy Roybal, Mary Lou Sanchez, Sara Hurtado, Belinda Laumbach, Greg Laumbach, Louis Lucero, Joan Maestas, Albert Martinez, Bernardo Martinez, Faustin Martinez, Lila Martinez, Phyllis Martinez, Matt Sandoval, Tammy Sproule, Consuelo Trujillo, Fabiola Trujillo, Florence Trujillo, Leroy Trujillo, Douglas Velarde, Charles, Rebecca and Robert Vigil. Two teachers who taught the year before, Orlando Arellano and Rosalie Regensberg were not hired at the time but promised to be hired pending vacancies in areas of their certification. Albert Martinez was the Athletic Director.

Board members were Jacob Regensberg, Juan Felix Archuleta, Samuel Olivas, Lazaro Garcia and Jose B. Sanchez.

Different programs available were Chapter I, Migrant, Headstart, Cafeteria, Ski, Upward Bound, Title VII and others. These programs and their appropriations made a big difference in the progress of the schools. $340,000 was appropriated to change the Annex Building into an Early Childhood Education Complex. In 1984, Automatic Bells were installed at the High School and the Elementary School by Daniel Espinoza Jr. and the school grounds were paved.

Leonard Aragon was appointed Independent School Superintendent in 1988 and he served until 1992.

Leroy Huero Sanchez, was appointed to the Superintendency. He served until 1995 when the board tried to oust him and had been replaced by Leonard Aragon who served for a few weeks when the board was ordered to reinstate Leroy Huero Sanchez.

The election of 1994 as many of the previous elections, was as uncivilized as can be. Tim Maestas and Felix Archuleta were elected board members and that changed the formation of the old board when Gino Maes, and Paul Garcia were ousted. Johnny Romero, Johnny Martinez and Benjie Trujillo remained. Johnny Romero was the outsider in the previous board. Together with Tim and Felix, he took over and tried to oust the incumbent Superintendent. They named Leonard Aragon as his successor but the department of State Education had other plans and Huero remained.

The old school building known as the Annex, built during Mr. Amadeo Aragon's tenure had burned down the previous year. Some dissatisfied students had lit a match to it. It was a total loss. Jerry Martinez was given the contract to remove the debris and to build another building in its place.

Enrollment 1950-51 was 1430.34. 1960-81 was 1,063.35. St. Gertrudes High School had 400 students enrolled.

In 1912 there were 61 school districts with some having more than one school houses.

Wood stoves were the only heating systems up to the late 1950 s when Pendelton Oil Company from Springer and Roy, New Mexico (Nivenes Flowers and Johnnie Montoya were the gas men.) came to the valley with propane gas and their stoves. Later Fermin Pacheco distributed propane under the Fermin Pacheco Oil and Gas Company.

In 1944 there were 64 teachers, 10 principals, 18 Bus drivers and 7 janitors. 1945 there were 66 teachers, 10 principals, 17 bus drivers and 7 janitors.

The names of people mentioned here are also a record in case of any one doubting their true positions and their being in the system.

MORA COUNTY SCHOOLS
SUPERINTENDENTS

1908-1909 Rafael Romero	1937-1938 Benjamin Gandert
1910-1911 Blas Sanchez	1939-1942 Mrs. Celia Ryan
1912-1916 Manuel Madrid	1943-1946 Mrs. A.J. Romero
1917-1919 Milnor Rudolph	1947-1948 Alfonso Medina
1919-1920 Alfred Lucero	1949-1950 Benjamin Gandert
1921- Grace Ogden	1951-1954 Canuto Melendez
1922-1923 Juan A. Pacheco	1954 Flavio P. Vigil
1924-1925 Cosme Garcia	1955-1956 Leonore Valdez
1925-1929 Antonia A. Sanchez	1957-1960 Amadeo Aragon
1930-1932 Levi Madrid	1960 Luz Gandert
1933-1934 Matias Zamora	1961 Manuel B. Alcon
1935-1936 Mrs. Phillip N. Sanchez	

MORA INDEPENDENT SCHOOLS
SUPERINTENDENTS

1961-1965 Manuel B. Alcon	1988-1992 Leonard A. Aragon
1965-1968 Cirillo D. Maestas	1992-1995 Leroy Huero Sanchez
1968-1970 Flavio P. Vigil	1995 Leonard A. Aragon
1970-1971 James B. West	1995 Leroy Huero Sanchez
1971-1979 Ernest B. Abreau	1996-1998 Leonard A. Aragon
1979-1982 Eufracio F. Vigil	1998-2002 Arthur Romero
1982-1988 Horacio B. Martinez	2002- Ruben Cordova PHD.

1961 was the year the Mora County School System gave way to the Mora Independent Schools and the term started July 1 of every year.

Levi Madrid was elected County School Superintendent in 1962 and Horacio T. Martinez was elected County School Superintendent in 1964 at the salary of $1 per year since there were no schools in that jurisdiction.

An interesting observation is that in 1917 there were 60 schools in the system. There were 4,791 scholars attending these schools. District #1 had 305, #2-212, #3-161, #4-120, #5-118, #6-80, #7-85, #8-46, #9-167,#10-70,#11-113, #12-239, #13-31, #14-55, #15-139, #16-73, #17-59, #18-55, #19-67, #20-176, #21-81, #22-80, #23-75, #24-74, #25-75, #26-60, #27-46, #28-88, #29-71, #30-68, #31-63, #32-55, #33-263, #34-40, #35-41, #36-no school, #37-44, #38-54, #39-57, #40-33, #41-36, #42-84, #43-35, #44-50, #45-29, #46-40, #47-41, #48-35, #49-38, #50-26, #51-56, #52-34, #53-117, #54-82, #55-28, #56-27, #57-43, #58-101, #59-73, #60-37, #61-40.

	High School Students	Grade School Students
1933	68	2,271
1934	134	2,517
1935	68	2,468
1936	94	2,520
1937	102	2,465
1938	91	2,455
1939	134	2,517
1943	117	2,055
1944	147	1,956
1945	130	1,863
1946	163	1,835
1947	178	1,612
1948	191	1,665
1949	200	1,616
1950	208	1,594
1951	235	1,406
1952	181	1,266
1953	203	1,140
1955	194	1,042
1956	185	1,116
1957	217	976.17
1958	177.3	927.17
1959	175	916
1960	195	901

ARTISTS, ARTISANS , BUSINESS ENTREPRENEURS ETC.
OF THE MORA VALLEY IN THE 1900 S

In the early days, by necessity, people had to depend upon themselves to survive. They made a living as farmers, ranchers, hunters, gatherers or artificers.

Some became artists, others artisans and still others artificers. Hunters and gatherers took less knowledge but quite a bit of practice and strength.

By the time the white man came to the Mora valley, there were hunters because of the many species of animals available and they had the guns to make hunting easier. The Indians were good at this since that was their main occupation as was gathering berries and plants.

The first humans who passed by the valley were the Indians, then came the trappers of different nationalities. Up to the early 1800's, those who passed through this valley were sojourners. In the early 1800's people settled here and built their homes. There were different nationalities such as French, Italian, English, Spanish and Indian. The majority were of Hispanic decent.

After 1846, the Anglos declared New Mexico part of the United States and so the culture took a change. Fences were invented and politics came to being. Before this time the only learned man was the priest and the church was where people got together and that was not too often. They worked all day from sun up to sun down. There were no known child labor laws, no child abuse, no jails or court houses. The men took the law into their own hands. A cattle rustler or horse thief paid his fine by hanging on the nearest tree.

Among the first business men were: T. Walton who ran a hotel, Roy and Co. ran a merchandise store and operated a sawmill, L. Chine had a sawmill, Combs and Bostwick ran a flour mill, H.H. Green a saloon, I.S. Holman dealt in livestock, Louis Kohn was the town butcher. B. Lowenstein had a general mercantile store, C. Menger operated a drug store, Ollendorf brothers were peddlers, B.M St. Vrain and Watrous had a general mercantile store and later a sawmill, Vanderwirth and May also had a general mercantile store. After becoming a United States Territory, the people became American citizens so it was that customs changed. A necessity for lawmen, judges, lawyers and jails as well as court houses came to be.

With all this politics came needs for sheriff, clerk, treasurer, and other officers. Politics brought people together at the court house. By now, the state was divided into counties then the counties to districts and precincts.

Meanwhile, the children had to attend school and learn how to read, write, and add. Before this time, the parents or guardians were responsible for the children's learning which was minimal. They were taught by proverbs and sayings. Later they learned to read and write by studying their catechism. The boys learned to work hard and the girls learned the arts of the kitchen and the home. Now they had to learn to figure accounts and count their animals and crops if they did not want to get ripped off by artificers. Maybe I am using this word carelessly but these were believed to be magicians and they took advantage of the poor who were very superstitious and believed in magic.

The older folks, as good American citizens, had to go vote during election time. New learning took place. They had to learn to vote, count votes and report. They also learned how to cheat and bribe so as to win the office they wish to control.

The schools became public and so there was a need for teachers to teach in the school districts, most of them were one room schools. A need for board members, superintendent, principals and janitors was created. A need for offices also arose.

Now that there were so many jobs created, money was more available and more needs came into being. Wood was needed to warm the school rooms and water needed to be made available as were the needs to satisfy the time that mother nature called so outhouses had to be built and wells had to be dug.

Money became the name of the game for that is what our type of democracy (Capitalism) stands for. A need for banks came to being so in the early 1900's. The Mora Bank and Trust was established at what used to be the J.M. Sanchez's residence and warehouse. Steve Sanchez was a teller in this bank. In the 1990's The Bank of Las Vegas started the Bank of Las Vegas branch at Mora. Josephine Vigil and Wanda Casados were the tellers and managers of this bank. It was situated at the old John Hanosh building, (the site of the old Butler Hotel which was razed by John Hanosh in 1948 to make place for his store). Here, Hanosh built his grocery store, rooms for rent and a theater.

Now that money was easily acquired, many people decided to get on the easy street. Being creative by nature or by experience, they took different routes to make money. The depression of the 1920's also had to do with what took place after. The government started some projects to help those who no longer depended on their lands to make a living. World War II was in progress.

Education was the answer the government came up and so it came to be that some ways to help were to start different programs. They would be run by the local school board.

Various crafts were considered. Weaving, because there were many sheep in the valley and the need for clothing, blankets and other uses for wool, was selected as one of the projects. To get a qualified and knowledgeable person to teach this course was a problem for some time but someone came out with a name of a person. The board hired this person, a beautiful girl by the name of Agnes Vigil from the Espanola Valley. She fell in love with the valley as well as with a young entrepreneur by the name of Joe A. Martinez and married him. She still resides in the valley.

Woodwork was the next craft selected since there was an abundance of wood, and the need for furniture. For this position, the job of searching for a good and learned man in this craft was not hard for in the community lived an already practicing carpenter with tools, shop and ready to teach his specialty. Mr. Frank Martinez, a very serious and disciplined person was hired. He was my woodwork teacher at the highschool and I knew him well. He used to call me "El

Hermano Javian" His favorite motto was "Un lugar para cada cosa y cada cosa en su lugar". He lived by this motto.

(One place for each thing and each thing in its place.) Many students learned the trade and practiced it. His two sons, Frank Jr. and Ernest E. make the most beautiful furniture and knick knacks.

Another craft that would benefit the community and material was very available was the craft of leather work and tanning of hides. At this time, there were three slaughter houses as well as most of the farmers slaughter their own animals. Mr. Peter Balland, Mr. Jose Martinez and Mr. Frank Trambley had custom slaughter houses. The need for leather belts, horse quarts, whips, leather jackets, some furniture was reinforced with leather or raw hide. Some stools and chairs were fixed with leather seats. To get a well qualified and disciplined teacher the board of education did not have to go far for in their midst was a tanner by the name of Benjamin Alcon.

To complete the programs, the board came with the idea that music is international and enjoyed by all so they set out to hire a music teacher. For this position, the board hired a Mr. Hernandez. I don't remember him very well but I do remember he was my sister's piano instructor. He, not only taught at the high school, but also to any student whose parents had an instrument at home.

These people contributed much to the Mora children. Besides the classes at school, the government came with the idea of a CCC camp where the older boys were taught and worked in landscaping and forest watch. The WPA was another project that the government invented. This was for older men. They built Court houses, outhouses, dug draining ditches and kept the valley clean.

A couple by the surname of White came to the village and started a movie house. They rented a house which was known as the Sosa's building. This building held the second drug store owned by Frank O. Meza some years later. This building no longer exists. It was situated east of Tio's bar. Later on, the movie franchise was acquired by Pat Trujillo and he and Melaquias Trujillo, moved it to a warehouse which was situated west of where the post office was, now, the parish hall. This was the site of Peter Balland's old warehouse.

Mike Montoya came to town and bought the movie franchise. By this time, the theater was situated at the Hanosh theater. Mike had a misunderstanding with the Hanosh and moved the movies to the St. Gertrudes Catholic school gym. This building burned down later. Soon after this move, the theaters had lost favor and people were not attending them to make a profit. The movie theater at Mora came to an end.

There was an artist, Frank L. Cantu who had moved to Cleveland. He was the best known artists in the valley. He had painted a portrait of Jesus in the St. Gertrude's Church. Later a priest had it painted over and then in the early 60's the church burned down.

Today's better known artist is Fred Olivas, who is very modest and doesn't crave recognition. He is a Vietnam veteran who is naturally talented. He had done many pieces of art for many people.

Other very talented artists: Rose Valdez, Sylvia Ortega, Rose Polaco, and Eligio Lujan.

Woodcarvers, furniture makers or remodeling and other wood workers: Frank Martinez Sr., Benjamin Alcon, Allan Nyss, Joey Casados, Robert Sandoval, Frank Martinez Jr. Manuel B. Alcon among others.

Ceramics and pottery makers: Mr. and Mrs. Tito Naranjo, Iona Fresquez, Genevieve H. Alcon, Alice Alcon among others.

Carpenters: Frank Martinez, Robert Sandoval, Leonard, Anthony and Victor Casados, Florentino Velasquez Sr., Florentino Velasquez Jr., Thomas Velasquez, Horacio T. Martinez, Noel Preston, Eli Romero, Thomas Martinez among others.

Plumbers: Ernest Montoya, Ron Alcon, Harold Nolan, Loren, Amos and Frank Romero among others.

Electricians: Matt Martinez, Ernest Montoya, Danny Espinoza among others.

Judges: Rafael Romero Y Valdez, Vicente Romero, Frank L. Cantu, Celestino Garcia, Rudy Montoya, Frank Martinez, Levi Alcon, Matias Zamora Jr. who also was a District Judge, and Dan Sosa, who was a State Supreme Court judge.

Priests who claim Mora as their hometown: Lupito Fuentes, Tito Melendez, Walter Cassidy, Phillip Cassidy, and the best known of them all was Fr. Angelico Chavez who was a well known author.

Doctors: Dr. Hoeg, Dr. Crane, Dr. Johnston who was brought to Mora by Phillip N. Sanchez, Dr. Husted, Dr. Vansickle among others.

Building contractors: Rumaldo Lujan, Andy Cordova, Anthony, Joey and Leonard Casados, Benjie Regensberg and his brother Travis Regensberg among others.

Saw mill owners and operators and loggers: Boney Gandert, Onesimo B. Gonzales, Antonio Herrera, Claudio Herrera, Feleciano Herrera, Phillip (Babo) Sanchez, Tito Melendez Sr. Andres Quintana, Gilbert Ortega, Ernest Lujan, Elias Hurtado Jr., Ernest Trujillo among others.

Propane Gas distributors: Fermin, Jacob, Paul, and Fermin Jr. Pacheco (Pacheco's Gas and Oil) Luke Gauna, Fidel Gauna, Nivens, John Montoya (Pendleton Gas Co) Arthur Martinez, Brian Pacheco, (Martinez Gas Co) and Earl Chavez (Ferrell Gas Co).

Drug store Pharmacists: Mr. Silva, Frank O. Meza. Garage owners and Mechanics: Lupe Trambley, Melaquias Trujillo, Peter Baca Sr., Willie Chavez, Levi Madrid, Joe Gallegos, Paul Berg, Edd Herrera, William and Ronnie Gandert, David Bonney, Amado Valdez, Andy Quintana, John Berg, Nestor and Nicholas Casados, Levi Madrid among others.

Service Station owners and/or operators: Joe A. Martinez, Alex Martinez, Nick Martinez, Alfredo Roybal, Orlando Roybal, Max Pacheco, Joseph Pacheco, Fermin Pacheco, Arnold Waxman, Pete Trambley, Phillip N. Sanchez, Levi Madrid, and Pedro Fernandez and Manuel B. Alcon.

Grocery store owners and/or operators: James Cassidy, Peter Balland, Benjamin Gandert, Celso Romero, Pete Trambley, Morris Back and Company, J.M. Sanchez and Sons, Florentino Sanchez, Steve Sanchez, Levi Madrid, Pete Trambley

Jr.. Lupe Fuentes. Mike Montoya. Clara Maes. Narciso and Rumaldo Fuentes. Antonio Herrera and O.B. Gonzales among others.

Butchers: Ernesto E. Martinez. Manuel Romo Jr.. Peter Balland and Thomas Martinez among others.

Bar owners and/or operators; Milnor Rudolph. Abran Chavez. Tommy Casados (El Tio). Esequiel Lucero. Manuel Padilla Jr.. Francisca Salas. Mr. Bruno. Paul Netzloff. Aurora Netzloff. Stevan and Frances Archuleta. Leo Rimbert. Joe and Luz Gandert. Dan and Adelina Tafoya and Candelario Lucero among others.

Restaurant . Cafe owners or operators: Mr. and Mrs. Kupp. Isabel Martinez. Ida Mora. Eugenio (Hatchas) Martinez. Theresa Marie and Gilbert Cruz. Mollie Segura. Emelina Martinez. David Rael among others.

Confectioneries: Roy Eagle. Paul and Consuelo Montano. Manuel and Genevieve Alcon owned and operated the Eagle confectionery at one time or another. Richard Branch and Grace owned and operated the Branch confectionery.

Clothing Store owner. Mary M. Pacheco. J.M. Sanchez and Sons. Morris Back and Company. Romero's Mercantile.

Gift Shop owners: The Gifthorse shop owned by Mr. and Mrs. Raymond Brown. La Casita Giftshop owned and operated by Mr. and Mrs. Manuel B. Alcon and the very first giftshop in Mora owned by Pablo C. De Baca.

Pool Halls: Rudolphs run by Don Quintana. Toms run by Eligio Lujan and also Gertrudes pool hall.

Post Masters and workers: Cosme Garcia. Phillip N. Sanchez. Rosalia Branch. Richard Branch. Albertito Romero. Trivinio Romo. Evangeline Maestas. May Olivas. Olivama Gutierrez Stella Olivas. among others.

Laundry or Laundromats: Mr. and Mrs. Anselmo Sedillo. run by Grandpa Garcia. and Doline Pando's Laundromat.

Dairy Mart: Mr. and Mrs. Anselmo Sedillo.

Hotel or Motels: Roubuello's. Walton's. Butler's Hotel. This one being one and the same but at different eras. By 1948. Mr. John Hanosh bought it and razed it. In its place. he built a big two story building which housed a grocery store. a theater. and some rooms. The Khan's Hotel owned by Julia Strong Khan. Katy Almanzar's Motel. Campgrounds owned by Mr. Ben Gandert. Campgrounds owned by Mr. Juan Casados and Pepe's campground.

Roller Skating Rinks: Tommy Casados. Esequiel Lucero.

Dance Halls: Trambley's. Tommy's. and Joe E. Gandert.

Farmers: Feleciano Herrera. Max Vigil and many others.

When Agnes Vigil later Mrs. Jose A. Martinez was weaving instructor. she taught the following courses: Two harness weaving. Diagonal Weaving. Rose path weaving. Herring bone weaving. Diamond weaving Monks Belt weaving Double width weaving and Double face weaving. Her class included the following in Group I: Adelia Rodriguez. Adelia Alarid. Erlinda Archuleta. Carmen Campos. Celia Chavez. Cres Espinoza. Elena Espinoza. Lupita Espinoza. Flora Garcia. Nestora Olivas. Alberta Romero. Lore Sandoval. Sofia Sisneros. Alice Valdez. Corina Valdez. Frances Valdez. Felonis Sisneros & Valentina Romero.

POLITICS IN MORA COUNTY

First recollections about politics in the County were in the early 1930 s when my Dad moved to Mora to take up the job as the Assistant School Superintendent. Mr. Matias Zamora who had won the 1932 election and the board had named my Dad, Benjamin Alcon to be his assistant. That year I became six years of age.

My recollections about the election are that the fights between the Democrats and Republicans were vicious. The leaders in either party acted as hostile to the leaders of the opposition. As I recall, the Democrat leaders were Barney Cruz, Benjamin Gandert, and Alfonso Sandoval .

On the Republican side were Milnor Rudolph, Eusebio Arellano, Arturo Romero, Vicente Romero ,and the Sanchez Brothers–Phillip N., Florentino and Steve.

In town, they acted as the worst enemies but as I learned much later, when they were in Santa Fe, or Albuquerque together, they were the best of friends. The followers were the suckers and the ones that suffered.

The teachers, there being no tenure or any other type of protection, had to do much brown nosing and shoe polishing. The game was to be on the winning side because if you were in the losing side you were out of a job. If one thought one could fool these masters one had another guess coming because the election officers were there to check that each one voted right. That is – what was right for the kingpin.

The ballots were made so that there was the number of the ballot on the top right corner that had to be torn and kept by the voter but there was another folded and blacked out corner in which appeared the same number. This number was the same number in the registration form so there was only the problem of checking the blacked out number by the masters and checked against the registration number before the ballots were burned. Secret ballot was secret for the sucker voter who believed that the evidence was in his hand as a torn piece of ballot with a number.

If the teacher voted one way and the spouse the other, chances were that if one were a woman teacher and she was favored by one of the masters, she would not have to travel too far to teach. If one were a man teacher and he voted for the winner while his wife voted for the loser, then it was La Armenta or any far removed school where he would have to move to teach in the boondocks but at least he had a job.

Fear was wide spread and fear, they must fear. Once you were placed in a position to teach you were still expected to trade for your groceries etc. in the Master's store. If one didn't and sometimes if one did, his or her checks could be held for two, three and even up to six months. The excuse being that the treasurer had not collected the money to pay those teachers they wanted to punish.

As we all know, the name of the game is money and you can go just so long without it. The teachers were no exception and after, two months they needed money. The masters were so nice that they would lend you the money or shall we say extended you credit until your check came through. But the catch was that the amount of one check was given to you and when you paid back you owed two checks. How does that grab you? You work two months for one month's salary. The scale of payments was anywhere between $40 and $65 a month. That depended on what year and what party we are speaking of.

Sisters of Loretto were teaching in the public school and were highly respected yet they also had to wait. The checks were held until the masters had gotten their share which they thought they had coming and then they would announce that their checks were ready.

The Board of Education was named by the county commissioners. The District Judge, the State School Superintendent. Each entity named one member a piece. The board members and the School Superintendent who served as secretary and was elected by the people completed the board.

These officers were not too concerned most of the time with the wishes of the people but the Party's interest.

The injustices done to the poor teachers were many and to attempt to name them, is a waste of time since nothing could be done about it. Politicians were in cahoots with the state officers.

You may be wondering where I received my information. The old teachers who went through this and were still teaching in 1952 used to tell me these stories. To name a few, Facundo Martinez, Josefita Baca among others and some that are still alive but to save them their dignity I shall not divulge their names.

To be a politician and last in there, you had to be supple, unsophisticated, two-faced and hard shelled and of course smarter that the average citizen so that you could steer clear from accusations on you and be able to blame the others for the bad decisions.

Fear of these people still exists to a lesser degree. I figure what I have written may be published long after I am gone and the only thing that they will be able to do is spit on my grave.

Paper ballots were the way that people voted at that time up to around 1970 when machines came to be used. I mentioned one way that an election was controlled. There were many ways that elections could change results and I will attempt to give you examples of what I learned while I was into politics.

I must make it clear that in either party, there were not very honest people and of course, the name of that game was to win at any cost with any trick worth trying being tried.

Once an election officer who among other schemers were bringing the ballot boxes from a certain precinct and it was around midnight, stopped by a junction where they met an individual who had been sent by one of the masters to pay all of them well, to change the results from that precinct because they were afraid they were way behind in votes. This person told me that around midnight they stopped and by the light of a farol (lantern), they took out the legal ballots and buried them where now there is a cemetery. As some of the members in that group dug a hole to bury the ballots, the others got busy and voted all over again. Those ballots were later challenged but it was too late for the right winner had lost almost a year.

Another trick, and I witnessed this in 1960 election, a person known to me, in the opposite party, was one of the judges during the counting of the ballots. I noticed that he was moving his right index finger and I wondered what was up. I noticed that the person who had filled the ballot had left empty spaces after the county senator's space and when it was announced, the space of the opposite candidate was filled. I waited for another ballot to pass by his hands and he started to do the same in another race. I slapped his hand and he made a long mark on the ballot. He had a piece of lead under his fingernail. I told him that if I caught him doing that again I would report him. The other officers calmed me down and told me I should watch my step for this was part of the game. Fear is bad company. That was the last ballot he marked that night. Needless to say, his candidate won.

That same election, soon as the polls closed, I called the Wagon Mound contingency to ask them how many votes had been in my favor. The officer said I had won by 91 votes. by the time the results got in, I had won with 21 in that precinct. What happened to the other 70 votes, I have an idea but there was no proof. Fortunately for me, they did not take enough votes to defeat me. I won with fourteen votes.

Another trick used by these smart people was the table where the ballots were marked were placed in a conspicuous place by a window where one of the master's puppets was paid to watch. These watchers could lie and make trouble for anyone. There were other tricks that were used, some so ridiculous that I am ashamed to even think about them.

No favors were bestowed by the masters on any miserable persons who had voted the wrong way. They went out of their way to punish them.

The master on the losing side would not bother to try to protect the sucker. He was on his own and by himself, he had to pay. The punishment was severe. This I know for back in 1954, I stuck my head out and did my civic duty out in the open and my candidate lost. I was kicked out of the school system and my friend stayed on the job. Later on the Board members defended me and I returned.

Voters were paid to vote as the master ordered and since Mora has never been affluent, people were willing to take whatever was offered. The more votes in the family, the greater amount was paid.

There were other tricks to that trade. Some of them down-right outrageous such as fist or knife fights.

Too many people were so naive that they believed the elections were honest and were satisfied with the results. The smarter ones just kept quiet and glad to survive.

During the 1960 election, I expected my friends and fellow teachers to vote for me, but even the County Chairman of my party was working hard to get me in the short end of the election. He went around telling people to vote for his Prima. He had more "Primos" than Carter had little Liver Pills however that did not sway them to vote his way. People had enough of politics. I ran under the promise to change the County Schools system into an Independent one. I did full fill this promise and so became the first successful superintendent of the system. Before, Mr. Amadeo Aragon had tried to change the system but was unsuccessful and had antagonized the politicians because they saw that they would lose prestige and power.

Most of the teachers voted against me for fear of losing their jobs. A fear that was real. I won by 14 votes. I was naive enough to let myself run for the position to better the school system. I believe that after my administration, which lasted until 1965, when I resigned, did affect many changes for the better. The politicians found other ways to survive and control the system. It became and independent school district during my tenure. I tried to practice what I had learned in college. The philosophy was that the school was for the benefit of the students and that the teachers were the second most important factor of the schools. I tried to make them comfortable but the fear that was instilled in them in the past years was too deeply engraved in their minds and they did not trust me. I decided that I was wasting my time and went back to being one of the sheep.

I retired in 1985 and am now a free agent. I doubt, I will ever go into politics again. My conscience would not allow me to try to cheat the people and the county. I am not saying that everyone who runs for an office becomes a crook. Fortunately, there are good honest people serving in the offices. It seems that if a person has been in a position for more than two years, that person is tempted at one time or another to do a dishonest thing or a favor for a less discretionary friend.

Democracy is a good type of government if it would work the way our forefathers intended it would, but they never figured that many people are smart enough or can stand on their two feet instead of depending on others for handouts or believe any unscrupulous persons who run for office.

It grieves me to see an honest person being elected and once in office, their personality changes completely.

Maybe our upbringing is to blame. Since everything can be interpreted to be ambiguous. Many people take a word in their meaning instead of in context. Take the quote "God helps him who helps himself", so many if not few help themselves to what does not belong to them.

As a young boy, I learned from the penitentes about forgiveness. A schoolmate of mine, undoubtedly a son or relative of a penitente, recited the following verse, "Penitente pecador por que te andas chiquotiando?" "Porque me robe una vaca y ahora la hando disquitando". (Sinner, why are you slashing yourself? Because I stole a cow and now I am redeeming it).

What I interpret out of this is that after flaying ones back once a year, the records are cleared of wrong doings and is ready to go out and do his thing. The coming year would forgive him for what he is about to do. Stealing is a matter of borrowing without the consent of the owner, without intentions to returning the thing.

Is it right to hate if you hate the right person or to screw your buddy before he does it to you. It is not ethically right but too many believe it is the only way to go.

In politics, life was of most importance. He that won was rewarded no matter what trick, or method he used even if the votes were recounted until he won. The important thing was to win. Many ballots cast by good citizens never were counted and since most people were honorable and had much faith, they believed everyone else was like them. The leaders had a different philosophy. They believed that God helps him who helps himself. Boy did they help themselves. Many unscrupulous people would stoop so low as long as the price was right or there was prestige in it.

These leaders had divided the people into two groups and played one against the other. These groups may be labeled as sadists and masochists. Sadists like to see and make people suffer. Masochists enjoy being made martyrs.

Teachers were afraid and that fear was so instilled in them that many died of old age with that fear still there. When I tried to show them, I wanted to free them from that fear, they would not or could not believe me. Yet there was a change for the better when they saw me stand up to these leaders. I know that many were applauding me yet they could not do it publicly because they knew what would happen to them. It took guts to try to do this or maybe it was just a fool who would dare.

When, in 1955, my career was supposed to have been ruined but not being very smart, I went on to get my MA degree and I came back for more punishment. I taught two years in Las Vegas and when I came back, I still thought I could change the way of thinking of these people but how wrong I was!

For over four years I tried to push politics out of the school system, not knowing or realizing that politics is our government.

There exist many infractions and injustices in our schools today but I am to believe that those things are part of the picture just as my nose is part of my face.

I have known the board of education advertise for building a fence (after it had been completed by a stout backer of the board members).

It is impossible for the one who has no backing while the one who does, there is nothing impossible.

Back in 1984, as principal of the High School, I was earning the same salary the grade school principal was. I had over 200 credit college hours more than the elementary principal and also had over fifteen years of experience more, and the superintendent would not treat me any different. I could probably have taken the board to court and won because the superintendent sent me a letter letting me know that I couldn't get the extra salary. I was asking for. The meeting he stated that the board had refused my request never happened or at least the minutes were never reflected in any meeting. The Chairman had signed the letter but I doubt that he ever knew of it. I did ask one member and he said that it never happened.

MORA COUNTY COURT HOUSE

BUILT 1889   MORA. NEW MEXICO

GAMBLING IN MORA

Humans, by nature, have always gambled whether by choice or by fate. It may be safe to state that the Indians who were here first were the first gamblers. Not the way we mean it today but they gambled their lives in finding game and berries in the valley. The first gambling that was reported was in the 1800 s. People used this type of entertainment since there were no such things as movies, television, V.C.R.s , bars, or another way to entertain themselves except when they got together in church or any other gathering place.

Much later when these people got more sophisticated, they would have horse racing, cock fights and much later card games were introduced. This was when bars and houses of ill repute came to the scene in greater numbers.

By the 1920 s, people were gambling to the point where the family suffered and laws were passed to abolish all gambling. This method has not worked for gambling keeps on. At first there were some arrests and some fines but there were more gamblers than those that wanted to enforce the laws. How many lost their lives doing that duty is not recorded nor reported except by word of mouth so many of these "facts" cannot be substantiated.

There was a bar called "El Tunnel" which was situated in what used to be the first old court house. Many are the people who came to gamble here. Later on it got so bad that these gamblers had to go underground. Underground is an understatement because they literally dug basements in their houses for this particular past time.

During fiesta time, there were horse racing, la pelea de gallo,(cock fights) and other games of chance that took place.

Some were caught but gambling continued. Even people from as far as Penasco made frequent visits to play cards in the village. The most frequent players, to mention two were Maximilliano Roybal and Manuel Casados from Rio Lucio. This information was given by Toni Atencio, who was Maximiliano's daughter. She claimed that they took home, their winnings quite often. Maximiliano died at the age of 84 in 1984 but others continued to come to gamble.

Many were the players from the village. Among the earliest ones was Dona Theresa who lived across the river and every morning she would wait until the bar tenders at "El Tunnel" would open for business. Weather meant little to her for she was like clock work. Came rain or shine, She was there daily. If there were cock fights, she would be the first to place her bet.

Every year for the Santiago-Santana Fiestas held on or around July 25 and 26, there would be the pelea de gallos. This was a game where horsemen would bury a live rooster, the legs protruding from the ground and they would ride past where the rooster was. Riders would bend down and whoever was supple enough to pull the rooster out while riding full speed holding himself by one hand from his saddle, would ride as fast as the horse could carry him. At first, the successful rider had a certain point to reach to be safe and to keep the roosters. Later, the rules were changed or were not followed and who ever had the rooster had to defend himself when the others tried to take it away from him. Sometimes it was a gory picture. The rooster's blood as well as human blood covered rider, horse and saddle. By the time the game was over, all the rider had left was the rooster's legs and maybe a torn shirt and a hat full of blood.

Bets on rider or horse were made. The winners of these bets had a hard time checking who won.

Horse racing was the most important sport where bets would be placed. Almost every Sunday there would be horse racing and, of course, betting.

Gambling was very serious business. There were many poor losers who saw to it that, that was the last time the winner would win. There were many poor losers who lost for the last time, too.

These villagers did not like to be in the looser's side and found a reason to justify their loss. Many were the ones who resorted to cheating. Once caught, cheating they usually ended with a bullet in their guts or swinging at the end of a rope.

Law and order were present and some times they were the biggest bettors.

During the early days, bartering was the way to do business because money was hard to come by. Because of lack of money, houses, horses, cattle or anything of value were used as collateral for their bets.

In the 1940's there was much gambling in town. It was usual for bets to go up to a thousand dollars and more. After this, the gamblers were more secretive about their games. Their hiding places became harder to find. Some went as far as Santa Rosa and Las Vegas to satisfy their need for gambling. To the present, gambling continues but at a much lower key for the fine is nothing to laugh at.

To mention a few persons who were heavy bettors, I will name them for most of them were nice to me: Alfredo Roybal, Lee Fidel, Nappy Sanchez, Frank Trambley, Agapito Montoya, Tomas (Tio) Casados, Steve Archuleta Sr., Juan Mora, and William Duran. The majority of this individuals are now dead.

The building to the left is the first court house which was abandoned in 1889. Later it housed the bar called "El Tunnel". It was the scene where much gambling took place. It was probably the first gambling gathering place.

ELECTRICITY IN THE VALLEY

In 1913, a contract was given to J.J. Fuss to construct and install electric-light works that would serve the most dense settled part of the county extending three miles on either side of the road in Mora.

Very few could afford the light which was about the only use for electricity at this time. Those who could afford kerosene and kerosene lamps used them while others had to do with candles or fireplaces for their night lights. Most of the people were sedulous and they went to bed right after dark and got up at sunrise hence, they had little use for lights. (This explains why most families were large. Just think, no T.V. a few radios which few owned and no other entertainment).

Two Las Vegas men ran the plant for some time. They sold to Fred and Ron Robinsons. A fellow who married one of Fred's daughters bought the plant. He later sold the plant to Seferino Lopez and a Mr. Williams from Taos. During this time, the big wheel on that plant broke and for some times there were no lights.

The power to run the generators was a big wheel run by the Agua Negra River and the Rio De La Casa River where they met below Cleveland to form the Mora River.

When water was low, a kerosine engine was used so that there would be no interruption of electricity.

The plant was later sold around 1934 to John Karavas from Taos. Mr. Karavas ran the plant until he sold it to the present R.E.A. in the late 1940 s. During Mr. Karavas ownership of the plant, Evaristo Trujillo was hired as the manager and Manuel B. Alcon as his lineman. Both had to take care of running the plant and line. Manuel's pay was the use of the electricity used at his home which at this time he had four lights each of 40 watts bulbs.

Wiring a house was an easy job since it took two wires and only for lights because there were no heaters, refrigerators, freezers, or televisions. Some had radios but batteries run them.

The ones that needed electricity for power were connected from a plug plugged into one of the light sockets.

Many times trees grew tall and shorted the electricity. One time these two industrious workers used bailing wire to connect a wire that had shorted out by some trees at Mr. Paul Netzloff's yard. The reason was that the copper wiring was scarce and at the time it was not readily available and they had to wait until the next shipment. Besides, their homes were the ones affected by the shortage.

The bulbs used were slightly brighter than a kerosene lamps and for sure than candles used .

The plant was at the bottom of a mountain on the North side of the Highway from Las Vegas to Taos. This place became known as La Cordillera. This plant was next to the flour mill owned by Daniel Cassidy. When Mr. Karavas bought it in the 1930s, he moved the plant to more or less the present site. It was a gym built by Mr. Albert Valdez who had built it to be used by the public school since there was no gym then.

In the 1940 s. the building became a warehouse because the R.E.A. organized and was buying the power instead of making it. It became known as the Mora-San Miguel Electirc Cooperative.

This is a photo of Joseph J. Fuss who owned and operated the mill at Cleveland, N. M. Mill later became the Cassidy Mill. He also set up electric power system at Mora. He was born August 1852 at Lansdale, PA. He died June 25, 1933 and was buried at Mora, New Mexico.

THE HISTORY OF THE TELEPHONE IN THE VALLEY

In 1914, the County Commission contracted with local businessmen to install six miles of telephone lines in and around the village.

It is not clear where or if the telephone lines were situated in Mora. What is clear is that a Mr. Fred Viles, who was a ranger situated at Holman, bought the telephone and worked out of Holman. Holman was known as the Agua Negra (Black Water) so the telephone entity was known as the Agua Negra Telephone and went by that name even after a line was connected to the main line from Las Vegas.

According to Mr. Levi Madrid, who was the last owner of that franchise, Mr. Viles stretched one wire to Penasco by himself (financially) with the help of some men who also helped him stretch another wire (One instead of two) to Mora.

At that time, there was only one telephone in Mora which was located at the Kahn Hotel. These were two wires that came to Mora from Las Vegas.

The Kahn sisters would receive the calls at the hotel and from there they would send a messenger to the surrounding hamlets.

Later, Mrs. Martina C. De Baca (who married Steven Sanchez later) was the operator. The office for the telephone had been moved to the Sanchez warehouse on the North side of the street. This is across the street where the Morris Back and Company as well as across the street from the J.M. Sanchez Mercantile Store.

Margaret Strong, later, became the operator. She had her office where the old C.U. Strong and Trambley Meat Market used to be. (Now the Lounge stands in this site). Margaret was Mr. Uleck Strong's daughter and was niece to the Kahn's sisters. Julia was the name of one of the Kahn's sisters which this author knew well.

Margaret moved to Santa Fe and her sister, Josephine, took the operators job. (Josephine was Mrs. Emma Sanchez and Margaret's sister. She was married to Frank Leon Trambley. Mr. Trambley was Mr. C.U.Strong's son in law and also his partner in the Strong and Trambley's Market).

Around 1950, Levi Madrid bought the telephone franchise (still known as the Agua Negra Telephone) Levi's wife, Laura and he were the operators and owners. Mr. Phillip N. Sanchez and a group of men from the R.E.A. in Washington offered to buy the franchise from Levi. A time was set to make the purchase. The time expired and since the family believed that nothing would come of this deal, Jacob Alcon, Levi's son-in-law had the idea of modernizing the Agua Negra Telephone Company by disposing of all the crank telephones and installing the dial telephone. He offered to buy the franchise and Levi, after weighing the situation, sold to Jacob. Jacob asked Mrs. Madrid if she would consider working for him, at least until he would set up the new phones. She said she would work with him for the time being.

Meanwhile, the people from the R.E.A came back to deal but Levi told them he had sold to Jacob. Jacob was willing to sell but at his price. The deal was made and the Agua Negra Telephone became the La Jicarita Rural Telephone Company.

The present Cooperative was headed by Mr. Phillip N. Sanchez for many years. At this writing, Mr. Benjie Vigil is manager.(1998).

The Levi Madrid Family

LEVI MADRID AND HIS WIFE LAURA WERE THE OWNERS OF THE AGUA NEGRA TELEPHONE COMPANY FOR SOME YEARS.

HE SOLD TO HIS SON IN LAW-JACOB ALCON WHO IN TURN SOLD IT TO THE LA JICARITA TELEPHONE COMPANY.

WHEN LEVI BOUGHT THE COMPANY IT WAS THE AGUA NEGRA TELEPHONE COMPANY AND HE KEPT THAT NAME.

HIS WIFE, AND DAUGHTER- PETRITA WERE THE OPERATORS UNTIL THE LA JICARITA COMPANY TOOK OVER.

HEATING THE HOMES IN ST. GERTRUDE'S VALLEY

Up to the 1950s, the only fuel to heat homes, public buildings or to heat branding irons to brand cattle, was wood.

By the time the village was settled in the early 1800 s, the forests were dense with pine, pinon and juniper trees. There were willow and other trees growing along the river which passed through the valley.

People used to climb the mountains in their burros and load them up with branches and easier wood to carry. There were no chain saws or gas tools to prepare the wood for their fireplaces except the ax and hand saws which came later. Some entrepreneurs would bring their loaded burros to town and traded their wood for corn, wheat, oat brand or whatever they needed.

As they became wiser, they brought wagons and horses so that they could carry more wood. By the 1920 s, the mechanized wagons came to the valley. Some tractors with iron wheels were making their appearance. Steam engines were making progress in making lumber and so more people became carpenters and furniture makers.

As more settlers joined the villagers, the forests were being depleted and by 1948, propane became the fuel of the future.

When wood became harder to get and expensive, it was necessary to find an alternate.

Meadow Gas from Las Vegas came in around that year (1948) and was slow in having people change their minds about using propane.

The Pendleton Gas and Propane Company from Roy and Springer came to Mora and before long the schools were changing their pot belly stoves for propane heaters.

By 1950, as more people got used to the easy life, the need for more propane was greater and became a necessity. Since the motor vehicles were plenty and affordable, carriers were easier to move and so it was that an entrepreneur with plenty of foresight got the idea that this was a good money making proposition. He bought a truck and transport and competed with Pendleton. His business succeeded and grew fast. This person was a local boy by the name of Fermin Pacheco Sr.

He made a business that when his three sons took over, the business was divided into three parts. Each son took his company to different parts of the state. One went to Las Vegas (Fermin Jr)
Jacob stayed in Mora and surrounding towns. The youngest (Paul) went to Penasco where he made his business grow and so he sold and retired at an early age. The other two kept on with their business and did very well. Fermin Jr. retired a few years later.

Jacob kept his business up to the present.

The Martinez Gas Company from Las Vegas came in and set an office in the valley. There were other companies, one from Texas and one from Raton who also came to do business in the village.

Up to the early 1990 s, people were getting their wood which was still used to heat many houses, from the National Forests. Wood was getting scarce and some people started fixing their homes with solar windows and plumbing and also there were others that used electric heaters or stoves.

Sometimes wood was hauled in pack burros.
Later on when wagons were used, men could carry logs not only for fire wood but for lumber.

MORA WATER AND SEWER

Mora was ideal for settlement when the first settlers came because of the abundance of water.

The valley had been a lake and there were many springs plus the river to accommodate that need.

One of the biggest problems at that time was the sewer. The only toilets available were what Mother Nature provided. As time passed, the outhouse was invented. What that first outhouse looked like is left to the reader's imagination. It probably was a hole on the ground with a shack built on top of it. What is known is that the well or spring was only a few feet from the house.

This situation created big problems which were magnified when the rainy season came.

The outhouses usually had two holes that accommodated two persons at a time. The holes were made to be comfortable however, by today's standards, the toilet remained very uncomfortable. One hole was smaller than the other. It was designed for the smaller persons.(with little butts).

Running out to the outhouse, specially in cold weather was a great inconvenience even to these people who were used to punishment. Some wiser person thought up an idea to save some suffering by inventing the pot or if the pot had already been invented, it was used as a convenience. The more affluent people had two or more. This created another job for some member of the family for each morning the pot had to be emptied. The children took turns at doing this job. The older children were ashamed to take turns and if no innocent, young kid was available or would not do the job at the request of the older siblings, they would get up earlier and perform this task in the darkness before dawn, as if the neighbors didn't have one!

To take care of their baths, a tub or a wooden half barrel would serve as a bath tub.

There was no running water except in the river or ditches so water had to be hauled from the nearest source, either wells, springs, ditches or the river. This created a big problem where the family was large and only bathed once a week. The water had to be heated in pans and so as many kids as possible were bathed in the same water. Usually the girls who were less dirty were the ones that got the water before their brother or brothers polluted it. By the time the water was passed on to the garden it was not clear by anyone's imagination. During warm weather and sometimes in not so warm weather, they would take a dip in the river.

Anyone who took a bath once a week (usually on Saturdays) was a clean soul.

Clothing was washed more often. To wash, the women would take few pieces of clothing they possessed and would meet by a ditch, spring, or river and scrubbed clothing on rocks.

Much later, when people became more sophisticated, scrub boards and tin tubs were used. People made their own soap from a combination of lye and rancid pig fat or lard. To wash their hair, they used the root of a cactus plant found locally.

Water got polluted only with human and animal excrement, or the dirt from their body. There were no chemicals so as to pollute.

Around the 1920 s, automobiles were made available in the village so gas stations begin to appear. Gas storage tanks were necessary to hold the gasoline. Gas tanks were buried underground and because of the formation of the dirt, the tanks rotted.

By 1949, the fathers of the valley saw a need to start a water association which they called "Mora Mutual Domestic Consumers Association"

On July 29, 1949, the Water Association articles of incorporation were filed at the County Court House. Alfredo Roybal was the county clerk. The board members named in this document are Phillip N. Sanchez, President, Fermin Pacheco, Vice President, Amadeo Aragon Secretary – Treasurer, Pete L. Trambley and Leo Rimbert members.

Levi Madrid billed and collected the monthly dues. Others who joined, to mention some, were Matias Martinez, Peter Balland, Eusebio Arellano, John Arnold, William Lujan, Frank L. Trambley, Florentino Sanchez, Isabel B. Sanchez, Waldo Trujillo, Pete Trambley Jr., Morris Back and Company, Mora Independent Oil Company (Joe A. Mrtinez), P.C.U. Sanchez, Margarito Maes, Anselmo Sedillo, Pete Baca, Tomas Gonzales, Mrs. Moises Valdez, Max Martinez, John Hanosh, Francisquita Martinez, Carlos Lucero, Milnor A. Rudolph, Juan Pacheco, Tomas A. Casados, Ernest F. Martinez and James Leger.

The board members had to sign a note to borrow money. Each signed a note for $500. Later on what was not paid by the Association, each member had to pay $134 on the note. The bank that loaned the money was the First National Bank in Las Vegas.

A well had to be dug. A place to dig it was bought. This was a piece of land belonging to the Catholic Church at China town.

To store the water, a deal was made with the Santa Fe Railroad. They furnished a big, long, black tank if the association would pay the transportation to Mora. This was a deal offered to the association and they could not refuse .

Levi Madrid mailed out the monthly bills at his own expense and was supposed to get paid $25 a month for collecting and billing. He did get paid for some months then the board decided that all the money collected had to be paid for transporting the tank so it was that Levi had to wait for his money. Meanwhile the pump gave out and the members went out collecting donations to fix it. P.C.U. Sanchez was in charge of setting the new pump. Levi never received his salary.

Collecting was a tedious job. Many subscribers failed to pay and around the 1970 s, a new board took over. Pete Trambley President, William Gandert,

Vice president, Willie Romero, Leo Rimbert, Michael Branch made up this new board.

In 1962, a group of people decided that a sewer system was badly needed.

There was opposition by a group of people. Progress has sacrifices and these persons were not willing to pay and besides they were not asked to be involved. Reasons given were that outhouses had served well for their parents and grandparents and what was good for pappy was good for them. Another reason was that to build an addition to the house would be hard for the poor people in the community. This was something they could not afford.

Facing a cold winter in an outhouse was not a very pleasant experience and these men had a long and miserable experience with these houses although the W.P.A had tried to improve the house during the 1930 s but it still was not heated and many were the colds caught in this place. Another factor was that many people had a taste of a better life while serving in the military during W.W. II or working in California factories.

The trend was to build bigger and better houses. Up to the 1930 s, no matter how many persons in the family, the house consisted of three rooms, namely a kitchen, a bedroom and a parlor. There were some homes that had more rooms but this was the exception.

World War II service opened many eyes and people wanted the best. With a bigger house came more progress. A bath room was designated and so with the running water installed, the sinks, commode and bathtub was an easy changeover.

With all these improvements, these men insisted in a sewer system and so formed the Sewer Committee. Selected as the acting board were Amadeo J. Padilla, a local barber as President. Manuel B. Alcon, Superintendent of the Mora Independent School System —Secretary Treasurer. Joe A. Martinez owner of the Independent Oil Company, Reverend Carpenter the local Presbyterian Minister and Pete Baca a mechanic and auto parts store owner.

Other subscribers were Benjamin Alcon, Amadeo Aragon, Michael Branch, Cresencio Cruz. Mrs. Raymond Casados, O. B. Gonzales, William Gandert, Eddie Herrera, John Hanosh, Juan B. Maes, Matias Martinez, Arturo Martinez, Ernest Montoya, Levi Madrid, Mrs. Gilbert Ortega, Fermin Pacheco, Damian Pacheco, Mrs. Celso Romero, Mrs. Dolores Ostrander, Albert Romero, Philip N. Sanchez, Joseph P. Trambley, and Frank L.Trambley.

Reverend Carpenter and Amadeo Padilla were the go-fers and made more trips to Santa Fe seeking all kinds of help for the project.

With the help of Frank L. Trambley, Joe C. Trujillo, John Hanosh, Damian Pacheco and a few others money was borrowed for the project. The First National Bank was the only bank who took the chance of lending the money. The only requirement was that each member who signed the note would be responsible for his share of the loan. In essence, this loan was loaned as personal loans.

For a few years everything went well. Reverend Carpenter got transferred to Penasco so Damian Pacheco replaced him as board member. The thing was that there was supposed to be an annual election but only the board members and a few others attended.

Monthly fee was set at $1.50 per month with the understanding that the members would be reimbursed whenever the association made enough money and a profit was realized.

To acquire the lagoon and a site for it was a problem. Once the money was made available, Arthur R. Romero consented to sell the association a 4.05 acres of land East of town.

The sewer line was installed from Malco Station down to the lagoon–about a mile in length. Powers Construction Corp. did the work.

Joe Martinez, with his backhoe and Manuel B. Alcon with his pickup would clean the lagoons at their expense. They also took care of plugged lines and any other jobs that had to be done as far as maintaining the lines was concerned. By now the loan had been repaid.

Up to 1970, the association worked well until the State Engineer decided that it should merge with the water association. This was well and good but the way he went about it was not right. The by-laws stated clearly that it had to be by mutual consent. The sewer association wanted to collect enough money to pay its subscribers back what had been promised but this was not to happen. By 1971, The Sewer and water associations became one. The board members of the Water Association took over. These board members were William Gandert, Willie Romero, Leo Rimbert, Michael Branch and Pete Trambley Jr, who was the president of that association.

Soon after the merging took place the fee went up to $3.50 a month and soon after to $6.00 a month. An additional well and an office building was built.

In the late 1980 s. the water lines were renovated and meters were installed and the sewer line from Edd's Garage to the lagoon was replaced. The lagoon was modernized and the bill for electric power became a burden as did the pills that were required to purify the sewer water before it was diverted into the Mora River. The fee was raised to $9.81 a month. It needs to be noted that before all the modifications took place, the electrical bill was around $13.00 per month. After the modifications, the bill went over a thousand dollars a month. A secretary had to be hired to take care of the bookkeeping and a manager to take care of maintenance. Mr. Pete Trambley was hired as manager and Mrs. Amelia Romero as secretary.

Because of lack of funds, Mr. Trambley was sent to school since the duties were getting so complicated that only a chemist oriented person would be able to qualify for the duties of checking the water and other duties that needed to be done according to the state and federal requirements. It seemed that lately the Federal Environmental Improvement Division and the New Mexico Environmental Improvement Division imposed on all water and sewer associations for health and sanitary reasons, more and more requirements. (The order was given but no money came with it.)

The new board was composed of William Romero President, Michael Branch secretary-treasurer, Eugenio Martinez, Manuel B. Alcon and Michael Cassidy, members.

All improvements made did not cost the membership anything. The work was done with the help of Senator Carlos Cisneros who helped get money from the state.

The new water project from State General Appropriation fund helped with $1.2 million and the sewer project was done at a cost of $660,000. The board was working to see if additional sewer lines could be added.

By March 5, 1992, there were 67 members using the sewage lines. There were 197 members using the water system.

With the coming of the Fish Hatchery, the board anticipated more problems and more need for additional sewage lines and additional water lines.

The Highway department resurfaced the state road #518.

The board at this time was composed of Manuel B. Alcon, president, William Gandert, Arthur Romero, Charles Vigil and Michael Branch.

The first water pump house of the Mora Water Association.
It is no longer in use.

MORA VILLAGE ROADS

Up to 1909, with the help of the 1904 flood, the roads were the ruts the horse drawn wagons had made. The very first road was a route from Las Aguitas and passed through El Alto del Talco. The road to Mora from El Alto was a swampy one even during dry weather and up to the 1940 s it was a corduroy road in part. The men had cut small trees and had laid them side by side. The swamps and the corduroy road were still evident in the 1950 s. About this time, the county commissioners hired Mr. Frank Trambley to gravel it. A rock foundation was laid. The ditch had been lined in the 1930 s with rock by the W.P.A.

In 1909, the county commission's attorney asked Governor Curry if he could supply territorial monies to build a permanent road. The roads continued to be bad up to well into the twentieth century when the area's primary automobile roads were some of the last to be paved.

The improvement of roads in the 1930 s was better since gravel was spread and later on paved. The road was made wider and this took some work in knocking trees at the west side of town since there were big trees that gave the appearance of a tunnel. From where the present school entrance up to where the Allsups now stand, there were big, tall willow trees which were removed around 1937 when the road was widened.

There was a swamp where the old road from El Alto Del Talco and the present road met. Even horse-drawn wagons would get stuck here.

The road was improved by graveling it and up to early 1940 s it remained so.

It was in the 1940 s that the road was first paved. The road was narrow and winding. By now the horse and buggy days were in their last agony. When the road was paved it was filled about two or three feet higher. The Court House's grounds were higher and there was a small incline as was there on the other side of the road where the Sosa's Hall was and what is now the Judge's office At this time some automobiles did not have a very good starter and so all they had to do is park up the incline and push the jalopy so that it would start.

By the 1980's, the road was made wider although it still remained a two lane. It was surfaced and filled with three feet of dirt, sand and gravel then black topped. A few sidewalks were made and some curbing was done as well.

In the late '90 s the road was filled and resurfaced with black top. The county commissioners also paved the road that led to the Catholic Church.

The road that leads to LeDoux and to the Murphy Lake was also paved.

The road at Juarez or the other side of the river remains unpaved. The two Caminos Del Medio, starting at El Ranchito and going East up to El Camino Del Alto Del Talco and the other starting at El Camino Del Alto Del Talco and going East up to the lands of Maes family have not been used much and never kept up as they should.

The Roads leading to El Alto De Los Herreras or El Alto de los Indios as was known ages ago, also has not been paved. Up to the year 2000, this road remains unpaved.

The road to Las Aguitas was paved by funds from the state. Thanks to Senator Carlos Cisneros and the other neighboring congressmen and the Legislature who appropriated $ 100.000 for this project.

The Main street of Mora in different years. Left top picture taken in the early 1910's. Top right picture taken in the 1920's. Bottom picture taken in the 1990's. The site is the same but the changes are very obvious.

HISTORY OF THE MORA POST OFFICE

Mora became the county seat in 1860 when Mora county was carved out of Taos county. At this time, Mora town was known as Lo de Mora or Santa Gertrudes after the patron Saint of the Catholic Church.

Mora Post Office was established in 1864. Charles Zimmerman was the first postmaster according to the stories passed on to the present generation. Mail was received once a week at this time.

Levi Madrid recalls, the route from Las Vegas had been established by the early 1900 s.

Among the postmasters Levi remembered or had been told were a Mr. Green, a St. Vrain, A Nolan, A Mary Kahn, and about the time he was born in 1895, Palemon Ortiz was the postmaster. After him, that he remembers was Jesus Maria Sanchez who was Steven, Florentino, and Manuel Sanchez's father. Eugenio Romero was another postmaster as was Phillip N. Sanchez whose wife, Emma, was the one who ran the post office. He believes Cosme Garcia was the next postmaster.

By 1934 or '35, Rosalia Branch was the postmistress and her brother, Richard was her assistant. She served until the early 1960 s. Joe Trujillo took over and later Alberto Romero was the postmaster. Trivinio Romo was his assistant. In the late 70's, Evangeline Maestas took over. Up to 1999, she is the postmistress.

Some buildings that have been occupied as the post office building are: in the early 1930 s at the present site of the Steve Sanchez home. Later it was moved to a two story house where Rosalie Branch was postmistress, later a small building was built in front of the old post office. A new prefab building was later set in the old site of the Balland Merchandise store which was razed years before. This building is in front of the Catholic Church and across from the old Butler Hotel site.

In 1998, a new building was built at the present location. A much bigger building was built. Many customers were up in arms because of the move to the new building. Before, the post office was conveniently situated across the Bank of Las Vegas Branch in Mora. The bank was across the post office building in the old Hanosh building.

The left picture shows the post office building 1935. Rosalie Branch was post-mistress. In the 1950's it was moved to the smaller building to its right. Albertito Romero was postmaster. In the early 1990's a new building was built across the Hanosh building.(center picture). The new post office building at the right was built in 1998. Evangeline Maestas was postmistress.

ROLLER MILLS IN THE VALLEY

The Gordon Mill as it was known by the villagers, was brought from Chicago by train in 1906. The mill was than transported from Las Vegas, New Mexico to Mora by J.B. Maes, his brother Leopoldo Maes and Mr. Gordon via horses and carriages.

According to Mrs. J.B. Maes, her husband Juan B. Maes, related they had a hard time bringing the mill due to the rainy weather. It had been raining the week they transported the mill. Two carriages used to transport the mill kept getting stuck in the mud. The mill was a pre-fabricated one. All parts were boxed.

The mill took one week to be transported from Las Vegas to Mora.

It was set in the eastern part of Mora where it still stands. (1997). By mid 1906, the mill was in full swing.

Mr. Gordon operated the mill up until he got sick in 1924. He used to smoke cigars, he bought a small machine to cut tip of his cigars. It had a little hole and a blade. He checked it out by sticking his finger into the hole and it did work. He cut his finger. He used to advertise for a mail order wife. Many came but lasted maybe a week or two. He owned race horses. He probably lost the Grist mill in one of his bets. The mill would run 24 hours a day. St. Vrain's mill stopped for a time but Mr. Gordon kept on going.

He told Mrs. Laura Casados, a neighbor, that he supposed all Mexicans took their wheat to Gallegos who owned the St. Vrain's mill. He died in 1926. Mr. Avendo Pacheco took over and ran it until 1930. In the late 1930 s Antonio Trujillo, his sons and Mr. Pendaries, a skilled miller from Rociada, operated it until it was sold in the late 1931 s to Mr. Sanchez. All operations of the mill ceased soon afterwards.

A Mr. Daniels lived in the old mill house in exchange of care taking services. Mr. Daniels died in late 1959 or early 1960 and the building was abandoned.

He claimed England to be his birth country.

He never married. He visited Mrs. Onofre Quintana quite often but she had lost her husband in the late '20 s or early '30 s and wished to remain a widow for the rest of her life.

Steve Sanchez claimed the mill and property until his death in the late '80 s and his nephew, Justin Valdez was his heir.

The St. Vrain's early mill was a wooden structure that was operated by Jacob Beard from 1850 to 1852. A Mr. William Bransford took Mr. Beard's place. Both Beard and Bransford wanted a greater share of the profits so St. Vrain fired them. St. Vrain turned over the business to his son, Vicente and to Theodore Mignault. This mill burned down on July 29, 1864.

Around that year, St. Vrain asked Oliver Smith to build a stone mill. Local people referred to it as El Molino de Piedra. The stone mill is a two-story structure constructed of rough-hewn, random ashlar set in thick mortar. The roof is covered with corrugated metal and the gables are wood frame.

St Vrain died on October 28, 1870.

He left the mill to his sons, Vicente and Felix and his daughter Felicitas. Vicente's wife, Amelia, traded the mill to her brother William Rohman. Frank Trambley acquired it later and operated it from 1912 until 1925.

During the late 1920's, Mr. Manuel Romo Sr. used to run the mill. Much of the products that were sold were used by the people in and around Mora.

The building has withstood the elements but at present (1997), is in dire need of fixing.

Louis Branch got a government stipend to fix it in the 80's but he died and nothing was done.

The Cleveland Roller Mill is attributed to J.J. Fuss, a blond, bearded German who emigrated to New Mexico from Pennsylvania in the late 1870 s. Fuss worked for saw miller, David Allen. Joseph J. Fuss was born on August 15, 1855 in Montgomery County, Pennsylvania to Henry and Elizabeth (Johnson)Fuss.

In 1913, the mill was purchased from J.J. Fuss by Daniel J. Cassidy. Cassidy was born on October 11, 1852, in Donegal, Ireland to Daniel and Margaret (Halferty) Cassidy.

Daniel Sr. later sold the mill to his eldest son Daniel J. Cassidy II who continued to operate the mill with the help of his sons, Walter, Albert and Daniel J. Cassidy III until 1947. He died in 1950. One of the current owners of the mill is Daniel J. Cassidy V son of Daniel J. Cassidy IV.

Mr. Dan Cassidy ran the mill for many years and much of the flour, bran and animal feed were used by local people.

As of 2000 A.D., Dan Cassidy V is owner and runs the mill once a year during the millfest which is held during the Labor Day holiday. This is just to demonstrate how it worked.

Ceran St. Vrain partnered with the first American business XX Carson trade, fought at Taos... 1802-56. (Century 1861.)

ST. GERTRUDE'S CREDIT UNION

In the early summer of 1946, Father McCarthy visited Mora and suggested that a Credit Union would help Mora. The people in the community were ready for something like this.

There had been the Mora Trust Bank in the 1920 s but it had closed during the depression. This bank had been situated at the old J.M. Sanchez warehouse building next to the Pacheco Fashion Shop which is now the Pacheco Propane Company office building.

The only places to cash checks or to get change was at the mercantile stores such as Strong and Trambley, Hanosh, Morris Back and Co. or J.M. Sanchez and Sons or at the bars. The nearest banks were at Las Vegas, thirty miles away.

With the end of World War 11, the automobile became the important mode of transportation and a Mora Stage Line was running between Mora and Las Vegas, not to mention a truck-line and the mail truck. Some had bought their own automobiles. Transportation was no longer a problem. People were earning a salary.

With all these facilities and happenings, it became apparent that a Credit Union's time had come.

On July 15, 1946, a group of prominent men gathered to organize and to sign a certificate of organization as the first step to start a credit union. All of these men were devout Catholics. It was logical that the credit union be named after the parish Patron Saint-Saint Gertrudes. So they all agreed that this should be the name-Santa Gerturde's Credit Union.

The persons who signed this certificate of organization were: Reverend George Boenninghausen, the Parish Priest at Holman, Benjamin Alcon, a tanner and farmer from Mora, Reverend John B. Peris, the then, St. Gertrudes' Pastor, Rafael Trujillo, a teacher in the Mora County Schools, Ricardo Pino, an office worker at the County Court House, Dan J. Cassidy, a grist mill owner, and Manuel Romo Sr., a farmer and mill operator from El Alto de Los Herreras. Gonzalo Archuleta, a notary public witnessed the signatures and notarized the certificate.

On July 18, Woodlaw P. Sanders, the State Bank Examiner approved the certificate.

The next thing that had to be done was to get members to join and so they started issuing books and collecting the $5.00 dues or shares. The first twelve members signed up. $83.75 was collected that day. this amount and number of members were the foundation of this credit union. On August 11, the first meeting of the membership was held. Rafael Trujillo was elected as the first President of the Board of Directors, Dan J. Cassidy was elected the first Vice President, Benjamin Alcon, Secretary-Treasurer, Juan B. Peris, Ricardo Pino, Gonzalo Archuleta, Manuel Romo Sr. and Guadalupe Fuentes were the other elected Board Members.

By October 14. The Credit Committee had been elected and the following composed that committee: Gonzalo Archuleta, Eliza Quintanilla, a very outspoken woman and Ricardo Romo.

The Supervisory Board members were Reverend John B. Peris, Reverend George Boenninghausen and Desederio Gallegos (who, in this author's opinion was the Benjamin Franklin of the village. (He could do anything).

On the October 13 meeting, J.R. Chavez came as a Board of Director's member and during this meeting a limit of $300 per member was set. Interest on loans was set as 1% on monthly loans and 8% on term loans. The first loan application was approved by the Credit Committee and was made to Santiago Mondragon. Eleven new members signed up and were approved, among them Reverend George Boenninghausen Book # 24.

On March 2, 1947 Gonzalo Archuleta moved to California and his vacancy was filled by Jose Rafael Gonzales.

On April 7, two new members were approved—Louis Ortega and Benerita Alcon. The limit on shares was raised from $300 to $500. Annual meetings were held at St. Joseph's Hall.

In 1948, annual meeting was held at Joe E. Gandert's Hall at 1:00 P.M. The following were elected: Rafael Trujillo—President, Louis Fernandez—Vice President, Benjamin Alcon—Secretary-Treasurer, Albert Cassidy, Miguel Romo and J. Rosendo Romero members. Eight new members were approved.

On March 7, the 100th member—Tillie Trambley was approved.

May 2, 1948, Dan J. Cassidy was elected Vice President, Rafael Trujillo remained President , Benjamin Alcon, Secretary-Treasurer, Ernesto Martinez, Louis F. Fernandez, Miguel Romo, and Albert Cassidy members.

On January 16, 1949, Albert Cassidy was elected Treasurer. On November 6, Rosaura M. Alcon and Roman Valdez were elected to the Board of Directors. Father Walter Cassidy and Benjamin Alcon urged all members to attend all meetings. They explained the advantages of being a member.

By 1950, Rafael Trujillo was still President, Albert Cassidy Secretary-Treasurer, Miguel Romo, Rosaura M. Alcon members. A resolution by Benjamin Gandert that terms of office be staggered was approved.

On February 10, 1952, Jose Leonore Manchego was elected President Desederio Gallegos—Vice President, Albert Cassidy Secretary-Treasurer, Rosaura M. Alcon, Olmedo Trujillo and Rosana Gonzales, members. Interest percentage changed from 1% to 8% per year.

In 1953, Dan J. Cassidy was elected Treasurer. Loans came up to $8,612.80, Shares $8,903.58. There were 191 members by the end of 1952. A motion was made that all members save no less than $.50 a month and it was passed. In 1954, a treasurer's salary of $30 a month was approved. In their November meeting which was held in the now non -existing Court House, the membership discussed the issue of bringing industries to the County. Delinquencies were bad. A $5 collection fee was advised. Supervisory Committee was asked to meet at least once every three months.

In 1956, Manuel Tafoya was elected President, Eddie Herrera–Treasurer. The Credit Committee Jose A. Martinez, Manuel Romo Sr. and Fidel Valdez. Frank Trambley had resigned. Supervisory Committee members were Manuel B. Alcon, Dan Espinoza, and Alfred Trammell.

Loan balance was $5,056.78 and Shares $5,079.85. The Credit Committee members were Fidel Valdez, Jose Alcario Martinez and Eliza Quintanilla. Mrs. Quintanilla was the best member to work on the credit committee. She would have made any banker proud!

On October 1957, Eddie Herrera was elected President, Alfredo Medina, Vice President, Manuel Tafoya Treasurer, Trivinio Romo Secretary, Adelaido Valdez and Tiburcio Martinez, members. The same persons as the previous year composed the Credit Committee, and D.R. Gallegos, Manuel B. Alcon and Alfred Trammel were elected to the Supervisory committee.

In 1958, The same Board of Directors as well as the Credit Committee as last year, were elected. The Supervisory Committee were Desederio Gallegos, Manuel B. Alcon and Ernest E. Martinez. There were 181 active members by the end of that year.

In 1959, Credit Committee members were Fidel Valdez, Manuel Romo Sr. and Jose A. Martinez.

In 1965, Ernest Montoya was elected President, Manuel Tafoya, Treasurer, Lucas Valdez, Adelaido Valdez, Alicia Vigil, members. Supervisory Committee were Desederio Gallegos, Pete Trambley, Eloy Valdez. Credit Committee were Fidel Valdez, Manuel Romo Sr. and Juan B. Olguin.

In 1966, Ernest E. Martinez was elected President, Adelaido Valdez, Vice President, Manuel Tafoya, Treasurer, Eufracio Vigil, Carlos Lopez, Lucas Valdez, and Alicia Vigil , members. Credit Committee were Desederio Gallegos, Eloy Valdez and Matias A. Martinez. Up to this time, membership had been restricted to members of the St. Gertrudes Church. On June 16, 1966, membership was opened to anyone living within the Parish boundaries, regardless of their religion affiliation. This action was acknowledged by Maurice Mathew, deputy State Banking Commissioner.

In 1967, members of the Board of Directors were Ernest E. Martinez, President, Adelaido Valdez, Vice President, Ida Valdez, Secretary and Manuel Tafoya, Treasurer. Manuel B. Alcon was named assistant Treasurer since Mr. Tafoya had a bad accident. Supervisory committee members were Eloy Valdez, Pete Trambley and D.R. Gallegos. the Credit Committee were Juan B. Olguin, Amalia Segura, and Manuel Romo Sr.

On March 1968, Manuel B. Alcon was elected President, Trivinio Romo Secretary.

On October 10, 1968, due to the untimely death of Manuel Tafoya, Mrs. Marie Tafoya, his wife, was appointed Treasurer.

The 1969 annual meeting was held at Molly's Cafe which was situated where Theresa Marie's now stands. Officers and members elected were Manuel B. Alcon, President, Mrs. Marie Tafoya, Treasurer, Adelaido Valdez, Vice President, Trivinio

Romo, Secretary, Benjie Vigil, Nick A. Martinez and Mike Garcia members. Credit Committee were Manuel Romo, Juan B. Olguin, and Amalia Segura. Supervisory Committee were Faustin Martinez, D.R. Gallegos, and Eloy Valdez.

1970 Same members on all three committees were reelected.

Trivinio Romo resigned in 1970 and Nick A. Martinez was elected Secretary. On November, interest on loans was raised from 2% to 7%.

In 1971, officers elected were M. B. Alcon , President, Benjamin Vigil Vice President, Nick A. Martinez, Secretary, Marie Tafoya, Treasurer, Mike Garcia, Adelaido Valdez, and D.R. Gallegos members of Board of Directors, Credit Committee were Juan B.Olguin, Rosalia Garcia, and Manuel Romo, Supervisory Board -Arthur Romero, Eloy Valdez, Pete Trambley. Shares amounted to $62,852.77 and loans to $66,413.

In 1972, same officers were reelected. Shares amounted to $81,885.36 and loans to $86,951. St. Gertrudes Credit Union was registered as an employer. A 5% interest on insurance was declared. 6% on uninsured shares and 3% refund. The same board officers remained in 1973 with the exception of Mike Garcia, Mary L. Montoya came instead.

In 1974, an alarm system was installed at the office. It cost $375. On May 9, borrowers must have in shares 5% of the amount they wished to borrow. In July 18, it was decided that St. Gertrudes Credit Union should have a fire proof file. Same members were reelected.

In 1975, minimum wage of $2.10 per hour was to be paid workers. Sapello Credit Union showed intentions of merging with this credit union as did the Guadalupita Credit Union. After a long discussion, it was decided that it was not to St. Gertrudes' credit union's advantage. The same board was elected. Bernie Arellano was elected to fill Louise Montoya's vacancy. Faustin Martinez was elected in Mr. D.R. Gallegos vacancy.

In 1976, a new adding machine was purchased for $217.86. Mary Lou LaRan was elected as Secretary of the board. The rest of the board and committees remained the same.

In 1977, Same members remained. Bernie Arellano was hired to help the Treasurer. A pin of appreciation and a plaque was presented to Benjamin Vigil for his loyal work to the credit union. The Board members elected were Manuel B. Alcon, President, Alex Medina, Vice President , Marie Tafoya, Treasurer, Mary Lou LaRan, Secretary, Adelaido Valdez, and Faustin Martinez, members.

In 1978, a 5% dividend was declared. Same set of officers was elected.

In 1979, motion to change mileage from $.12 to $.17 per mile was made and it was approved. Manuel Romo Sr. resigned from the credit committee and Charles Vigil was elected to fill that vacancy. On the 29th of August, the by-laws were up-dated.

On May 13, 1980, interest rates were raised from 12% to 14% effective June 1980. The same set of officers was elected. Board of Directors and the Supervisory Board members were Arthur R. Romero, Sam Martinez and J.D. Olivas and the Credit Committee consisted of Charles Vigil, Bernadette Arellano and Juan

B. Olguin. Loan balance for November was $176,076.63 and share balance was $155,135.77 and there was cash on the bank $5,850.07.

1981 There was no change in board and committee membership with the exception of Nick A. Martinez. Leroy Blea was elected in his place.

In 1982 The same staff as before was elected. Manuel B. Alcon resigned as president of the board after serving in that position since 1968. A plaque was presented to him for his faithful service in this credit union.

On December 19, 1983, employees of Luna Vocational Institute were given the privilege of belonging to this credit union. The Board of Directors were Faustin Martinez President, Mary L. Sanchez Secretary , Maria Tafoya Treasurer, Tonie Trujillo, Leroy Blea, J.M. Cadom, and Joseph Valdez, members. Credit Committee were Charlie Vigil, Bernadette Arellano and Juan Olguin. The Supervisory committee were Moise Medina, Arthur R. Romero and J.D. Olivas.

1984 The same set of officers remained with the exception of Arthur Romero and J.D. Olivas who were replaced by Ivan Roper and J.J. Valdez. Dennis Chavez replaced J.J. Valdez in Board of Directors.

1985 No change of officers.

1986, elected were Mary L. Sanchez, President, Dennis Chavez Vice President Tonie Trujillo Secretary, Bernadette Arellano Treasurer, Charles Vigil, Leroy Blea and Jose M. Cordova were elected Board of directors. Frank J. Martinez, Marie Tafoya, and Juan B. Olguin were elected Credit Committee members and Moise Medina, Ivan Roper and J.J. Valdez remained Supervisory Committee members.

1987 There was no change of Officers.

1988 Dennis Chavez was named Vice President of the board of Directors and Carlota Gutierrez replaced Jose M.Cordova. Emenencia Romo replaced Juan B. Olguin in the Credit Committee. The Supervisory Committee remained the same.

1989 Same officers remained. Frank J. Martinez resigned and was replaced by Catherine Martinez.

1991 and 1992 Same officers were reelected. Joseph J. Valdez was replaced by Andrew Valdez in 1992. Mary L. Sanchez resigned after 16 years of service.

1993. Elected were, Jose M. Cordova, President, Dennis Chavez, Vice President, Carlota Gutierrez Secretary, Bernadette Arellano Treasurer, Charlie Vigil, Leroy Blea, and Ella Arellano were elected Board of Directors. Emenencia Romo, Marie R.Tafoya, and Catherine Martinez composed the Credit Committee and Moise Medina, Ivan Roper, and Andrew Valdez composed the Supervisory Committee.

There were 553 active members by 1992 of the 200 members who had signed up to 1952, only Manuel B. Alcon book #3, Fidel Valdez Jr. #30, Ernest E. Martinez #49, Fred Sanchez #76, Jose F. Martinez #98, Teresa Tafoya #103 Francisco M. Martinez #104, Marie R. Tafoya #107, Daniel Espinoza #113, Mrs. Laura G. Madrid #170 and Jose E. Bustos #191 remained.

Ben Alcon was the first treasurer. He served until the 1950's when Dan J. Cassidy took over. In 1957 Manuel Tafoya succeeded Dan J. Cassidy. He served until his untimely death in 1968. Manuel B. Alcon served the rest of that year and then Mrs. Maria Tafoya served from '1969 until 1987 when Bernie Arellano took the books. She is the present treasurer.

Membership was restricted to members of the St. Gertrude's Catholic Church until June 16, 1966 when membership was opened to anyone living within the boundaries of the Parish regardless of religion affiliation. At this time Manuel Tafoya was treasurer and Ernest E. Martinez was president of the Board of Directors.

The By-laws were updated in August 29, 1979 when Manuel B. Alcon was president and Mrs. Marie Tafoya was treasurer. On December 19,1983 Employees of Luna Vocational Institute were given the privilege of becoming members. Faustin Martinez was president and Toni Trujillo was Secretary while Mrs. Tafoya was treasurer.

In 1986, the constitution was amended when the fee to become a member was raised to $25. Mary Lou Sanchez was president and Toni Trujillo was secretary.

1392 members had been assigned books up to the present time. Many of them have died but their book numbers were never reassigned.

Acknowledgment is hereby given to Mrs. Maria Tafoya and to Bernie Arellano for the help and support they gave the author in acquiring most of the information included in this work as well as helping the author in doing research and to Eddie Herrera for verifying the story of the credit union.

The following are the members who have belonged to the Saint Gertrudes Credit Union at one time or an other:

The list is in the book number order: Book #1 Rev. Juan B. Peris, 2 Benjamin Alcon, 3 Manuel B. Alcon, 4 Gonzalo Archuleta, 5 Albert L. Cassidy, 6 Miguel Romo, 7 Manuel Romo, 8 Manuel C. Romo, 9 Dan J. Cassidy, 10 Rafael Trujillo, 11 Guadalupe Fuentes, 12 Ricardo Romo, 13 Delfinia A. Romo, 14 Peter L. Trambley, 15 Pedro Claudio Gonzales, 16 Eduardo Romo, 17 Elaiza C. Quintanilla, 18 Fidel Valdez, 19 Lucia Romo, 20 Enefe Bernal, 21 Julian Olivas, 22 Rafael E. Martinez Jr. 13 Annie M. Herrera, 24 Rev. George Boenninghousen, 25 Santiago Mondragon, 26 Dionicia R. Romo, 27 Jose Rafael Gonzales, 28 Miguel V. Romo, 29 Rafael Trujillo Jr. 30 Fidel Valdez Jr. 31 J.R. Chavez, 32 Emilia (Lila) Alcon, 33 Cecilia Cassidy, 34 Desiderio R. Gallegos, 35 Severo Lucero, 36 Eloisa Archuleta, 37 Emilia C. Vigil 38 Jose B. Valdez, 39 Jose A. Vigil, 40 Jose Rosendo Romero, 41 Erlinda Gutierrez, 42 Rosaura M. Alcon, 43 Margarito Maes, 44 Adela Serna, 45 Guillermo Gonzales, 46 F. Fernandez, 47 Stella Chavez, 48 Ricardo Pino, 49 Ernesto E. Martinez, 50 Louis F. Fernandez, 51 Terecina Mondragon, 52 Erminia Mondragon, 53 Juanita S. Mondragon, 54 Mary L. Mondragon, 55 Cesario Castillo, 56 Juan Paul Castillo, 57 Salomon Castillo, 58 Louis P. Ortega, 59 Jose N. Valdez, 60 John Paul Berg, 61 Isabel Romo, 62 Louis R. Romo, 63 Manuel Tafoya, 64 Mrs. Severo Lucero, 65 Bennie Alcon McNeff, 66 Delfinia Pauline Romo, 67 Nieves D. Romo, 68 Nestor Gonzales, 69 Edubigen E. Bustos, 70 Alfredo Medina, Ernestina Trujillo, 71 Amalia Montoya, 72 James A. Leger, 73 Rev. Henry J. Rael, 74 Candido

Valdez, 75 Guadalupe Trambley, 76 Fred Sanchez, 77 Nick Bustos, 78 Amado Valdez, 79 Andres Quintana, 80 Beniberto Quintana, 81 Pablo A. Romo, 82 Edith Veronica Berg, 83 Yolanda Romo, 84 Louis Bustos, 85 Teofilo Esquibel, 86 Anselmo R. Sedillo, 87 Eliza Romo, 88 Celia M. Campos, 89 Ricardo Adolfo Romo, 90 Alberto N. Valdez 91 George F. Berg, 92 Raymond Martinez, 93 Alfonso Romo, 94 Demetrio R. Martinez, 95 Jose U Lucero, 96 Jose Leonor Manchego, 97 Celina M. Manchego, 98 Jose F. Martinez, 99 Victor J. Casados, 100 Tillie Trambley, 101 Ernestine Marie Trambley, 102 Teresina Romo, 103 Teresa Tafoya, 104 Francisco M. Martinez, 105 Epifanio Montoya, 106 Abel D. Maestas, 107 Maria R. Tafoya, 108 Joe Ignacio Garcia, 109 Alfred F. Trammell, 110 Roman Valdez, 111 Bertha Martinez, 112 Jose F. Hernandez, 113 Daniel Espinoza, 114 Rev. Albert Chavez, 115 Rafaelita T. Archuleta, 116 Rosanna Gonzales, 117 Michael Patrick Cassidy, 118 Rafael E. Martinez, 119 Frank Segura, 120 Celia Segura, 121 Sinforosa M. Espinoza, 122 Hilaria L. Martinez, 123 Manuel Quintana, 124 Ramon Martinez, 125 Mrs. Pablo Romo, 126 Fernando Naranjo, 127 Nicomedes Romero 128 Jacobo Naranjo, 129 Delfinio Lujan, 130 Juan A. Espinoza, 131 Delfido Sanchez, 132 Alfonso P. Roper, 133 Maximinio Valdez, 134 Filadelfio Garcia, 135 Juan J.C. Esquibel, 136 Livorio A. Vigil, 137 Aurora Serna, 138 Servando Bustos and wife, 139 Olmedo and Constancia Trujillo, 140 Jose Maria Valdez, 141 Florencio Gonzales, 142 Frank L. Trambley, 143 Eugenio D. Romo, 144 Carlos D. Romo, 145 James J. Cassidy Jr. 146 Carlos Romero, 147 Mrs. Abelino Lucero, 148 Eduardo Rimbert, 149 Betty Ann Rimbert, 150 Francisco Leopoldo Rimbert, 151 Adelaido Valdez, 152 Jose A. O. Sandoval, Jose M. Marrujo, 154 Dulcinea A. Serna, 155 Juan Medina, 156 Alfonso Medina, 157 Juan J. Trujillo, 158 Rose Mary Ann Valdez, 159 Vera Espinoza, 160 Manuel and Otilia C. Kemm, 161 Mrs. Antonia A. Romero, 162 Mrs. Frank (Toni) Gauna, 163 Gilbert L. Ortega, 164 Armida G. Ortega, 165 James J. Cassidy Sr. 166 Alejandro Martinez, 167 Celia Serna, 168 Mary R. Kemm, 169 Emelinda Martinez (Abeyta) 170 Mrs. Laura C. Madrid, 171 Simon B. Maes, 172 Jose B. Valdez, 173 Mary Grace Yolanda Alcon, 174 Ricardo Gonzales, 175 Marcelino Pacheco, 176 Jose Santiago Bonney, 177 Matilde Ernestina Romo, 178 J.F. Valdez, 179 Jose E. Valdez, 180 Onofre Quintana, 181 Trinidad M. Lopez, 182 Mr. and Mrs. Peter Balland, 183 Tiburcio J. Martinez, 184 Orcelio L. Romero, 185 Felipe DeHerrera, 186 Jose E. Archuleta, 187 Cirilio Maestas, 188 Frank Gauna, 189 Juan Pablo Trujillo, 190 Belarminio Tenorio, 191 Benito Enrique Valdez, 192 Jose E. Bustos, 193 Jose Alcario Martinez, 194 Albert Williams, 195 George Sandoval, 196 Adelino (Edd) Herrera, 197 Trivino Romo, 198 Mora Festival St. Gertrude's. The following registered after 1952: 199 Alberto Romero, 200 Ted Gutierrez, 201 Mary Apodaca, 202 Robert R. Alcon, 203 Vidal Benavidez, 204 Mrs. Vidal Benavidez, 205 Mary Louise Montoya, 206 Tiburcio B. Martinez, 207 Francine J. Martinez, 208 Lawrence Martinez, 209 Frank Leon Martinez, 210 Mrs. Frank Trammell 211 Juan D. Leon, 212 Irene D. Cruz, 213 Mary Ann Cruz, 214 Perfecto Duran, 215 Prescilla L. Romo, 216, Richard K. Martinez 217 Andres F. Martinez, 218 Raymond A. Ruiz, 219 Juan A. Martinez, 220 Juan Salgado, 221 Floraido Valdez, 222, 223 Manuel Garcia, 224 Amadeo Gallegos Jr., 225, 226 Nick Martinez 227 Ida S. Archuleta, 228 Luisita Viola Martinez, 229 Salomon Bustos, 230

M.S. Melendez, 231 Max Pacheco, 232 Severo Aragon, 233 Gilbert Gallegos, 234 Tony Vigil 235 Adolfo Sandoval, 236 Candido Montoya, 237 Teodoro B. Montoya, 238 Fabiola G. Valdez, 239 Sam and Dora Romo, 240 Mr. and Mrs. Frank E. Lucero, 241 Jose or Deluvina Rodarte, 242, Rafael Edward Martinez, 243 Ernest F. Martinez, 244 Isabel C. Martinez, 245 Antonio Romero Jr., 246 Eloy J. Blea, 247 Martina B. Sanchez, 248,Orlando Valdez, 249, Angelina Archuleta, 250 Marcella Lopez Gallegos, 251 Mr. Carlos Trujillo, 252 Johnny C. Sandoval, 253, 254 Ernesto Serna, 255 Jose Antonio Bustos, 256, Franklin D. Branch, 257 Carlos De Herrera, 258 Cesario Torres 259 Emenenciana T. Valdez or Candido Valdez, 260 Julian Romero, 261 Wilfred Casias, 262 Ralph Lopez, 263 Anselmo Chavez, 264 Harry Nolan, 265 Juan O. Salas, 266, 267 Eddie S. Martinez, 268 Emilio T. Martinez, 269 Aurora Borrego Gonzales, 270 Judy A. Pacheco, 271 Nick A. Martinez, 272 Julia L. Martinez, 273 Luisa Lopez, 274 Agnes V. Martinez, 275 Holy Name Society, 276 Lucas Valdez, 277 Jose Maria Pacheco, 278 Elaine Lucille Herrera, 279 Marion M. Olivas, 280 Rev. John S. McHugh, 281 Alicia Vigil, 282 Filadelfio Vigil, 283 Alfredo Roybal, 284 Porfiria N. Valdez, 285 Gabriel Bustos, 286 Joseph P. Trambley, 287 Jose I. Velasquez, 288 Carlos A. Garcia, 289 Thomas Velasquez, 290 Epifanio Vigil, 291 Our Lady of the Most Holy Trinity, 292 Secundino Aragon, 293 Ninfa R. Valdez, 294 Juan J. Leyba, 295 Maria Carlota Gallegos, 296 Marcelino Herrera, 297 Onesimo Benjamin Gonzales, 298 Elmer F. Valdez, 299 Tony Vigil, 300 Ambrocio Montoya, 301 Florencio Trujillo, 302 Guillermo Casias, 303 John P. DeLeon, 304 Carlos Domingo Lopez, 305 Jose Rafael Quintana, 306 Manuel Garcia, 307 Eufracio Vigil, 308 Manuel D. Garcia, 309 Jacobo D. Martinez, 310 Josephine R. Serrano, 311 Ernest A. Montoya, 312 Rufina Maestas, 313 Celso Lovato, 314   Daniel Maes, 315 Carlos Martinez, 316 Joseph Gerald Martinez, 317 Estevan Dominguez, 318 Theresa J. Garcia, 319 Ida Jane Valdez, 320 Maria Angela Valdez, 321 Mike Garcia, 322 Salomon Vasquez, 323 Gregorio J. Cordova, 324 Livorio A. Vigil, 325 Fermin B. Vigil, 326 Leandro Mondragon, 327 Sipreano Trujillo, 328 Dennis D. Escobedo, 329 Benny J. Escobedo, Jesse Benjamin Esquibel, 330 Frank Leroy Valdez, 331 Ernest A. Martinez, 332 Paul Pacheco, 333 Martin Sandoval, 334 William Fahey, 335 Martha C. Trambley, 336 Dennis J. Trambley, 337 Josephine Maestas, 338 Onesimo Salazar, 339 Fileberto B. Sanchez, 340 Samuel Lovato, 341 Amalia Segura, 342 Billy J. Ortega, 343 Manuel C. Maes, 344 Felix Maes, 345 Jose G. Martinez, 346 Victor Garcia, 347 Edmond Ortega, 348 Jose A. Lopez, 349 Helen L. Valdez, 350 Emenencia H. Romo, 351 Jose Maria Rudolfo Garcia, 352 Guadalupe A. Garcia, 353, 354 Bernabe Cruz, 355 Rubel Medina, 356 Marcella C. Valdez, 357 Samuel L. Valdez, 358 Patricio Trujillo Jr., 359 Ben Lujan, 360 Pedro Abeyta, 361 Juan B. Olguin, 362 David R. Martinez, 363 Cecilia Campos, 364 David Joseph Maestas, 365 Luis Polaco, 366 Mrs. Frutosa L. Romo, 367 Joe Adan Garcia, 368 Jose Benino Espinoza, 369 Florencio Olguin, 370 Richard John Radmacher 1-4-65, 371 Maria Guadalupe Olivas, 372 Mrs. Alex Gonzales, 373 Alex Gonzales, 374 Fermin De Herrera, 375 Agustina Arellano, 376 Carlos Garcia Jr., 377 Alex Elauterio Mora, 378 Dora and Reynaldo Mascarenas, 379 Isabel Rudolph, 380 David A. Valdez, 381 Rosalia Garcia, 382 Frank C. Trambley, 383 Matias A. Martinez, 384, 385 Glen R. Martinez, 386 Mrs.

Pete Abeyta, 387 Mary T. Martinez, 388 Paul R. Duran, 389 Esequiel Romero, 390
William Velasquez, 391 William Velasquez, 392 Mrs. Larry Gutierrez, 393 Theresita
Irene Gallegos, 394 Carmen Gallegos, 395 Rosita Gallegos, 396 Daniel Garcia, 397
Modesto Borrego, 398 Carolina G. Garcia, 399 Laurencio Gonzales, 400 Joe A.
Florence, 401 Mora Public Library-Carlos Lopez, 402 Agapito Martinez, 403, 404
Sylvia De Leon, 405 Juan F. Romero, 406 Josephine Trambley, 407 Benjamin Vigil,
408 Nicomedes Romero, 409 Faustin O. Martinez, 410 Ernesto Lovato, 411 Juanita
M. Garcia, 412 Genevieve R.I. Alcon 413 Onofre Martinez, 414 Eric Martinez, 415
Arthur V. Romo, 416 Feloniz Torrez, 417 Milnor Romero, 418 Miquela Martinez, 419
Evelyn Romo, 420 Ambrocio C. Rivera, 421 Darrel E. Vigil, 422 Dante E. Vigil, 423
Leroy Chavez, 424 Dennis J. Chavez, 425 Danny Chavez, 426 Joe N. Romero, 427
Urbano Trujillo, 428 David Leo Maes, 429 Andy E. Valdez, 430 Samuel Romero, 431
Robert Bradshaw, 432, 433 Michael Martinez, 434 Kenneth W. Martinez, 435 Juan A.
Casias, 436 Joseph L. Garcia, 437 Julius Garcia , 438 Tommy E. Martinez, 439
Manuel A. Romo, 440 Ida Trujillo, 441 Genevieve H. Alcon, 442 Agustin Padilla, 443
Monica Garcia, 444 Rudy J. Romero, 445 Beatrice Tafoya, 446 Victoria Gonzales,
Stephenie Martinez, 447 Mrs. Ernesto Serna, 448 Rudolfo Trujillo, 449 Dolores
Martinez, 450 Charles E. Vigil, 451 Corinne Baca, 452 Fidel E. Valdez III, 453 Manuel
De Leon, 454 455 Dante Vigil, 456 Robert DeHerrera , Del Rio Water Association by
Gloria Maestas, 457 Tomasita Valdez, 458 Donnie Gandert, 459 Mary R. Florence,
460 Peter Abeyta Jr. 461 Anna Marie Abeyta, 462 Miguel Cordova, 463 Leo Mestas,
464 Nick Martinez Jr., 465 Leonor Silva, 466 Stephane Martinez, 467 Mrs. Gregorio
Cordova 468 Leo Romero, 469 Karen Rimbert, 470 Valerie Rimbert, 471 Flosha
Sanchez, 472 Breena I. Sanchez, 473 Emilio Roland Sanchez, 474 Marcella R.
Sanchez- Dineen, 475 Mora Moonlighters Town Team, 476 Janet Garcia, 477 Bert
Garcia, 478 Meliquias Pacheco, 479 James Gutierrez, 480 Rolanda Gutierrez, 481
Florence Olguin, 482 Annette Olguin, 483 Jody Lynn Olguin, 484 Ignacio Maestas,
485 Adela Maestas, 486 Fabiola F. Esposito, 487 Eloisa DeHerrera, 488 Rene Dion
Vigil, 489, 490 Edwin Leonard Vigil, 491 Julia Antonia Rogers, 492 Dante Vigil, 493
Miguel Jose Gallegos, 494 Andres A. Gallegos, 495 Camilo Modesto Gallegos, 496 Jose
N. Martinez, 497 Agustine Mares, 498 Paul John Pacheco Jr., 499 Tiffany M. Starr,
500 Yevette Rimbert, 501 Gary Rimbert, 502 Manuelita Rimbert, 503 Mary Abeyta,
504 Carmela Romo, 505, 506 Flora Cordova, 507 Epifanio Vigil, 508 Susie Martinez,
509 Mary L. Sanchez, 510 Damian Pacheco, 511 Charles Cassidy, 512 Arthur R.
Romero, 513 Anita Romero, 514 Edith Romero, 515 Letitia Romero 516 Tony
Cordova, 517 Josefita Herrera, 518 Carla San Roman, 519 Cipriano Mondragon, 520
Joseph Pacheco, 521, 522, 523 Ignacita Espinoza, 524 Raymond Duran, 525 Alvin R.
Vigil, 526 Morada De San Antonio by Stevan Sanchez, 527 Norman Leslie Vigil, also
Anthony B. Vigil, 528 Leonila N. Valdez and Jerry Trujillo, 529,530 Elma and Urbano
Trujillo, 531 John Abeyta, 532 Theresa Romero, 533 Joseph Abeyta, 534 Samuel M.
Romero, 535 Samuel Olivas, 536 Mrs. Juan B. Maes, 537 Aurora Netzloff, 538
Victoriano Silva, 539 Gilbert R. Valdez, 540 Raul T. Valdez, 541 Samuel and Lupita
Romero, 542 Jose N. Mares, 543 Arleen T. Garcia, 544 Eileen C. Garcia, 545 Moses
Mares, 546 Magdalena Ortega, 547 Charles L. Garcia, 548 Robert Trujillo, 549

Eugene R. Mares, 550 John T. Romero, 551 Manuel B. Martinez, 552 Gilbert Valdez, 553 Robert Ortega, 554 Raymundo Villa, 555 Arcenio Gutierrez, 556 Elvira Pacheco, 557, 558 Donnie Gandert also Monica Ann Lovato, 559 Dominga Mares, 560 Leon Anthony Martinez, 561 Dennis W. Sanchez, 562 Justine Garcia, 563 Arthur J. Romero, 564 Johnny N. Romero, 565 Pablo Garcia, 566 Lilly Jaramillo, 567, 568 George Lemmons, 569 Samuel Aragon, 570 Frank C. Cordova, 571 Emilio Brizal, 572 Joseph J. Valdez, 573 Susie Ash Vigil, 574 Florence Romero, 575 Antonina Valdez, 576, 577 Max Olguin, 578 James DeHerrera, 579 Gloria B. Griego, 580 Policarpio Torres, 581 Fidel Gauna, 582 Leo Mondragon 583 Jacob Regensberg, 584 Joseph Luke Gauna, 585 , Rudy W. Montoya, 586 Jose O. Cruz, 587 Viola Duran, 588 Anna Margarita Pacheco, 589 Cayetano Cordova, 590 Clarita Sanchez, 591 Eduardo Cordova, 592 Louise Sanchez, 593 Johnny Mondragon, 594 Luis Elias Martinez, 595 Judy Vigil, 596 Wanda Lou Vigil, 597 Maria Salome Lopez, 598 Robert Martinez, 599 Amy Lynn Martinez, 600 Jose Leandro Leyba, 601 Mary Frances Martinez, 602 Theresa Ann Martinez, 603 Elizabeth Dina Martinez, 604 Diana May Martinez, 605 Denise Marie Martinez, 606 Frances Romero, 607 Jose R. Sanchez, 608 George Sandoval Jr. 609, 610 Ida Q. Lujan, David L. Romero, 611 Josefita Martinez, 612 Dora Olguin, 613 Erica Martinez, 614 Charlotte Duran, 615 Jose C. Lucero, 616 Pauline Mares David D. Romero, 617 Edwina Celestina Valdez, 618 Raquel Elena Valdez, 619 Trini Cordova, 620 Oliver F. Martinez, 621 Max Gutierrez, 622 Flavio Vigil, 623 Maria Theresa Gallegos, 624 Anna Maria Gallegos, 625 Maria Lucia Gallegos, 626 Thomas Mateo Gallegos, 627 Martina B. Sanchez, 628 Lucille Garcia, 629 Stacey Marie Trujillo, 630 Antonio Mora, 631 Kathleen L. Marquez, 632 Salomon Olivas, 633 Pete Mares, 634 Robert G. Mares, 635 Floyd Trujillo, 636 Della Olivas, 637 Franklin Regensberg, 638 Jake Regensberg Sr., 639 Guadalupe Torres, 640 Ray Cordova, 641 Mercedes Martinez, 642 Robert Raymond Abreau, 643 Rumaldo Trujillo, 644 Benancio Trujillo, 645 John N. Martinez, 646 Caroline Trujillo, 647 Manuel Montano, 648 Carolina Olivas, 649 Arthur S. Romero, 650, 651 Debra Gonzales, 652 Donald Abreau, 653 Larry E. Maes, 654 Guillermo Romero, 655 Theresa Conchita Vigil, 656 Marcella T. Gonzales, 657 Kenneth Valdez, 658 Leroy Vigil, 659 Mary Louise Abreau, 660 Carlos Salazar, 661 Lucille Vigil, 662 Elizabeth Romero, 663 Art Pacheco, 664 Sandra Branch, 665 Darlene Alcon, 666 Eddy Alcon, 667 Jimmy Dunlap, 668 Ursula Vigil, 669 Antonio & Lupita Olivas, 670 Clorinda Griego, 671 Lorenzo Lujan, 672 Leo Rimbert, 673 Michael Branch, 674 Jose D. Vigil, 675 Eugene Hanosh, 676 Rosemary Villa, 677 Marvin Martinez, 678 Pearl Ann Martinez, 679 Myra Martinez, 680 Christina Lee Martinez, 681 Carlos Martin Lopez, 682 Lupita Silva, 683 Martha Martinez, 684 Priscilla Romero, 685 Moise Medina, 686 Jimmy Weber, 687 Gail Martinez, 688 Jose T. Espinoza, 689 Clyde Regensberg, 690 Joseph Branch, 691 Nora Lopez, 692 Adrian Herrera, 693 Apolonio Martinez, 694 Bella Joan Blea, 695 Arthur Martinez, 696 Jose V. Grine, 697 Donald LaRan, 698 Eliseo Alcon, 699 David Velasquez, 700 Josephine Garcia, 701 Tito Pacheco, 702 Deon Phillip Maes, 703 Sebastian Maes, 704 Gene Maes, 705 Paul Valdez Sr., 706 Bernadette Arellano 707 Barbara Vigil, 708 Avenicio Maes, 709 James Griego, 710 Angela Romero, 711 Antonio Abeyta, 712 Samuel G. Martinez, 713 Duane Frances

Maes, 714 Iris Maes, 715 Dale Anthony Maes, 716 Rachel Lynn Vigil 717 Paul Griego, 718 Drucilla Romero, 719 Lorraine Gutierrez, 720 Sydney Regensberg, 721 Aragon Espinoza, 722 Edmund Salazar, 723 Pete Blea, 724 Bernice Rusk, 725 Frances Barela Martinez, 726 Margarito Martinez, 727 Anita Martinez, 728 Ambrocita Lovato, 729 Margie Lujan, 730 Andres Maes, 731 Berna Griego, 732 George Sandoval, 733 Leslie D. Vigil, 734 Juan E. Casados, 735 Bercy Espionoza, 736 Reynaldo Martinez, 737 Paul Lujan, 738 Virginia Romero, 739 Elsie Romero, 740 Tamara Trujillo, 741 Olivia Archer, 742 LaDonna LaRan, 743 Richard L. Martinez, 744 Mary Jane Medina, 745 Frank Medina, 746 Anna Marie Esquibel, 747 Louis Martinez, 748 Simonita M. Valdez, 749 Raymond Sanchez, 750 Julia Martinez, 751 David Angelo Sanchez, 752 Eloy Roybal, 753 Anita Roybal, 754 Arthur J. Romero, 755 Mrs. Alois Martinez, 756 Manuel Velasquez, 757 Walter Griego, 758 Michael R. Esposito, 759 Acianita Chavez, 760 Grace Chavez, 761 Michelle Carrie Vigil, 762 Fidel J. Trujillo, 763 Nelson Trujillo, 764 Gilbert Olguin, 765 Lorraine Medina, 766 Filimon Vigil, 767 Tom R. Paiz, 768 Maria Rita Gallegos, 769 Jose Alex Medina, 770 Jose Eulogio Maestas, 771 Reina Cordova, 772 Lorraine Romero, 773 Anita Lucero, 774 John Frank Serna, 775 Adelaida Trujillo, 776 Ernie Olivas, 777 Albert Martinez, 778 Adelina P and Frank Medina, 779 Flavio B. Duran, 780 Susan Muniz, 781 Moises Maestas, 782 Veronica Trujillo, 783 Anthony Trujillo, 784 Andrew R. Jaramillo, 785 Fred Romero, 786 Alvin Duran, 787 Juan L. Vigil, 788 Inez Abeyta, 789 Adolfo Sandoval, 790 Rosie Vigil, 791 Qurinita Martinez, 792 James A. Abreau, 793, 794 Luis Chavez, 795 Lila Maes, 796 Florence Trujillo, 797 Nancy Garcia, 798 Peter Vigil, 799 Leo Pacheco, 800 Leroy L. Polaco, 801 Mary Lou Sanchez, 802,803 Isabel Pacheco, 804 Doris Casados, 805 Georgia Pacheco, 806 Ricky B. DeHerrera, 807 Mrs. Frank Padilla, 808 Ted Anthony Gandert, 809 Fiddy Gonzales, 810 Antonio D. Lopez, 811 Christina Barela, 812 Andrew Pacheco, 813 Roy Regensberg, 814 Frank L. Cordova, 815 Joseph DeHerrera, 816 Pablita Lucero, 817 Patrick Ash, 818 Daniel Espinoza Jr., 819 Debbie Ann Ortega, 820 David Madrid, 821 Albinita E. Garcia, 822 Alejandro Montoya, 823 Crucita Casados, 824 Teresina Roper, 825 George DeHerrera, 826 Frank G. Padilla, 827 Carlota Gutierrez, 828 Velma Vales, 829 Ronald Lujan, 830 Christina R. Gallegos, 831 Nick N. Hernandez, 832 Jerry Mares, 833 Cyrus Martinez, 834 Emilia Trujillo, 835 Nora Olguin, 836 Rudy C. Chavez, 837 Marina Pacheco, 838 John Berg, 839 Ivan Berg, 840 Jose B. Sanchez, 841 Juvencio Gonzales, 842 Emma Casados, 843 Juan W. Martinez, 844 Emily Lujan, 845 Matilda S. Martinez, 846 Manuel R. Montoya, 847 Theresa or George Herrera, 848 James P. J. Maes, 849 Jack Roper Sr. 850 Leroy M. Martinez, 851 Ernest Alcon, 852 Arnold Trujillo, 853 Claudio Chacon, 854 Rudy Montoya, 855 Irene T. Valdez, 856 Sarah Abeyta, 857 Herman Lujan, 858 Pedro Mares Gloria Weber, 859 Isabel Romero, 860 Catherine Martinez, 861 Ursulita Vigil, 862 Morada de San Antonio, 863 Gloria D. Lujan, 864 Antonina L. Vigil, 865 Juan R. Maes, 866 Joseph D. Olivas, 867 Jose M. Montano , 868 Edwin M. Lovato, 869 Ida Torres, 870 Mildred Sandoval, 871 Iris Leyba, 872 Danny Roper , 873 Patricia E. Leyba, 874 Filbert R. Trujillo, 875 Diana Gonzales, 876 Henrietta Martinez, 877 Senior Citizens by Claudio Chacon, 878 Eddie Mares, 879 Eddie Vigil, 880 Gary E. Martinez, 881 Scott G. Martinez, 882 Scottie

Martinez, 883 Marcia Biddle, 884 Jimmy Garcia, 885 Joan Espinoza, 886 Lucille Alcon, 887 Nestor Casados, 10-8-79, 888 Maria Lupita Casados, 889 Leroy B. Blea, 890 John E. Martinez, 891 Sammy Chavez, 892 Mary Ida Branch, 893 Ida Martinez, 894 Lorenzo Olivas, 895 Regina Vigil, 896 Robert E. Ortega, 897 Johnny B. Mares, 898 Jane Valdez, 899 Alfonso Valdez, 900 Kevin Espinoza, 901 Albert C. Romero, 902 Emilio Olivas, 903 Willie Olivas, 904 Robert Yee, 905 Stevan Yee, 906 Jose R. Sandoval, 907 Doloritas T. Velasquez, 908 William Abeyta, 909 Sam Mascarenas, 910 Robert Sandoval 911 Susie Vigil, 912 Rose Marie Yee, 913 William J. Weather, 914 Brother Thomas Coleman, 915 Theresa Marquez, 916 Magadelena C. Montoya, 917 Robert Weather, 918 Roger Mora, 919 Robert Romero, 920 Rev. Douglas Raun, 921 Floyd Griego, 922 Natalia Chavez, 923 Ernestina Garcia, 924 Joclyn Trujillo, 925 Horacio B. Martinez, 926 Ruben Cordova, 927 Linda M. Montoya, 928 Viola Berg, 929 Darlene Romero, 930 Nancy Lujan Hurtado, 931 Lily M. Mares, 932 Raymundo A. Villa, 933 Annabelle Griego, 934 Tonie Trujillo, 935 Jose D. Olguin, 936 James Sandoval, 937 Mary P. Vigil, 938 Jose Ignacio Maestas, 939 Evangeline G. Herrera, 940 Theresa M. Cruz, 941 Edwin J. Herrera, 942 Patricia Medina, 943 Elizabeth Maestas, 944 Mardia Trujillo, 945 Carlos & Francisquita Martinez, 946 Luis or Elvira Martinez, 947, 948 Luis Garcia, 949 Mary Elaine Valdez, 950 Clauta Sanchez, 951 Yolanda Lovato, 952 Emily Roybal, 953 Reina Roybal, 954 Christopoher N. Roybal, 955 Benjamin Trujillo, 956 Gabriel Jentette, 957 Robert Craig, 958 Randolpoh Espinoza, 959 Timmy Espinoza, 960 Isabel Duran, 961 Alfredo Sanchez, 962 Richard Casados, 963 Mathew Cassidy, 964 Raymond Pacheco, 965 Paul Daniel Gallegos, 966 Sammy C. Lopez, 967 Arleen Romero, 968 Elmo Romero, 969 Erlinda Valdez, 970 Elsie Trujillo, 971, 972 Berna Lovato -9-13-79, 973 Mary Ann Vigil , 974 Gilbert Vigil, 975 Mathew Valdez, 976 Priscilla Silva, 977 Carlos Duran, 978 Jose M. Cordova, 979 Jeannie Mondragon, 980 Albert or Frances Martinez, 981 Jesse Vigil, 982 Michael Benavidez, 983 Frances Roybal, 984 Charlie Trujillo, 985 Patricia Moreno, 986 Oralia Dominguez DeHerrera, 987 Frank J. Martinez, 988 Valerie Villa, 989 Thomas Sanchez, 990 Fernandita Valdez, 991 Johnny Johnson, 992 Charles Vigil, 993 Grace Branch, 994 Christobal Herrera, 995 Justin Alcon, 996 Marcos Medina, 997 Richard N. Olivas, 998 Joyce Romo, 999 Tonita Martinez, 1000 Guadalupe Santistevan, 1001 Loretta Vigil, '1002 Victor Villa, 1003 Lucy Mares, 1004 Isabel Lovato, 1005 Julia Lovato, 1006 Anthony Esquibel, 1007 Fidel Duran, 1008 Robert & Elizabeth Vigil, 1009 Dennis Romero, 1010 Eliza Cardenas, 1011 Dolores Valdez, 1012 Lillian B. Martinez, 1013 Debra M. Alcon, 1014 Johnny Trujillo, 1015 Debra Whicher, 1016 Arlene Romero, 1017 Olivia Vigil, 1018 Dennis Trujillo, 1019 Michael Trujillo, 1020 Ivan Roper, 1021 Wanda Dale Roper, 1022 Thomas A. Sanchez, 1023 Alfonso Romero, 1024 Archie DeHerrera, 1025 James E. O'Connell, 1026 Mary Helen Romero, 1027 Michael Griego, 1028 Celso Romero, 1029 Feliberto A. Casias, 1030 Herman Vigil, 1031 Noyola Abreau, 1032 Florence Maestas, 1033 Pauline G. Espinoza, 1034 Kenneth W. Padilla, 1035 Bertha Martinez, 1036 Michael Serna, 1037 Donald Wright, 1038 Virginia Griego, 1039 Bobby R. Biddle, 1040 Adam Olivas, 1041 Vanee Lynn Lujan, 1042 Margaret Alcon, 1043 Floyd Lovato, 1044 Mary A. Garcia, 1045 Deborah Lynn Lujan, 1046 Antonio G. Esposito, 1047 Alex Guzman.

1048 Paul Gallegos, 1049 Lee Griego, 1050 Sharon Santistevan, 1051 Francisco A. Montoya, 1052 Anthony Griego, 1053 Nazario Montoya, 1054 April A. Romero, 1055 Denise Medina, 1056 Angelina M. Arellano, 1057 Johnny A. and Charlott Romero, 1058 Michael Griego Jr., 1059 Arthur Yardman, 1060 Carol J. Regensberg, 1061 Darren Craig, 1062 Dolores Casados, 1063 Louis Casados, 1064, 1065 Elauterio Trujillo, 1066 Carol Regensberg, 1067 Feloniz Hernandez, 1068 Helen Espinoza, 1069 Debra Alcon, 1070 Paul C. Maestas, 1071 Lorenzo Lujan, 1072 Vidilia Trujillo, 1073 Robert M. Cassidy, 1074 James I. Branch, 1075 Ernestine Pacheco, 1076 Max Pacheco Jr. 1077 Alicia Lujan, 1078 Michael Herrera, 1079 Sally Esposito, 1080 Tomas L. Martinez, 1081 Alberto A. Martinez, 1082 Gene Vigil, 1083 Antonia Luci Roybal, 1084 Mike Romero, 1085 Debra Trujillo, 1086 Remigio Trujillo, 1087 Cathy Martinez, 1088 Leroy Martinez, 1089 Alberta Pino, 1090 Sarah E. Romo, 1091 Lydia Griego, 1092 Martha Chavez, 1093 Patrick M. Romero, 1094 Paul R. Duran, 1095 Cleo Bernal Valdez, 1096 Amanda Lynn Vigil, 1097 Ronald L. Cruz, 1098 Doris Pacheco, 1099 Christina C. Olivas, 1100 Rita Cordova, 1101 Dennis Cordova, 1102 Doris Mae Sandoval, 1103 Juan Floyd Duran, 1104 Pauline Duran, 1105 Margaret Tafoya, 1106 Paul Anthony Garcia, 1107 Geraldine or Raymond Pino, 1108 Margaret E. Romo, 1109 Patrick Griego, 1110 Ray Cordova, 1111 Steve A. Herrera, 1112 Leo Amos Espinoza, 1113 Rosalia Romero, 1114 Cindy DeHerrera, 1115 Joe E. Gandert, 1116 Angela Candelaria, 1117 Elizabeth Maes, 1118, 1119 Marissa Cassidy, 1120 Fares Martinez, 1121 George Trujillo, 1122 Yvonne Montoya, 1123 Samuel Vigil, 1124 Dr. Jose A. Perea, 1125 John Sanchez, 1126 Evangeline Villegas, 1127 Ralph E. Sierra, 1128 Frances Lucero, 1129 Doris Velarde, 1130 Joe Gene Pacheco, 1131 Leroy Abeyta, 1132 Eli M. Duran, 1133 Vera S. Sanchez, 1134 Anthony Trujillo, 1135 Andrea Anna Martinez, 1136 Tobias I. Montgomery, 1137 Sisto E. Martinez, 1138 Christopher J. Vigil, 1139 Kristen Medina, 1140 Joseph Tafoya, 1141 Peter Cordova, 1142 Frank J. Leyba, 1143 Winter Weather, 1144 Charlene Chacon, 1145 Daniel D. Craig, 1146 Charles Anthony Vigil, 1147 Manuel Chavez, 1148 Steve M. Hernandez, 1149 Lorraine Lujan, 1150 Pauline D. Biddle, 1151 Janice Biddle, 1152 Julia Griego, 1153 Loretta Tafoya, 1154 Odilia J. Casados, 1155 Jessie Romero, 1156 Antonio Mares, 1157 Nichole A. Sanchez, 1158 Marcella Palomino, 1159 Ella Arellano, 1160 Joanne E. Padilla, 1161, 1162 Fred Montoya, 1163 Jason Trujillo, 1164 Fidel Trujillo Jr., 1165 Benjamin Cruz, 1166 Juan and Evelyn Sandoval, 1167 Roma H. Rivera, 1168 Diane G. Vigil, 1169 Jerry Garcia, 1170 Vicente Duran, 1171 Sofie Sandoval, 1172 Julia Romero, '1173 Rudy Wm. Montoya, 1174 Margie Williams, 1175 Bonney Williams, 1176 Lila Martinez, 1177 Jimmy Lee Weathers, 1178 Jesse Vigil, 1179 Larry or Shirley Romero, 1180 Martha Yardman, 1181 Adam G. Roybal, 1182 Anita LaRan, 1183 Bertha Moir, 1194 Frank L. Martinez, 1185 Arnold Trujillo, 1186 Johnny Medina, 1187 Duane Martinez, 1188 Bianca Carla Esposito, 1189 Jesus Romero, 1190 Orlando Vigil, 1191 Theresa M. Garcia, 1192 Dorothy Aragon, 1193 Clyde Quintana, 1194 Rodney Lee Cordova, 1195 Ida Valdez, 1196 Paul and Theresa Herrera, 1197 Jose H. and Elizabeth Montoya, 1198 Erlinda Fernandez, 1199 James Mondragon, 1200 Mary Jane Sandoval, 1201 Sofia Archuleta, 1202 Carmelita Olivas, 1203 Ernie Olivas, 1204 Victor Sandoval, 1205 Carl A. Vigil, 1206 Ryan Vigil, 1207

Linda Trujillo, 1208 Daniella Romo, 1209 Patsy Lucero, 1210 William E. Abeyta, 1211 Pauline Tapia, 1212 Viola Garcia, 1213 Teodorita Regensberg, 1214 Nicomedes Romero, 1215 Andrew J. Romero, 1216 Stella Saiz, 1217 John Louis Martinez, 1218 Mavrina L. Sanchez, 1219 Daniella Medina, 1220 Judy Padilla, 1221 Elidoro Vasquez, 1222 Wayne J. Roper, 1223 Elaine Montano, 1224 Michael Romero, 1225 Jose Fidel Gurule, 1226 Randolph A. Espinoza, 1227 Nathan Espinoza, 1228 Anthony R. Olguin, 1229 Daniel A. Garcia, 1230 Rose Tapia, 1231 Praxedes F. Martinez, 1232 Andy Alcon, 1233 Susie R. Vigil, 1234 Lorraine Hurtado, 1235 Clarissa Sue Espinoza, 1236 Dolores Roper Romero, 1237 Samuel Muniz, 1238 Paul Olivas, 1239 Mary R. Romero, 1240 Johnny Romero, 1241 Theresa A. Leyba, 1242 Frank E. Leyba, 1243 Kristy Nicole Martinez, 1244 Edmund Romero, 1245 Mary Jo. Cordova 1246 Julius C. Garcia, 1247 Mary C. Roybal, 1248 Marlyn Valdez, 1249 Francine H. Trambley, 1250 Frank Fred Trambley, 1251 Mary P. Romero, 1252 Paul Valdez Jr. 1253 Nicolas Casados, 1254 Rudy Romero, 1255 Johnny J. Martinez, 1256 Paul David Sanchez, 1257 Tara Valdez, 1258, 1259 Charles H. Osuchowski, 1260 Mary Ann Osuchowski, 1261 Charles L. Osuchowski, 1263 Isabelle D. Arman, 1264 Sam J. Aragon, 1265 Lori Garcia, 1266 Matilda Padilla, 1267 Santana Flor Sanchez, 1268 Lucas Diego Sanchez, 1269 Zachery A. Montgomery, 1270 David Salcido Jr., 1271 Telesfor Abeyta, 1272 Stella Renee Olivas, 1273 Yolanda A. Chavez, 1274 Kristen Lee Duran, 1275 Fabiola Vigil, 1276 Daniel and Herminia Flores, 1277 Lorenzo Gonzales, 1278 Dolores A. Martinez, 1279 Rita Griego, 1280 Pete Martinez Jr., 1281 Bo Jacob Sanchez, 1282 Delores S. Maestas, 1283 Jose T. Roybal, 1284 Joshoa N. Padilla, 1285 Lawrence Espinoza, 1286 Estella Romero, 1287 Valiente Ruiz, 1288 Corrina Ruiz, 1289 Teodorita Serna, 1290 Patricia Serna, 1291 Rev. Walter Cassidy, 1292 Josephine Cruz, 1293 Marcia Vigil, 1294 Roy Louis Gallegos, 1295 Josua Chad Martinez, 1296 Mathew M. Mares, 1297 Anastacia DeLeon, 1298 Erlinda Fernandez, 1299 Edward Romero, 1300 Frederico Gonzales, 1301 Richard L. Medina, 1302 Carlos Romero, 1303 Robert Vigil, 1304 Greg N. Medina, 1305 Joe L. Arellanes, 1306 Julie Nichole DeLeon, 1307 Rachel Lopez, 1308 George J. Sandoval, 1309 Rene E. Padilla, 1310 Rosie Lucero, 1311 Martin B. Serna, 1312 Marian T. Vigil, 1313 Cresencio E. Espinoza, 1314 Belinda Lee Blea, 1315 Rebecca D. Martinez, 1316 Matias Eloy Roybal, 1317 Richard C. Maestas, 1318 Crystal Padilla, 1319 Douglas Velarde, 1320 Denise Tafoya, 1321 Dan Cassidy, 1322 Francisca Martinez, 1323 Julian Quintana, 1324 Lucas Manuel Romo, 1325 Dominguita Sanchez, 1326 Marvin B. Cordova, 13427 Angelica Espinoza, 1328 Domecinda Trujillo, 1329 Alicia Garcia, 1330 Elsie M. Tapia,1331 Joe Valdez Jr. 1332 Michelle Espinoza, 1333 Simonita Cardenas, 1334 Donald D. Valdez, 1335 Del Ivan Roper, 1336 Branden Roper, 1337 Brandie Roper, 1338 Lorren A. Montgomery, 1339 Sammy Chavez Jr., 1340 Agustin Padilla Jr., 1341 Joe Valdez III, 1342 Rumaldo Pino III, 1343 Susan Maes, 1344 Jessalyn T. Espinoza, 1345 Elias M. DeLeon, 1346 Pearl Rose Romero, 1347 Mallory Slark, 1348 Genevieve Rivera, 1349 Cecilia Medina, 1350 Mary Sandoval, 1351 Steve A. Martinez, 1352 Esperanza Home Health Care, 1353 Priscilla Cruz, 1354 Melvin V.Cordova, 1355 Carmen Cordova, 1356 Christopher Montoya, 1357 James Montoya, 1358 Peter Rudy Padilla, 1359 Lorena Griego, 1360 Tiffany A. Medina, 1361 Judith

Ann Martinez, 1362 Nazario Romero, 1363 Brianna Roper, 1364 Anselmo Chavez Jr. 1365 David A. Meserve, 1366 Damian E. Gallegos, 1367 Daniel Roper, 1368 Frances Torres, 1370 Adriana Stark, 1371 Genevieve Vigil, 1372 Juan Carlos Romero, 1373 Rita E. Sandoval, 1374 Edward Sandoval , 1375 Monica Landovago, 1376 Frank S. Padilla, 1377 Juanita B. Martinez, 1378 Roberto S. Martinez, 1379 Evelyn H. Sanchez, 1380 Rita P. Duran, 1381 Carlos Martinez Jr. 1382 Flavio Elias Romero, 1383 Martha Martinez, 1384 Justin Garcia, 1385 Maria Louisa Padilla, 1386 Frank A. Padilla, 1387 Michael Trujillo Jr. 1388 Nicolas Olivas Jr. 1389 Manuel A. Medina, 1390 Antonio Medina, 1391 Agnes Padilla, 1392 Franchesca Stark, 1393 Theodore Esquibel.

AMERICAN LEGION POST # 114
MORA NEW MEXICO

Most of the veterans who have made this history are now gone. and many records have disappeared. The only surviving members who have kept their membership since inception of this post are Amadeo J. Padilla. Manuel B. Alcon. Levi Espinoza, Pat Romero, Joe C. Trujillo. Alfredo Roybal and Phillip C.U. Sanchez. Levi Madrid who was the last veteran of World War I died this year.

There are many who have failed to continue their membership or have moved away. Many have belonged and then dropped out. To name them would be a tremendous job because documentation has been miss placed or lost.

The World War I Veterans had organized the Trammel Post #6 of the American Legion around the 1920 s and it lasted up to the late 1930 s. Among their members were Levi Madrid. Alfredo Medina. Phillip N. Sanchez. Alejandro Martinez. Agapito Montoya. Celestino Garcia. Samuel Brooks. Juan B. Maes. Matias Maestas. Emilio Martinez. Frank Nolan. Canuto Sandoval and Charles Williams who. all of them, later joined Post #114.

By the latter part of 1946. most of the World War II Veterans had been discharged from the armed services and a group of them gathered to organize themselves. Among this group were Albert Cassidy. Amadeo J. Padilla. Manuel B. Alcon. Ricardo Pino. Candelario Lucero. Samuel Romo. James Roy Eagle. Gomisindo Espinoza. Joe A. Florence. Florencio Gonzales. Claudio Gonzales. James Leger. Elfego Lovato. Delfinio Lujan. Frank A. Maestas. Samuel Maestas. Leo Madrid. Ernest E. Martinez, Nicolas Martinez, Paul Montano. Jose B. Montoya. Tony Mora. Levi Pacheco. David D. Romero. Napoleon Sanchez. Patricio Romero. Pablo Romo. Anselmo Sedillo. Dan Tafoya and Joseph P. Trambley Jr.

Many of the soldiers who had died during World War II were being brought back and this group would give them military funerals. Most of them were buried in the local cemeteries.

The decision of organizing all veterans into one group that would not be biased. took some time. At first. it was decided that the Catholic War Veterans would be the organization to join. There were others who belonged to other churches and they would not be comfortable in such organization. The Veterans of Foreign Wars was opened for those who had been overseas and there were some who had not been overseas. The one organization that would take all persons who had been discharged in 1946 was the American Legion. The qualifications were that a person must have served during war time. had served at least 90 days. and had been honorably discharged.

Everyone mentioned above qualified and by December of 1948 these thirty veterans had applied to join.

Ricardo Pino was elected as the first commander of the post. Suggestions as to what name be given to the post were many. finally it was decided that the name Pacheco-Romero be given in honor of Jacobo Pacheco and Guadalupe

Romero. These two men were the first to be World War II casualties from this county. The post was assigned Post #114 by The Department of New Mexico.

Ricardo Pino submitted the 30 names of those who had applied and so the post was organized. As the first Finance officer, James Roy Eagle was elected while Joseph P. Trambley was named adjutant.

There was no set place to meet so the membership met in different places. Among the places they met were the old Kahn Hotel which belonged to Pete Trambley at the time. The old Elementary School Building built in 1923 was another place where the Legionnaires met as was the court house.

The fiscal year ended June 30 and started July 1st. The terms of each Commander covers half of one year and half of the next. The first Commander elected in 1948 was Ricardo Pino.

The Legion took over celebrating the Santiago and Santana annual Fiestas that year. The FFA under the instructions of James Leger had rented the grounds from Mr. Juan Casados and had a few stock and he, being a member of the post, loaned the grounds and some of their animals not to mention the crudely made corrals for this purpose.

Ricardo Pino served up to June 1950 when James A. Leger took over. Amadeo Padilla was elected Finance Officer and Joseph P. Trambley was chosen adjutant.

June 1951 Sam Romo was elected Commander and J.P. Trambley was elected Finance Officer while Pat Romero was chosen adjutant. During Sam's tenure, the membership showed the need of a home and started negotiating for a place to buy.

Rocke Romero, Pat's brother, had several parcels of land and as a member of the post, his arm was twisted to sell the Legion, a few acres. Under pressure of his peers, he relented and sold the Legion 11 ½ acres for $325 with the provision that he would be allowed 15 feet path in the East side for passing his cattle from one pasture to the road. J.P. Trambley, A.J. Padilla and Sam Romo among others, were in the committee to purchase this land.

In 1952, Harry Sandoval was elected Commander and A.J. Padilla was elected Finance Officer while Pat Romero was named adjutant.

1953 James A. Leger was elected Commander.

1954 Joseph P. Trambley was elected Commander. Pat Romero was named adjutant.

1955 Sam Romo was elected Commander and Pat Romero was named adjutant. Pete Trambley was elected Finance Officer. 1956 These same people were railroaded into serving another term. During this year, on May 31, the post was incorporated, and talks about a home were rumored. A 40 'x 60' wooden pavilion was built.

In 1957, Manuel B. Alcon was elected Commander, Pat Romero was named adjutant. In 1958 Manuel was reelected commander and Floyd Maes was named adjutant while Ernest E. Martinez was elected Service Officer. In 1959 Manuel was reelected as commander and Pat Romero was named adjutant. This same year

Manuel was elected Commander of District I. On May 8, 1960, the first District Convention was held at Mora. The doings were held at the Old High School Gym. At this time it was the new Gym. In 1960 Manuel B. Alcon was reelected Commander, Horacio T. Martinez was named adjutant and Nick A. Martinez was elected Finance Officer. By mid year, Manuel had to resign since the by-laws stated that the Legion was non-denominational and non-political and he had entered into politics. He was seeking the Mora County School Superintendency. The first Vice Commander, Joe C. Trujillo, took over as Commander. Nick A. Martinez was the Finance Officer and Horacio T. Martinez was adjutant. In 1961, Joe was reelected Commander and Nick A. Martinez was reelected Finance Officer and Arthur R. Romero was named adjutant.

The American Legion Auxiliary was organized since the early days of the post but by now, they were inactive. During Joe's term, on April 9, 1962, Arthur Romero moved that the American Legion sponsor the Mora Fire Department and the motion was seconded by Noel Preston. It carried and the post took up the task of running the Fire Department. A new fire house was built by the Post. Nick Martinez was named as head of that committee. Manuel was named Treasurer and Pete Trambley Sr. was named Fire Chief.

The 1962 election was a re-run of 1961. Joe stayed as Commander, Nick as Finance Officer and Arthur R. Romero as adjutant.

By mid 1962, Joe had the ambition of becoming County Clerk and like his predecessor, had to resign and his first Vice-Commander, Pat Romero took over. The finance officer and adjutant remained the same.

In 1962, Pat Romero was railroaded into being Commander, as were Nick A. Martinez as Finance Officer and Arthur R. Romero as adjutant.

In 1963, Philip C.U.(Babo) Sanchez was elected Commander, Pat Romero as Finance Officer. This year, talk about a new pavilion was the issue. The old wooded pavilion had been moved in pieces to the neighboring lots by a strong wind. March 11, 1963 minutes read that Manuel moved to rebuild the Pavilion and Matt Martinez seconded the motion and it carried unanimously. The motion stated that a 40' x 60' dance hall be rebuilt. The following Sunday, many members showed up in their work cloth and started the work. They worked until the wee hours of the morning. There was plenty of booze and lunch to keep the laborers awake and in a good mood. Nappy Sanchez had never driven a truck but he sure could push a wheelbarrow as could Alfredo Roybal and Manuel. Ernest Martinez, Pat Romero Arthur Romero and Nick Martinez were the cement mixers. A long shot from Ernest's profession as the town's butcher, Arthur's, Nick's, and Pat's profession of school teachers. Alfredo's as Service Station owner, and Manuel's as School Superintendent. There were many more who contributed to the work as well as to imbibing.

In 1964, Nappy Sanchez had proven himself a hard worker so he was railroaded into becoming Commander. Matt Martinez was elected Finance Officer and Ernest E. Martinez was named adjutant.

1965 and 1966 saw the same administration railroaded to the same positions.

During 1967 election, Eddie Herrera was elected as the Commander, Manuel B. Alcon was elected Finance officer. It was during Eddie's tenure as commander that a well was dug. The well never produce much water but it was usable as it still is.

In 1968 Amadeo J. Padilla was elected Commander and Manuel B. Alcon Finance Officer. By now the membership became apathetic to the point that very few were attending meetings and fewer volunteering to do the work.

From 1969 to 1973, Amadeo and Manuel, in the same 1968 positions they held, ran the Legion sponsoring the fiestas. To their amazement, they succeeded in getting queen candidates, musicians, bar tenders, dance collectors, gate collectors etc. In the early 1970 s, Damian Pacheco joined and now there were three. It is necessary to know that there were more members but they did not help or attended the meetings.

The election of 1973, Damian Pacheco was elected Commander by the total of two votes. Damian did not vote for himself. There were only three members in that meeting. Manuel B. Alcon kept his job as Finance officer as he did up to 1986.

In 1974, Damian was reelected by the same majority as the election before since the same fellows were the only ones present. By 1975, Damian figured he had enough, so A. J. Padilla was hoodwinked into being the commander. 1976 was a replay of 1975 with the difference of a couple more votes. By this time new faces had shown up in the club. Harold J. Dineen was very active, had a lot energy and was willing to use it. Harold intrigued the others. By now , Alex Gonzalez had re joined the club. Since Harold had so much energy and was willing to be a martyr, the 1977 election was a snap . He did put up a front but all the excuses he gave were not taken seriously and besides he was outnumbered. He received the total votes cast(3).

Again in 1978 Harold was railroaded into being commander for another year. His chaplain was Luis Lucero and finance officer was Manuel B. Alcon service officer was Matt Martinez, first vice was Luis Martinez, second vice was Carpito Torres, historian was Joe C. Trujillo and sgt. at arms was Luis Romero. Commander Dineen was very energetic and was willing to suffer another year as commander so he and his slate were reelected . On the December 12, 1979 meeting Commander Dineen sold land to The V.F.W. Commander Manuel B. Alcon for $500. The lot was less than one half acre.

By 1980, New members were becoming active and so it was that Fares Martinez, A Vietnam Veteran, and a neophyte at Legion matters was hoodwinked into the honor of heading such outstanding organization. By the end of the term, he had learned much and so it was up to the conspirators to find another neophyte who had joined the club. Amadeo J. Padilla was elected District I Commander and again in 1980 and 1981 .

The following election, a new member by the name of Moise Medina was easy prey. He accepted and was elected by acclamation. That year Moise offered his air compressor so an addition to our spook house during the Halloween season was added. Also Bud Williamson, who had, the years before been Frankenstein, (He is tall and heavy set and is just perfect for that role) again played the role and that was one of the best Halloween parties, the Legion had ever given to the children of the valley. Moise did such a good job during his administration that he deserved another. He was reelected and needless to say, by acclamation. That year, the New Year's party was such a big success. Even Baudy Martinez participated. In the December 10, 1980 meeting, the Auxiliary unit was reestablished with 10 members joining. On February 11, 1981 Bleachers were ordered to be built by Luna Vocational Tech School at a cost of $250 for welding, $41.40 for metal plates, $57.10 for welding rods. April 8, 1981 dues were raised to $14. A second set of bleachers were bought for $1250 in Albuquerque. The slate elected during the April 14, 1982 meeting were: Commander Moise Medina, first vice commander–Tomas Martinez, second Vice Jose M. Marrujo, Sgt. at arms Luis Romero, Chaplain Joseph W. Valdez, Historian Red Haskins, finance officer M. B. Alcon, Service officer A.J. Padilla, adjutant H. J. Dineen. The District 1 meeting was hosted in Mora April 25, 1982. The exhaust fans were bought October 13, 1982. Red Haskins was elected Historian in 1981 and served until 1985.

The election 1983 was when Moise sat back and could not be convinced to another term so the search for another good candidate was underway. A good candidate showed up by the name of Emilio Thomas Martinez. The prestige of becoming Commander was nothing to sneer at and he was convinced to run. Thomas was elected Commander by acclamation. By the end of the term Thomas had his fill and no love or money would make him a candidate to succeed himself.

1983, no one was willing to take the responsibility of becoming commander. But M.B. Alcon had been friends with Harold Brock who had joined not too long before. He was sickly and did not attend meetings too often so in his absences, he was elected Commander. When he was confronted with the news, he gave all kinds of excuses why he couldn't be commander. Manuel, being his friend and giving him such news found himself in a dilemma. The only solution was that he would act as Commander in the absences of Harold. This was approved and so Harold missed some meetings but the Legion moved on. Air conditioner was installed may 13, 1983.

The election of 1984 found the Legionnaires in a desperate situation. No one wanted to tackle the job. Moise Medina was asked or should the word be begged? He couldn't take it any more and finally relented. Cabinets and an ultra violet light were acquired during this year.

In 1986, few showed up election night. No one wanted the position. So, as usual, railroading was the only solution. These railroaders picked on Manuel B. Alcon. He gave the excuse that he would hate to relinquish the finance office job. It was working well until there came a volunteer to be finance officer. Samuel Muniz promised he would take care of the books and so there went the last good excuse. Manuel was elected Commander and Samuel Muniz became the Finance Officer First-vice Jerry Martinez, second-vice John B. Martinez, service officer A.J Padilla, chaplain Ernest Chavez, sgt. at arms Levi Espinoza, historian Joseph Valdez, adjutant Fares Martinez. This year the bar windows were closed. Firing squad uniforms were purchased. the District meeting was hosted.

1987 There was competition for the Commander's post. Sam Muniz was nominated as was Bud Williamson. Sam declined and Bud was willing. No questions were asked and Bud was elected Commander as was Manuel Alcon returned to his old post of finance officer.

1988 A new member and a very active one at that came in. This fellow had the stamina, and willingness to work for the organization. Ben V. Bustos came in willingly and no questions were asked. He was elected by acclamation. Manuel was elected Finance officer.

1988 and 1989 and 1990, was a repetition of the previous year. Ben had done a good job of running the organization but like all good things must come to an end, Ben found a job that he could no longer attend the meetings and the work that had to be done in the Legion. The Legion sponsored a Mud Bog in the summer of 1989 and again in 1990. By then, the members thought that the arena was being destroyed and so it was suggested that the Mud Bog be held out of the arena. This was not acceptable to J.D. and Joe Weathers who were running such sport.

To find persons who are willing and can do the job is not an easy task. The search for a good commander was underway once again. This time, a member of a long time ago, returned and had rejoined the Legion. He like, Manuel and Amadeo was a glutton for punishment and was willing to serve if Manuel would help him out. Manuel couldn't say no so Levi Espinoza was elected commander and Manuel was elected finance officer-adjutant. in the election of 1991.

The District meeting was held in Mora that year and the Ladies' Auxiliary was reinstated.

The election of 1992 was a replay of the 1991. During Levi's tenure the bleachers were re-roofed with a tin roof. 1993 elected officers were Levi Espinoza, commander, Richard Ponzer, vice-commander, Finance officer, Manuel B. Alcon, Service officer, Amadeo J. Padilla, Chaplain Raymond Brown, Historian, Sipreano Trujillo and sargent at arms, Nerio Martinez.

A few highlights must be mentioned here.

The post has been sponsoring the Mora Fiestas and Rodeo since the inception of the post.

The first pavilion was built of lumber and a wind storm blew it down.

The present brick building was built by E. Sandoval and Andres Espinoza. Ernest E. Martinez directed the brick addition now used as a bar.

Harold J. Dineen, Manuel B. Alcon, and Ernesto Alcon made the addition now used as the meeting room. Later on the addition that covers the well house was built by Harold J. Dineen, Manuel B. Alcon, Ernesto Alcon and Fares Martinez.

Damian Pacheco, Manuel B. Alcon, Max Pacheco and Edd Herrera built the well house.

The electric wiring was done by member electricians, Matt Martinez and Jose Frank (Pelon) Martinez.

The bleachers were brought from Albuquerque by Harold Dineen and set up by the membership.

The arena was first built with the crow's nest facing west and with wooden poles and hog wire as were the chutes. Later the crow's nest was moved to the southern part of the arena and steel was used to make the stalls and chutes.

For many years Pat Romero and Manuel B. Alcon were the rodeo announcers, that is until the post was affluent enough to pay a professional.

The first rodeos were held in town when stock was not available, contests were held and prizes were awarded.

One year the Rodeo was held at Buena Vista.

In 1979 the Legion sold land to V.F.W. In 1980 The legion bought pipe and sucker rods to build corrals. Camp Luna did the welding.

Two legionnaires of the fair sex that joined the legion at one time or another are Leonore Maes Valdez and Juliette Sanchez Van Sicklen. Juliette has been a loyal member for many years and is still a member. She is the only female member of this post, at the present time. (1990)

Dues were raised to $14.00 January 1, 1982.

The second set of bleachers were bought for $1250 in Albuquerque. They are 60' long and are 10 seats high. Harold Dineen did the negotiating.

District meetings have been hosted, 1959,1982,1985 and 1991.

Cooling Fans for the pavilion were bought in 1982 and were installed by Harold Dineen and Manuel B. Alcon.

Cabinets were acquired in 1984 by Harold Dineen.

Firing Squad Uniforms Purchased in 1985.

The post had many honorary members. At one time all prominent men in Mora were honorary members. To name a few, Ernesto Lujan, Flavio P. Vigil, Frank L. Trambley, Ernesto Alcon, Pete Trambley Sr. and Fermin Pacheco.

Every year, the Legion sponsors girls to be queen of the fiesta; Among the queens were: 1957 Lorraine Cassidy, 1968–Catherine Pacheco, 1969 Patty Van Sicklen, 1972 Ruby Zamora, 1975 Kathy Grine, 1976 Iris Leyba, 1977 Bernice Velasquez, 1978 Margaret Medina, 1979 Hanna Chavez, 1980 Linda Porter, 1981 Nancy Ruiz, 1982 Renee Zamora, 1983 Margaret Duran, 1984 Clarissa Espinoza, 1985 Kiki Arellano, 1987 Lillian Martinez, 1989 Lori Lucero, 1990 Cindy Vigil, 1991 Denise Martinez, 1992 Isla Jo Montoya, 1993 Angelica Castelon, 1994 Nancy Martinez, 1995 Bernadette Maestas. There are some girls whose names do not appear in this work because the records are missing. Author regrets this fact.

This post has sponsored two boys to Boy's State and two girls to Girl's State every year since its inception.

It has sponsored the annual Oratorical contest and made available scholarships to students of Mora High School.

In the early day's of rodeo, horse racing was one of the main attractions.

Members of this post who have been District officers are: Commanders, Manuel B. Alcon and Amadeo J. Padilla. Matt Martinez has served as District Chaplain and Manuel B. Alcon as District Sargent at Arms.

Many of the members have served in the different offices and to mention them by name could, in itself fill enough information for a book.

Fares Martinez, Baudy Martinez and Alberto Abeyta joined 12/13/1978, Jose Maria Marujo joined 1-10-1979, Moise Medina, and Paul J. Pacheco joined 9/10/1980.

Three prisoners of war have belonged to the post. Willie (J.G. Lucero – Batan Death March) Feleciano Herrera and Jose Maria Marrujo who were Hitlers workers for a long while.

Picture at left shows the American Legion Rodeo Grounds. The crow's nest is at the center of picture.
The pavilion and office building is at the right..

V.F.W. POST 1131
OLIVAS-VALDEZ POST
MORA, NEW MEXICO

The post was organized on March 19, 1967 in Mora. In order to start a new post a minimum of 25 members was required.

The post started with 32 veterans. The post was organized as Olivas-Mascarenas. In 1978-79, Commander Ricky De Herrera recommended to change the name of the post to Olivas-Valdez the name was to honor Lorenzo Olivas from Holman who died in the Korean War and Leroy Valdez from Mora (Las Aguitas) who died in Vietnam.

The following veterans organized the post:

Modesto Borrego	Leandro Mondragon
Charles Louie Garcia	Alfonso Olivas
Jose Benito Grine	Jose Manuel Olivas
Jose A. Lopez	Levi G. Ortiz
Felix Garcia	Albert Romero
Eddie Herrera	Ramon G. Romero
Elfego Lovato	Frank A. Padilla
Juan B. Maes	Carlos Salazar
Matias Maestas Sr.	Feliberto G. Sanchez
Daniel Maes	Jose Bengie Sanchez
Sam Maestas	Rudolfo Trujillo
Horacio T. Martinez	Juan J. Duran
Nick A. Martinez	Elias Duran Jr.
Frutoso Martinez	Joe M. Garcia
Victor Nestor Martinez	Arturo H. Ledoux
Ismael J. Mondragon	Lucas Valdez

The perpetual post charter was obtained after a gain of 25 or more life members. This happened when Ricky DeHerrera was elected commander in 1977-78. That year and the following year, Ricky worked aggressively in committing 20 new life members and so the Mora Post earned the Perpetual Charter #3489 with a total of 30 life members on March 10, 1978.

Charter Life Members include:

Manuel B. Alcon	Nick A. Martinez
Helmut "Pete" Beck	Victor Nestor Martinez
Juan Richard DeHerrera	Antonio Montoya
Harold J. Dineen	Rudy C. Montoya
Elias Duran Jr.	Alfonso Olivas
Andres Espinoza	Frank A. Padilla
Sam Garcia	Albert Romero
Arturo H. LeDoux	Arturo R. Romero
Demetrio E. Lucero	Ramon G. Romero
Matias Maestas Sr.	Phillip C.U. Sanchez

Sam Maestas
Frutoso Martinez
Horacio T. Martinez
John E. Martinez
Louis E. Martinez

Jose Bengie Sanchez
Rudolfo Trujillo
Joseph J. Valdez
Lucas E. Valdez
John B. Vigil

V.F.W. Post Commanders have been:
Feliberto G. Sanchez
Jose Bengie Sanchez
Horacio T. Martinez
Andres Espinoza
Harold Dineen
Manuel B. Alcon
Eloy Leyba
Joseph J. Valdez
Alfonso Olivas
Robert Romero
Elias Duran Jr.
Ricky DeHerrera

Harold Dineen made All State Commander in 1974 for bringing membership over 100 % and submitting all reports to state. Dineen was one of the top 10 post commanders in the state.

Ricky DeHerrera made All State Commander in 1978-79 for bringing up membership over 100% and submitting all reports required by the state.

DeHerrera was selected as Veteran of the Year in 1978 by District 5 Veterans.

In 1978-79 DeHerrera was also selected as National Aide-De-Camp for recruiting over 100% in post membership and up to 64 life members in the two years as commander of post #1131.

DeHerrera came back from teaching tour in Penasco and was elected commander of Post 1131 in 1984-85.

He, again, made the all State Commanders Team in 1984-85 for bringing the post over 100%. For the third time, he made the All State Team in 1996-97. Horacio T. Martinez made the All State Quarter Master's Team 1996-97. That year the post membership was 130 veterans with 108 of them life members. The post finished with 139 members and 109 of them life members.

DeHerrera was commander from 1984-2000. At the end of the century and beginning the new century Horacio T. Martinez has been Post Quarter master and adjutant. This is over 20 years.

By the beginning of the century, DeHerrera had brought the post up to 153 members with 116 of them life members. For the fourth time, DeHerrera made the All State Team of Commander and Horacio T. Martinez made the All State Quartermaster Team. The author expresses gratitude to Ricky for the above information.

MORA COUNTY ENVIRONMENT

Mora County was carved out of the Taos County in 1860, which at the time it was a county that covered all the north eastern part of the state. Later on, Mora County gave part of its land to Union, Colfax, and Harding Counties.

Mora County has had a very rich history starting since its beginning.

It has had its part in good and bad things. The only military exercises it had was in 1847 when a contingency of the U.S. Army leveled it down in revenge of the Brent assassination. Many raids by Indians and some by white men have happened in the county.

The beautiful scenery has changed but very little. The mountains are still beautiful. However, the mountains had very few trees at the time the white men came. At this time, Indians and maybe a few trappers and hunters approached the county. There were some buffalo in the Eastern part of the county. There was a salt lake called "El Salitre" where the first settlers and those after them went for salt. There were deposits of different color of dirt which were used as source to give their homes a different color.

The houses were mud or adobe huts with a flat roof and had a thatch roof with sod which leaked when it rained. Later the roof was made out of lumber with a pitch roof. Most of the roofs are made out of plywood and tin because of the climate. Some roofs have asphalt shingle but because of the hail storms, they have been re roofed with tin or pro panel.

The people are beautiful as far as looks are concerned and the vast majority are good people. Like any other group, there are a few bad apples that spoil the good name of the place.

There have been many fiestas, two centennials and many weddings performed in the county. The Centennial was held in 1935, the Coronado Centennial was held in 1940. The Mora Fiestas and Rodeo held the closest weekend of Santiago and Santana which fall in July 25 and 26 of each year.

The rodeo was added when the American Legion took over. At first, the rodeo was local. Steers, cattle, sheep and contestant were all local boys. Pat Romero and Manuel B. Alcon were the announcers. Later individual persons like Eloy Zamora took the contract. Much later, Wiseman Rodeo Inc. took up the management of the rodeo.

The Centennial fiestas was attended by many people from near and far. They had a king who was called "El Rey de Los Chivatos" (the king of the goats) and that was Don Pedrito Trujillo who had the best grown beard. The Queen was Gertrudis Cruz who was Barney Cruz's wife. Ice cream was a fad at the time. There were Matachines Dancers with violin and guitar music which was about the only music used for dances. Thomas Martinez played the devil's part in this dance and forever he retained the name of Thomas Diablo. Adelina "Huera" Romero was the Malinche. Then there were others who completed the Matachines.

The Coronado Quarto Centennial was not as colorful as the Centennial.

The Santiago and Santana Fiestas were held annually. In 1948, the American Legion Post #114 took up the sponsorship and started their fiestas with a parade. At first, the fiestas lasted two days. A dance was held the first night of the fiestas where the coronation of the queen was crowned. At first there were three dances during the fiestas but in later years only one was held. This was due to the competition of the other town halls.

The Wagon Mound Bean Day was and is celebrated during the Labor Day Holidays. It starts with a dance. They have two dances at the gym and a rodeo. They also have a parade that makes the town proud . People who make it possible are the Zack Montoya family, The Alfred Romero family, the Wiggins, the Garcias, the Schmitts, and others. The people are treated with a meal of beans and BBQ meat. They also may attend the rodeo which in the past few years is managed by the Wiseman Rodeo Inc.

Mora, as the county seat, has the Court House and Jail situated right in the center of town. The first Court House was built across what was the Butler Hotel, later the John Hanosh Grocery store. The building had the court rooms on the top floor and the jail on the first floor. 1898, a beautiful building was built by some Italian builders at the present site of the court house building. There, also was a smaller building that looked like the main building. This was the jail house. It was razed before 1938 when the court house was abandoned and a new courthouse Southwestern style was built. The jail was on the second story. Much later an addition was made in the north side of the building. This became the present jail.

Incidents that have happened during this period of time are many and it would be impossible to name most of them since there is no record written.

Suffice to mention a few of those incidents: The Gavia (gang)de Silva, Los Gorras Blancas and other less famous gangs worked Mora County . There have been many murders committed. Some hangings, and shootings as well as many accidents. The 1904 Flood which made a rut out of the street and made the people think twice of getting better roofs.

The mysterious county may be peaceful for a time and all of a sudden it can change to something very different. The weather can also play these kinds of tricks.

The reputation of the county is as diversified as anything else. It being agricultural center and the states' breadbasket for years in the 1900 s to almost a ghost town in 1982. The population of over 15,000 down to 2,000+ in 1990, the closing of business, the moving out of the cream of the crop for lack of industries are just a few examples how the county has changed.

During the second World War, many people went to work in defense factories and many of the boys and girls went into the service, voluntary or otherwise, went to war and proved how good and loyal citizens they were. Many never made it back and some survived the most cruel treatment humans can dish out to their fellow men. Guillermo "Willie" Lucero was one of those who refused to die in the Japanese prisons. Jose Maria Marrujo and Feliciano Herrera returned back after being held by the Germans and many more like these two boys went through hard times to keep our country free. Many were decorated for valor.

Arts and Crafts and progress had been experienced in the County. Many crafts persons have gone through this county. The same thing goes for buildings. Many have been razed and newer buildings built however there are some buildings that need to be replaced or repaired.

The top picture is the site of the Butler Hotel
The house to the left is the first court house in
Mora. Picture is of the 1920's
The bottom picture is same site but in 1948
John Hanosh razed the Butler Hotel to take the
place of the Butler Hotel. Picture taken 1990.

MORA FIESTAS

We know that Mora was founded in 1835 and that the county was carved out of Taos County in 1860 and later on Union, Colfax and Harding Counties were carved out of Mora County.

Also, we know that this County had a very rich history starting since its inception. It has had its good times and bad times. But we do not know when the first fiestas were held.

In the early 1900's, people did celebrate what we believe, was the St. James (Santiago) and St. Ann's birthday which fell on July 25th and 26th of each year. This celebration has been celebrated since the early days.

Other celebrations held are The Centennial held in 1935. This was the first big occasion that this author attended. As a young boy, he remembers the first ice cream cone he ever tasted.

Also, it was the first time he witnessed the Matachines dance. The part of the devil was played by Thomas Martinez. Until his death a few years ago, was known as Tomas Diablo. The Malanchi was performed by Adelina "Huera" Romero. She died as a young woman a few years later. The other performers, the author does not remember their names. He did attend some of their funerals.

The main attraction was held in front of what is now the Lounge. Across the street was the old Court House built in the 1800 s which now no longer exists. There were outside steps to the top story. It was a two story building. It was on these steps that the coronation of the King and Queen of the Centennial was held.

Pedrito Trujillo was crowned the King of the Chivatos. (Rams) He sported the best looking and more complete beard of all the contestants. Gertrudis Branch who married Barney Cruz was the Queen. Her throne was a big Chair on the right side and on the left was another chair which was the King's throne. In between covered with a blanket was nothing underneath and who ever the King or Queen wanted to punish for some dastardly deed he or she had committed according to them, would have to sit between them. Needless to say they landed on the floor.

In 1940, The Coronado Quarto Centennial was held. It was not as colorful as the Centennial. The people had a very good time dancing and visiting.

The St. Gertrudis Catholic Church had its share in presenting other fiestas such as the day that commemorated St. Gertrudis day.

This gatherings took place at the church yard. The church at that time was a beautiful church with a steeple and bell tower. Many tents were set up and much action took place. Mr. Pablo Baca played the part of a Chinese emperor who spoke a language that only he could understand if he did understand. People went to hear him speak. He made a good profit for the church. Another tent held a fortune teller who foretold the future. She also made a good profit since there were quite a few souls who were superstitious to believe what she foretold them. Such as "If death did not take you when you were young it will take you when you are old".

There were food concessions, game concessions, gambling concessions, bingo, and many other entertainments. The priest and the nuns put up plays and many healthy entertainment was had by the people.

During some fiestas, the bells were ringing while the members went on a long procession.

The choir would play during the mass. There was a very nice organ that need to be pumped so that with the air the person turning the wheel that did the job would make it play. It had many pipes that made the most beautiful music. This author, as a boy, pumped that organ many times and many times, the nun in charge got after him as well as after the others that goofed while working the pump. As soon as the wheel did not turn the music would stop and many times it was very embarrassing to the organ player because she missed some notes.

The Santiago and Santana Fiestas were and annual affair. The church was mostly in charge. Then in 1948, the American Legion took them over. They started out with children's races, sack races, dress races, fat men's races, egg races and any other race they could think of.

Later on, they began to include a rodeo in their fiestas. The first rodeo was held in a field that belonged to Don Juan Casados where now, Larry Garcia lives . The front of that field housed Don Juan Casados' camping grounds. There were three or four buildings.

During these rodeos, Pat Romero and yours truly were the announcers. Later on in the 1950 s, the Legion bought eleven acres from Pat's brother, Roque, and so the rodeos were moved to the present Legion Arena. The first rodeos were local. Steers, cattle sheep and contestants were all from the valley. A pavilion was built of lumber by the members. A heavy wind moved it to the next field piece by piece.

The membership was set in continuing the dances as well as the rodeo and they took it upon themselves to build one of bricks. This has withstood the test of time. Most of the members were World War II veterans and were not afraid of work or of debts.

They became more sophisticated and started to hire a rodeo company to bring the stock and put up the action. The Wiseman Rodeo Co. From Clayton took over the rodeo.

Up to the late 1990 s, the Legion was the sponsor of the parade, fiestas and rodeo. It became a heavy burden to the few members and so the responsibility of the parade was passed on to the County Commission then the following year it was passed on to a group of people and later on to the Chamber of Commerce.

Many other fiestas have been held in the valley. Weddings, and birthdays, and when there were no excuses for one, they had a prendorio. A prendorio was when one or more persons were caught and for any reason they had to redeem by paying the musicians to play for a dance. Dances were held in private houses, in the dance halls when it did not cost any rent. The music was guitar and violin and sometimes a saxophone. When someone with much gusto was the one to redeem himself would bring a bigger band. maybe with a drum and maybe an accordion.

The last of these prendorios. this author remembers is in the 50 s. when he singled out the then sheriff. Leonor Manchego. He charged him of stealing his wife from her parents. The jury found him guilty. As usual, he pleaded guilty and he paid the fine. Unfortunately the author could not attend this happy occasion and that was about the last of the prendorios ever held.

Top picture is a 1918 end of first World War celebration.

Bottom picture is an early 1900 Santa Ana and |Santiago celebration.

SOME HIGH LIGHTS IN SPORTS IN MORA

The Mora Rangerettes with coach Mark Cassidy and assistant coach Salcido won the 1998 state tournament class AA in March 7, 1998. The first team to make to the top in the Mora history.

The boys (Mora Rangers) had made it since back in 1964 - 1965 when Doroteo Vigil was coach. They beat Santa Rosa for that honor. Manuel B. Alcon was the superintendent of the school at that time. Santa Rosa had a unique team but Coach Vigil used his knowledge to outsmart them. Later Coach Arthur Romero also made state.

These facts bring back memories of the sports in high school back in 1940 when this author was in high school. He was in the basketball team. Flavio P. Vigil, Ignacio Maestas and John Cassidy were the coaches. Flavio was Doroteo's father and John was Mark' Uncle. These families have been into sports both basketball and baseball since the early days.

The high school had a basketball team of boys who were the only ones allowed to play. Girls were not allowed to even play with the boys because it was very unlady like.

Sister Marie had baptized our team the "Mavericks" and Flavio took this team to play in Santa Fe at the Sweeney gym. It was the first time the team ever played in a gym. For that matter the first time they ever played another school team. Needless to say, the team was royally beaten.

To let the reader know, the team did practice in the field later the coaches got the politicians to lend the school the court house which by now had been abandoned.

The windows were broken and the court room was in the second story. the court room was about 30 x 30 which was not suited for a ball court. Every time a bad pass was made, someone had to run downstairs and out for the ball. It took the runner a good four minutes or so to recover the ball.

These teams to win a state tournament was almost impossible save by a miracle.

Later, Albert Valdez built a gym in his property and loaned it out but it was too far away to go practice and besides the players had to get home to do their chores before it got dark.

Mora and Cleveland had a very good baseball team. The persons this author remembers are the Cassidy brothers (John, James) Feleciano Herrera, Crecencio Barela, Francisco (Pancho Ganchete Pelon) Martinez, and the author. The last game they played was in the latter part of 1940 s.

WHY HISPANICS HAVE SUCH A HARD TIME
MAKING DEMOCRACY WORK

To understand the philosophy in comparison of the Anglo culture in the early days, the author offers the following:

Hispanics, if not all most of them, are or were: Catholic, authoritarian, rule by one, poor, hard laborer. They believe that it is easier for a camel to go through the eye of a needle than for a rich man to go to Heaven.

He has much pride. He is a macho-man and as head of the family is the boss. His children are reared in strict discipline. Child abuse was not considered as such. Parents and older people are treated with great respect whether they deserve it or not. They believe that he who bosses cannot be wrong. What he says is the law and must be obeyed.

Money is only to satisfy his needs. Bank and other financial institutions have little or no place in their lives.

Loyalty is a virtue which is to be practice. If a wife double crosses the husband and leaves him for another, he will follow both and more likely kill them if he ever catches them. He is very emotional. On the other hand the man can mate as many woman as he desires and it is fair game. The animal instinct is there.

Laws are made to be broken and he breaks them. Laws that are not to his advantage, he will break.

Jails were made for one purpose and unless he has been in one he is not a man.

He can love with a degree that compares only with the degree he can hate. He wants to be king. Everyone wants to be king so no one wants to follow. They are very jealous. They do not like for the neighbor to have as much as he does. He will help the underdog. He will go out of his way to help those under him.

Laws are made for the neighbors. His pride is his down fall. Enforcing the law on others is the reason laws were made.

Education is secondary to his physical health. He believes that the less he knows, the less he will have to account for when he faces his maker. He asks God not to give him anything just to put him where he can help himself. Help himself, he will if the opportunity knocks at his door. The consequences do not matter. He likes to suffer. He also likes to see others suffer. They have been excellent soldiers during war because of this characteristic. He does not fear death. La vida no vale nada. (Life is worth nothing) He can withstand punishment without flinching.

Now a few characteristics of the Anglo culture: They instituted Democracy. All humans were created equal, most are Protestant, middle class, business men, educated and used their head to rule them instead of their heart.

Freedom, love and right of life, pursuit of happiness equal justice were their virtues according to their interpretation.

They believe that there must be laws and they must be for everyone although when it hits home, it becomes a different story (politics). They believe that every one was born equal. However, some are more equal than others as it was proven when Spanish, Negroes, and Indians were treated as less than equal.

The above was true up to the time that the Anglo culture took over and still today, many Hispanics fit some of the above descriptions if not all. It is very hard to change after so many years believing as they did.

Top picture is a scene of the court house steps with a group of office workers in the 1900's. Bottom picture is a scene at Rio De La Casa in the early 1900's.

The following sections of this report covers incidents that the author experienced in the valley.

A TOUR OF THE VALLEY IN THE 1930 S

You need to picture a town with little electricity, no paved roads, and the only running water was found either in the ditches or the River. Plumbing was a thing of the future and gasoline was 12 cents a gallon. (Drivers eat your heart out).

This tour would have taken place in the early or mid 1930's.

I was around nine years of age and just had learned to drive. My father had a 1925 Star Touring car which he trusted me to drive. If there are any State Policemen, they are none stationed in Mora. Most of the transportation is done in horse drawn wagons or horseback, on foot or on Tin Lizzies and Chevrolets and other makes.

We are riding the above mentioned Star Car. The road is graveled and in riding any automobile, one would think one is running over a washboard. Excuse me, you young ones would not know a washboard from a rolling pin, but I'll try to explain. A washboard was used to scrub clothing while washing it. The washboard was a one woman power. It had a corrugated side used to rub clothing.

There were no sidewalks except the one at the court house. The stores had wooden platforms in their front. The Butler Hotel had stone instead of wood walks.

We are at the Romero's Bend which today is the sharp curve at the East end of town. You will notice the steep hill behind us. No trees exist here.

There is no bridge to cross the Mora River towards El Alto, except a big long log farther up so that the people walking could cross. Any of you who would try to cross better not look down or you will fall into the river.

We will start the tour at this point. This is known as State Road #3. The bend is where cars can turn to go back to town with out backing up. It made a large loop and was wide enough for the automobiles of the time.

We can see the village about a mile up towards the West. This sharp bend was called the vuelta de los Romero's because the Romeros owned the land around it.

That road that crosses the river on our right as we travel towards town, is the road to El Alto de los Herreras or El Alto de los Indios. As I mentioned before, there is no bridge for cars, wagons or horses. To our left is the Romero's ranch. Right at the foot of the hill is their house and corrals. Vicente Romero, the judge lives here alone.

As we proceed the road to our left leads to Las Aguitas, El Carmen and on towards Rociada.

Next, we cross a bridge which will cross us over drainage ditches.

This next road you see to the left leads to Vicente Maes' house

(With Vicente live his wife, and two children) as well as Don Toribio Maes who lives next door with his wife, and then to Alfredo Medina's ranch where he lives with his wife and two daughters, Celia and Lupita.

Back on the main road, to our right is Damian and Adelia Lujan's residence where they live with their sons Elijio and Willie and daughters, Magdalena, Mela, Lourdes, and Vangie.

Right next lives Don Isidoro, wife, Mariaita Campos' and my pal Ernesto who is their grandson. Ernesto and I used to take care of our parents cattle or should I say we were supposed to watch them? Many are the times my dad kicked our butts for letting the cows into his cornfield or the neighbors cornfield or wheat fields. I remember the time we built a fire in a small cave and were roasting corn on the cob when dad happened to check up on us and the cows were in the middle of the cornfield. The snack was not enjoyed by us. There were few fences and none, where they planted.

The next house to our left there are no houses until we get to Juan Maes' house. Mr. Maes lives with his wife and their two daughters, Mary and Jennie and sons Gilbert, Floyd and Charlie. We travel farther into town. Farther up to our left is the old grist mill which at this time belongs to The Sanchez's brothers. Mr. Ben R. Daniels lives here. He is the mill's caretaker. The mill is not in use anymore so he takes care of the mill and the ranch.

Farther up to our left is the Laura Barnum's house and property. She lives with her granddaughter Adelaida. Mrs. Barnum owns the property up to the next road.

There are no houses on either side of the road for a good while. The next road to our left is the El Alto Del Talco town. It is not much of a town. We could get stuck on the mud for this is a road built in a swamp and has logs along some spots. It is rough riding.

I will tell you who lives there. First you see the chapel, it faces east. On the house to our left lives Don Tomas Ortega, his wife, two sons and daughter Lola. Next door lives Don Leandro Muniz, his wife, son Waldo and daughter Annie. Behind the chapel lives Mrs. Medina, and two sons, Jose and Martin and a daughter Adela.

We move on ahead and the next house to our left is the Raymond Casados residence where he, his wife, Crucita, son Victor and daughter Ramona live. Victor is my friend. Raymond is Mrs. Laura Barnum's son.

Next door lives Don Quintana, wife, Natividad, with their daughters, Mary, Rosita and Cora.

Next door lives Mrs. Onofre Quintana, her daughter Magdalena, and sons, Pat, Andres and Pablo. Pablo is my friend.

Next door lives Mr. Cooper and next to him in the house with the orchard lives Dona Franke Salas and her daughter, Mariquita.

Across the street from Dona Salas lives Dona Veneranda Valdez with her son Acorcinio, and daughters, Viola and Maria.

Next door is the Manuel Rodarte's blacksmith shop and just behind is his residence. Mr. Rodarte lives with his wife, and two sons, Frank and Jacinto and a daughter. Both boys are my playmates.

To our left, right across the street of the Rodarte's residence and next door to Franke Salas live Dona Elena and Erminda. Next to them is the Paul Netzloff residence where he and his wife, Aurora live. They have no children.

Next to the Netzloff's is a two story building (El Palomar) at this time no one lives there. Next door lives Mr. Arturo Romero, his wife, Sofia, daughters, Connie and Bea and Son, Arthur.

Still to our left, next door to Mr. Romero's live Mr. Arturo Medina, his wife Dolores with their children, Sam, Moise and Nancy.

Next door to the Medinas live Mrs. Leonore Maes and her sister. Next to them in the same property lives Don Leandro Maes with his wife and their sons, Rumaldo, George, and daughter Lucia. George is my friend.

Across the street is the empty house of Don Jorge Martinez. Next lives Eloy Martinez, his wife Refufito, sons, Eloy Jr., Ernest and George. With them is Annabell Martinez who is Mrs. Martinez's babysitter.

Next door to them, lives Manuel Melendez, his wife, and two sons, Manuel Jr. and Frank.

Next to the Melendez's lives Don Antonio Pino , his wife, Perfecta, sons Ricardo and Arturo and daughters, Leonore and Dolores.

Across the street from Eloy Martinez's lives Don Martin Medina, his wife, son Edwardo, and daughters, Seralia and Fabiola.

Next to them lives Mr. Isaac Castillo, wife, Juanita, daughters, Angelina, Emelina, Veneriza and Clorinda and their son Vidal.

Next door to them lives Don Pedrito Trujillo, his wife, Maximianita, and grand son Waldo, a poet.

Next is the two story house where Don Palemon Ortiz, his wife Dona Anita and their two daughters, Adelina and Dolores live.

Across the street live Mr. and Mrs. Solano, sons, Arturo and Floyd and their daughter. Next to them lives Dona Piedad Archuleta and her daughter. The Trambley Twins, Ernestine and Tillie spend much time with them. Mrs. Archuleta is their grandma.

Next door is the residence of Benjamin Alcon, his wife, six daughters, Aurora, Erminia, Viola, Benerita, Adelina, and Lila and his son Manuel (yours truly).

Across the street to our left, live Benito Mora, his wife Isabel, and son Willie, my playmate.

Next door, lives Dona Genoveva Casados. She is a regular church goer and is very religious. She has her own little chapel with many statues.

Next to her house, live Mr. Tomas Jacquez, his wife, Rosa, sons, Henry, Tomas Jr., Arturo, Floyd and daughters, Mary and Amelia. Arturo is my classmate as well as my friend.

Next to them live Mr. Celso Romero, his wife, Antonia and daughters, Tillie, and Simonita. Right next door is Mr. Romero's candy store. Here is where we kids buy our blackies, brownies, and whities. With a nickle, we can buy a big bag of candies and my friend Willie can buy a bar of chewing tobacco. Mrs. Romero was County Superintendent from 1926 to 1929.

Across the street live Mr. Cosme Garcia, his wife, and sons, Beltran and Nelson.

Next to their place is an alley that leads to Don Cesario an his wife, Felipita. They live right by the edge of the river.

Next to the alley is the Khan's Hotel. Mrs. Julia Strong owns and manages it. The building is a long one. The back yard is a square with a patio within. Mrs. Strong is Gaily, Decky and Jeanine's grandmother.

Across the street is the Peter Trambley's residence. Here live Mr. Trambley, His wife Anita, sons Pete Jr., Fred and daughters, Cecilia, Twins— Tillie and Ernestine and Maime.

Next is the road to LeDoux and across to your right is the Trambley's store, garage, and on the second floor is their dance hall. Next is the Bruno's Bar.

Next to Bruno's Bar is the Jose Martinez's residence. Here live Mr. Martinez, his wife, Francisquita, their children, Mary, Margaret, Nasha, Adelina, Joe, Pablo and Nick. Mr. Martinez's slaughter house is right behind Bruno's Bar. Mr. Martinez's Meat Market is adjoining his residence.

Next door is the Hanosh residence where Mr. John Hanosh, his wife, Rosa and sons Jojo and Eugene live. His store is next door. Next is the Sanchez warehouse and Dr. J. Johnson's office. He is the only Doctor in town. Next door still under the same roof lives Mrs. Isabel Sanchez who is the wife of J.M. and mother of Florentino, Steve, Manuel and I do not know the names of the others.

Across the street from Mr. Martinez is the Waxman residence. Next is a long house then The Morris and Back Mercantile store then an alley then the J.M. Sanchez Mercantile store. Next is the road that leads to the Catholic Church.

Across the street and next to Mrs. Sanchez is an alley that leads to a vacant lot where carnivals and other tents are set once in awhile.

Next is the Milnor Rudolph's Mercantile Store, Bar, and Mr. Pablo Baca's Curious shop.

The big long building next to the Curious shop is the Butler Hotel. Behind it is now a vacant lot where there used to be a barn and a place for keeping the horses and wagons of the clients who frequented the Butler's Hotel. Next is the road that leads to Guadalupita.

Across the Butler's Hotel is the Peter Balland Meat Market, store and antique shop as well as a warehouse.

Between the J.M. Sanchez and Sons store and the Peter Balland store is the road that leads to the Catholic Church. This neighborhood is known as China. The town is divided into imaginary sections. China is one. Juarez which is across the river and La Vega or La Rana (Frogville) down below in the swamps. El Ranchito which is between the road to LeDoux and the China road.

Let's take a tour to China. To the left is, as I mentioned before, the J.M. Sanchez store. Behind the store lives Florentino, his wife Stella and their two sons, Napoleon and Gilbert Bierbaum.

Next is the Rimbert's residence then the Marcelino Pacheco's meat market.. Then there is the two story building belonging to Don Blas. The other four houses follow but I do not remember the names of people living there.

Across the street is the St. Gertrude's Catholic Church and farther on is the Priest's Rectory. Father Juan Perez is our priest and he lives here. The road turns East here to meet the road that leads on to Ledoux.

To our left, is the Archuleta's residence. Mrs. Odelia Archuleta, a widow, lives here with her children, Polo, Angelina, Philomena, Evelyn, Joe and Emilia.

On the corner, two story building Dona Guillerma and her children, Willie, Federico, Viola, Margaret and Ida live.

The road turns East and still to our left next to Dona Guillerma is the Pablo Martinz's residence and next is the San Jose Parish Hall. The alley after the San Jose Parish Hall leads to the houses in that block. Don Tomas Olivas, his wife, Son, La Ganza and his daughter, Maggie live here. Farther down and to your left lives Tomas Diablo Martinez, His wife and sons.

Let us turn back the way we came. Across from the San Jose Parish Hall and to our left is the empty lot where the Christian Brothers started their Boys school back in the middle 1800's. The ruins you see at the end of the lot is where their residence used to be.

Next is the School which is two story high and built in 1922, I believe. The only playground equipment in our school is a fire escape which we used as a slide. I have no recollection of ever using it for the purpose it was constructed for.

There is a fifty foot deep well in the South side of the playground and in the boy's side. The lumber wall separates the boys and girls playground. The apple orchard is on the boys side. Each side has and outhouse with accommodations for two at a time. You know, I wonder if the teachers are human and need this facility and if they do where do they go?

Next is the priest's orchard and car garage then the Rectory then the Church and to the West at the end of the alley next to the church is the Sisters Of Loretto Convent which also in part is the High School.

The Church's front yard has seen much action. Back in the 1920's the Mora Town Band had Sunday's concerts here. There have been concession stands and other activities as well.

To the West side of the parking lot, is Florentino Sanchez's rental house. Then farther South is the Frank Trambley's corral and slaughterhouse. Then we are back to the Peter Balland Mercantile Store. We are back to the main street.

Traveling West, on the left side, the next building is the Balland's warehouse followed by the Trambley's Yard and then the Strong and Trambley Meat Market and Grocery Store.

The big long house that follows is the residence of Mr. Frank Trambley who lives with his wife, Josephine, Son Frank, known as Decky, his twin sister Gayle and baby sister Jennine. The alley that follows is the entrance to the fort like old Presbyterian School yard, which existed back in the 1800's. This school was later relocated in Albuquerque. It is now known as the Menaul School.

The next long building across the alley is the Madrid's property. Father Angelico Chavez, his parents who were Mr. and Mrs. Fabian Chavez, and brothers and sisters lived here at one time.

Across the street of the Trambley's store is the first court house in Mora County. You can still see the steps that lead to the second story of that building. That building was also the jail house. It is said that here, quite a few men were sentenced to hang by a judge. Later it became a tavern. Behind it towards Guadalupita is Macario Segura's blacksmith shop and behind the blacksmith shop and towards the Juan Mora's home is the first Public school in Mora. This alley is along side of the Mora River. The road to the South leads to Guadalupita.

Back on State Road #3 starting at the old court house is the P.N. Sanchez's Service Station followed by his residence. He lives with his wife, Emma who is Mora County School Superintendent. With them, lives their son Phillip C.U., daughters, Juliette and Patsy. It is said that John Dougherty who at that time was sheriff of Mora County was shot through that window facing East. He was sitting on his easy chair with two of his grandchildren on his lap, one on each side, and a member of the La gavilla de Silva shot him dead.

Next is another alley. On the other side of the alley is a string of houses that look like one long house. Mr. Romero, his wife and daughter Viola live in the first section. Then there is a bar then more residences followed by the residence of Benjamin Gandert who lives with his wife, Isabelita, sons Joe, William, Ben, Robert and daughter Ida.

Then there is another alley which leads to the Gandert's camp grounds.

Next is the Sosa's property. Here is the first movie house. Next is Don Juan Casados' Bar followed by an alley that leads to Dona Rodarta's, a Curendara lives, next to her is Juan Mora's residence, where he resides with his wife, Dorotea, son, Arturo and two daughters, Ignacita and Adelina.

On the other side of the alley is another long house. In part of one of this house lives Dona Felicitas Gallegos, daughter of Ceran St. Vrain and her son Jose.

Next is the two story house which is the old Sosa's residence and now is the U.S. Post office. The house is now owned by Richard Branch who resides in part of the house with his wife, Grace, sons, Richard Jr. Benjamin, and daughter, Eva. Mr. Branch is the assistant postmaster. His sister, Rosalia Branch is postmistress.

Across the street from the Sosa's property is the Court House and the Jail House. Both buildings were built with stones from La Cueva. These two beautiful buildings were built by an Italian company.

Next to the court house grounds is the two story house where Frank Vigil and his parents live.

Next to the Vigils is the two story house where Mr. Leo Maes, his wife Jesusita and son Margarito live.

Across the street is the Peter Balland's residence where he lives with his wife, Martha, their sons, Louie and Peter Jr. and daughters, Marcella, Martha and Margaret.

The corrals and slaughter house is just behind the residence.

Next is a road that leads to the other side of the river. On the other side of the alley is the Juan Casados residence where he lives with his wife, two daughters, Frances and Jenny and son Tomas.

Next is a renting house where Salvador and son reside. These people came from San Salvador.

Next to this house and in the same property lives Matias Zamora with his wife, Antonina, daughter Maclovia and sons, Stevan, Luis, and Matias Jr. Mr. Zamora was Mora County School Superintendent recently.

Next is the Levi Madrid residence and his store.

Across the Zamora's residence to our left is the Presbyterian Church. There are cotton wood trees from here to the alley to Don Bonney Gandert's road towards his saw mill.

Let us turn back and go across the river through the alley by the Balland's residence.

As we cross the wooden bridge to our left is the residence of Mr. Rafael Gonzales who lives with his wife, sons, Laurencio and Florencio and daughter Dolores. Next to him live Macario Segura with his wife Amalia, daughter Consuelo and son Manuel. Next door to them live Juan Segura and wife and family.

Traveling East we get to another group of houses. To our left is the residence of Eddie Williams where he, his mother and sister Julia live. Dona Carolina Martinez lives next door with her son Demetrio and daughters, Anne, Antonia and Bessie. Farther on down live Mr. Molinar with his wife and children, Anastacio, Gregorio and Jovita. Mrs. Molinar is a good story teller. She can keep children entertained for hours with her stories.

Farther on is the Rudolph's Mansion where the two Rudolph sisters, Bella and Josephine, Josephine's son Rudy and Milnor, the owner, live. Next to them live Mr. Joe Florence, his wife Cuca,(Milnor's sister, and children, Joseph (Pee Wee), Caroline, and Johnny live. (The house at the corner is a photography shop.) Caroline is small for her age and plays the Child Jesus in our Christmas plays.

Next is the St. Vrains Mill where wheat is turned into flour.
We are now in the road to Guadalupita. As we take the Guadalupita road, to our right is the Pablo Baca's residence where Mr. Baca, his wife, daughters, Martina, Corina and sons, Pablo Jr., Louis, Frank, and Anthony live.

Behind the Baca's residence is the Trambley's residence. Here live Charles, Milnor and their parents.

Continuing the trip towards Guadalupita, we pass the bridge that crosses the ditch which drains the water from the St.Vrain's mill which turns the big wheel. To our right is the Guadalupe Fuentes residence where he lives with his wife, Stella, sons, Lupito, Rumaldo, Narciso and daughters, Felecitas and Emilia.

Across the street from them, lives Mr. Milnor Rudulph Sr' sister. Mr. Rudulph changed the spelling of his name as you may notice.

As we move on, we come to the junction where the road to El Alto de los Indios turns. To our left as we face the road towards El Alto live two sisters. I believe their last name is Romero. People refer them as the Leonardas. One of them is named Leonarda.

At the distance, to our right we see the only two houses. In the one to our right live Mr. Pedro Maes, his wife, Luz, daughter, Donicia, and son Nestor. Next door to them lives Pablito Martinez and his mother, Antonia.

We shall return to the main road. As we get to the river, you will notice the iron bridge. This was built after the 1904 flood. It is said that some cattle rustlers paid with their lives under this bridge.

As we cross the bridge, we see the Segura's Blacksmith shop. The alley you see before we get to his shop is the road that goes by the first school house in Mora and on to the Juan Mora's residence, as I stated before. We are now back to the main road right next to the first Court House and Jail of Mora.

To our right was the old Butler parking place.

We will end this tour here.

Next, we will take the Ranchito tour.

As we leave State Road #3, we turn South between Peter Trambley's residence to our left and the Morris Back and Company warehouses to our right. We are on the LeDoux road. This road we will follow up to the hill where the Catholic and the Protestant cemeteries are located.

The houses to our left belong to Mr. Peter Trambley. This used to be the sight of the first camping ground in Mora. Here live Mr. Peter Trambley and his family as I mentioned on our town trip. To our right is the Morris Back and Company houses and at the big building behind them is their warehouse. We pass a ditch and still to our right is Mr. Romo's residence where he lives with his wife and sons, Nono (Antonio) and Dee Dee (Popeye)real name is Gilbert.

Next to the Romos is the long house where Mrs. Donaciano Romero lives with her two daughters and granddaughter Frances. Mrs. Romero was dubbed Dona Chana after her husbands nickname whose real name was Donaciano.

Next to Dona Chana is Mr. Maximiliano's shoe shop and his residence. Mr. Maximiliano Lucero lives with his daughter, Adelina. Behind Mr. Lucero's residence and across the alley, is the San Jose Parish Hall. Next is the road leading to China and the Catholic Church.

To our left is another road that goes clear down to Vicente Maes' property at La Vega. There are no houses from Mr. Trambley's up to this road.

To our left is the next house. Here live Alfonso Sandoval, his wife, Regina, son David and daughter Sandy. Next door to them is Don Daniel Maes' residence where he, his wife and daughters, Tina and Annie and son Daniel (Guzano) live.

Next to Don Daniel's residence live Don Benjamin Romero, his wife, daughters, Dora, Tita and sons Ben Jr., Louis (El Conejo) and Lorenzo (La Rata).

I need to clarify the nicknames of these wonderful people. At this time, these nicknames were used as a loving gesture and if any of them objected, nothing was ever said and they answered to this names whenever they were called. As a matter of fact, this was the only way to identify most of them. It seems that the people in the village thought they could baptize these people with a more popular name. The strange thing is that those names stuck.

The next building is a two story house next to Ben Romero's saw mill and residence is where Mr. Esquibel and David Vasquez, known as Dave Cookie and his two sons, Dave Jr. and Lupe also known as Dave Cookie and Lupe Cookie.

Across the street from the road up to here is the site of the old Christian Brothers School Campus.

To our left after the Cookie's residence, live Don Fernando Pacheco and next to him live his brother Marcelino, Marcelino's daughter, Mary and son Frank.

Next to Marcelino live Jose Pino, his wife, Margaret, son Joe Jr. and daughter, Frances.

Next is Don Candelario Lucero's residence where he resides with his wife. He is a good curandero, whenever anyone's bone goes out of place, he can reset it easily.

Next to Mr. Lucero live Don Agapito Abeyta, his son Max, granddaughter, Adela, and grandson Tony. Don Agapito was Mora Co. Sheriff some years back.

Next door neighbor of Don Agapito live Don Placido Romero
(El Charita), his wife, daughter Julia and son Christopher (El Chape).

Across the street and to our right is where Don Arturo Maes, his wife, Adela, daughters, Leonore, Viola, Praxedes, Nina and his sons Arturo Jr., George and Eugene live.

The last house in this street to the left live The Cosios family.
If we keep on going, we climb part of the hill where, to our right is the Catholic Cemetery and behind it is the Presbyterian Cemetery.

Trambley's garage, station, and store. Thomas Jacquez residence.

ATTENDING SCHOOL IN SECOND GRADE AT THE MORA ELEMENTARY SCHOOL

These incidents happen in 1933. Miss Ophelia Florence was the second grade teacher. She was a beautiful young lady and loved her students and treated them as her own children.

The building and rooms are big and nice for the times. The building is a two story building. It had four rooms in the first floor and four rooms in the second floor. The room to the Southwest was the second grade room. The room to the North West was the third and fourth grade room. The Northeast room was the fifth grade and across the second grade room was the first grade room.

The top floor was where the sixth, seventh and eighth graders took their classes. One room was empty and used as an extra to save books, desks and things that were not used.

The desks are large. They had an inkwell and each desk sat three kids. All desks were the same size except in the first grade room. They had small chairs and tables for the students.

There was a wood stove, the teachers desk, ten student's desks and a table in each room. There were two blackboards in each room. They were black until the janitors painted them green.

The top floor had steps on the north side of the building. The second floor had a big culvert which was called the fire escape. It served as a slide since there was no other playground equipment.

The playground covered about half of an acre. Part of it was an orchard which had many apple trees. The apples were removed from the trees by the time school went into session. In the Southern direction was the adobe wall that separated the neighboring land. By the wall, among the trees was a 50 foot well with a rope and a bucket. This was our drinking fountain. It had walls so as to keep adventurous kids from trying to explore the inside or the bottom of it. On an easterly direction stood two outhouses for the use of the girls. To the west stood two outhouses for the use of the boys.

Healthful conditions had not been invented at this time. Toilet paper in use were a sheet out of the big chief tablet or a rock or a stick. There was little if any privacy.

What was left of the playground was small and the bigger students would spend their recess in front of the building. Some would congregate at the opening of the fire escape. The recess was of a fifteen minute duration and all students went by the same bell.

It was tough for the little ones to gain entrance to the outhouse or to get their turn at the bucket at the well. It needs to be said that this playground was a part of the old Jesuit Boys College.

The schedule of the second grade class and the rules that had to be obeyed are as follows:
If you need to go to the restroom or for a drink of water raise your hand until the teacher acknowledges you.

Only one at a time must be out.
You need to wait until whoever is out comes back. (Sometimes this took time and many an accident occurred in the room).
No gum chewing or eating candy or pinion nuts are permitted during classes.
Coats and overshoes are to be placed on the spots provided. (Some were in the hall and sometimes those who had no coat would borrow one without the owner's consent).
If one had an answer to a teacher's question, raise your hand until the teacher calls on you otherwise keep your mouth shut.
No monkeying around, talking or laughing will be permitted during the class.
Keep the floor clean at all times.

Punishment was severe. One might make the first mistake but would, for a long time, behave. That is until that one forgot the anguish, embarrassment, and hurt he or she suffered. There were many who had a short span of memory and would get a repetition of punishment the very same day. Chewing gum was one of the worst offenses and some students were caught often. The punishment was where the teacher would paste the gum in the students nose and parade him or her to the next room. The students got a big kick when they saw the culprit with a big wad of gum on their nose.

This was the best and about the only entertainment the kids had and it was daily if not every period.

The day started by saluting the American Flag and reciting the pledge of allegiance. Then our daily, morning prayers. (Separation of church and state were not heard of at this time and in our school or if the elders knew about it, they never paid attention and no one complained).

Arithmetic was a hard subject and since our minds were fresh early in the morning, it was the first class. Learning addition basics was hard but some had little trouble and went on to subtraction then to multiplication and on to division. Some waited until they passed on to third grade to learn subtraction not by their choice but because they had a hard time mastering it. One had to master the time tables from two through twelve before he went to multiplication and division. Many were the fourth graders who learned them in that grade or in a higher grade. There were some dropouts because the tables or division was too much for them and the computers were not invented then. Many were retained in the second grade until they learned to read and some had been there more than three years.

Spelling followed Arithmetic. Again it took more memorizing. This was fun because the teacher would line up the kids and whoever misspelled the word on the first try had to go to the tail end of the line. Some kids had trouble even to spell jump or even hop. English was most of the kid's second language. The rule for spelling was to say the word after the teacher, spell it and pronounce it again. Any one who broke the rule even if they spelled the word right, had to go to the end of the line. Kids got a kick out of the poor sucker who failed to follow instructions. It was fair game to make fun of the poor child.

After Spelling came recess time. Fifteen minutes were allowed. The only thing one could do during that span of time was go get a drink of water at the well and maybe use the toilet.

By the time one would get there, a long line was waiting, usually the upper class persons had a monopoly of the bucket. Some creative kids would take there containers and get some water out of the bucket before a bigger kid put the bucket in his mouth. If one was lucky to get the bucket, he or she would hand it next to a friend. Some went to the outhouse and met the same problem. A big line waiting to get in had developed. Some would be late to class and they would be punished. Punishment by some teachers was kneeling or standing on a corner or behind the door. If there were not enough corners or doors they would stand facing the wall. The upper class teachers sent their students to stand on the hallway. Sometimes the County School Supervisor would pay a surprise visit and as he opened the door, the kid behind would get smacked on the face or head with the door. That did not hurt as much as the ostracism that followed. All of this in front of ones peers. Then there was that fear that parents would find out.

After recess came Science. There was only one theory as to how the earth and everything in it came to being. God had created everything in six days and on the seventh day he rested. The seventh day was Sunday and the kids looked forward to that day. So that they could rest but resting meant rest from school for most of the time kids were kept busy or had to attend church. The rule was "Idle hands are the tools of the devil", and no one wanted to be his tool.

After Science, came the noon recess. There being no such thing as hot lunch, all students went home to eat or ate in the classroom if they brought their own lunch. This was the time to eat candy, pinion or whatever they had in their possession. The lunch hour was short for some and it seemed that when one had barely started to chew on his bubble gum, the darn bell rang. The gum was still sweet and one hated to throw it away so the kid would hide it in a cavity in his mouth or behind the gums. This action proved to be fatal most of the time for children tend to forget and started chewing it during class or it would drop from its hiding place and the teachers were very sharped eyed. Punishment for chewing gum was mentioned before and here is where the entertainment came. At least it broke the monotony of studying and was a lot of fun except for the one who had been caught. The teachers were not selfish and shared the fun with other rooms. Now that was punishment! After that, the teachers sent word to the parents and that meant the woodshed and it wasn't for a load of wood. Here, the child got a good ole fashion whipping.

There were other novel punishments that were utilized for the different infractions. The teachers excelled in their creativity of forms of punishment and they must have been accepted for the stricter the teacher or punishment, the higher the rating was of being a good teacher. (Now I believe it was discipline they were after).

First class after lunch was geography. Learning the capitals of the forty eight states was a task. Fortunately there were only forty eight states at this time. Learning the topography was harder to some. Learning anything consisted of memorizing whatever was taught. Never mind if you understood what you were learning.

Catechism was the last subject of the day. Here we learned about God, His angels, saints etc. We also learned that the devil was on our backs every minute of the day so that would get candidates for his hot hell so that we better straighten up and fly right.

The end of the day came. The three people who were assigned to clean the erasers stayed after school. (No buses to transport the children to school were available—they came after the school was consolidated – students walked to school every day).

The ones assigned to bring in wood that was to be burned that day, had to be at school early before the classes started.

Kids, at this time were afraid. Some were afraid of their own shadow. Of course, there were few who, if they saw the devil, they would ask him to let them touch his horns or to pet his tail but most were modest, fearful and helpful.

As you have noted, back in those days what we call child abuse today was called discipline and if anyone was being punished, woe to whoever put in his two cents worth to try to help the culprit.

There was no doubt the child was guilty for the teacher, parent or any adult used his or her discretion and punishment. Parents would side with the teacher, principal or whoever was in charge.

Aside of the bad times there are many happy and nostalgic moments.

I mentioned that the second grade teacher was understanding, and I don't recall of any one receiving brutal punishment by her.

A WEDDING IN MORA UP TO THE 1950'S

Girls were betrothed at a very young age and either died or married the fellow her parents (usually the father) had chosen, no matter if he was twice the age of the bride. In few instances, the girl was stubborn and ran away with the one she loved. Chances were, she would stay away forever if not during the parent's life time.

Later on as the folks became more sophisticated, the girls were given more freedom to choose. When they became engaged, the groom to be would tell his parents what his intentions were and they would write a letter to the bride to be's, parents, praising them for the good and honorable job they did in bringing their beautiful and hard working daughter. In a week's time, the bride to be's parents would return the visit with the message that the girl had considered the proposition and was willing to marry their son.

The couple, if not underage, would visit the priest and the priest would look up to see if the parents were not delinquent in their premisas which were $1.50 dues a year. Having cleared this business, he would check to see if the kids were qualified to marry. That is, if they had received all the sacraments of the church, if they attended Mass every Sunday and holidays of obligations and had done their Easter duty, and were not half brother and sister. The priests were well informed on these matters.

The priest, through the peoples' confessions, knew who was a legitimate son or daughter and so he checked to see that they were not related within the third degree.

He would also decided if the couple were compatible and after this exhaustive research, he would either approve or disapprove that marriage. (Many of these disapprovals ended by the couple being married outside the church and so they were no longer members).

Once the priest agreed, the announcement of the banas (bans) would be announced every Sunday for a month's time, in all Masses that this couple were to marry at such a date. These bans were just in case the priest had made an incorrect decision and had missed a thorough investigation of the couple or had overlooked some of the reasons why the couple should or could not be married.

When everything had been cleared, the prendorio (engagement) took place. The padrinos (Bride' maid and groom's best man), flower girls, and all the personnel who would take part in the wedding were chosen and the party continued to the wee hours of the morning.

The couple would go to the court house to purchase their marriage certificate. There were no blood test or other requirements to be made. If the priest had said everything was fine then it was.

The parents of the bride had the more costly part for they furnish the pig, cow, sheep or whatever poor animal would become the main course for the wedding fiesta.

Marriages took place in the morning, however, this was optional.

The church was crowded to capacity for this was one of the high lights of the town. There were no formal invitations and everyone in town was welcome. Pictures were taken, the feast was served usually at the bride's home. There were no catering services.

The feast was an all afternoon gathering with music, usually violin and guitar. At night a big dance was held. In the early days it would take place in a home since dance halls were not usual. Later on, the dance halls were built and the dances became more sophisticated. Drums, accordions and maybe pianos were added to the band. There were no laws as to what time the dance would start or end.

The entriega took place at the end of the dance. This was when the couple were told that there were no more parents and they were on their own. This was a sad occasion specially to the mother of the bride and her sisters. Many a tear was shed. I assume that the fathers saw it in a different light. They had to show they were machos and saved their tears to be shed in private. The entriega was a litany of verses which, after the good time was had, the reality set on.

After the dance and the crying were over, the groom took his bride to his house which he had prepared for both. In the early days, there was no such a thing as a honeymoon.

The following Monday was work day and the schedule for both was imprinted in their minds for that would be the future for both. In this early days, there were no televisions, electric lights, few telephones (none private) or any other entertainment, and the custom was to have as many children as possible. Many young brides never realized this dream for they died young. There were few doctors and so parteras (ladies) were the ones who helped during child birth. The rules of cleanliness were not adhered to if there were any. The reason for having a big family was more help in the farm or ranch. There were few office work, or easy jobs to do if any.

OBSERVING A LENTEN SEASON

Lent was the holiest season of the St. Gertrudes Parish. It started on a Wednesday set aside as such by the church. This Wednesday was known as Ash Wednesday.

Early in the morning, parents would get their children up, wash and dress them and took them to church. While in church, everyone walked up to the communion railings where ashes were placed on the forehead of each one. This was a reminder that he or she was earth and that to earth he or she would return.

Everyone would be fasting. Anyone who had reached the age of 7 which, supposedly, was the age of reason, had to fast. To fast meant nothing solid could be taken as food until the noon meal. The age of reason I mentioned above was for everyone. There must have been no retarded kids born. If there were some they were treated as being normal.

Once out of church, everyone went home. The mother and older sisters went straight to the kitchen to make torta de huevos (egg omelet) with chile, panocha (wheat pudding), bunelos (now called Indian fried bread). By anyone's standard of that time, this was a feast. No one was permitted to over-indulge in food but with that temptation, it was hard to do anything else. So it was back to confession again. Since it was time to make penance, the devil had to tempt the poor innocent and hungry kids. This was the stones after the sticks as the saying goes.

After Mass, the kids had nothing to do and in their nice Sunday-go-to-church clothing could not play. This was done for a reason. The church, according to the parents, could not throw rocks during the holy season (all forty days of it) because if they did, they might hit Jesus and he had suffered enough. Throwing rocks was a no-no.

One could not play touch games because if one touched your playmate too hard (kids always pushed, pulled and touched hard) one would hurt Jesus.

If one used foul language (some language was considered foul) it was said that one was cussing Jesus. If one would get dirty hands, one would not be able to touch Jesus. If one had to take a leak (pee) one better not do it in water for Jesus would never forgive you. Anything that was fun was barred, for somehow would do damage to Jesus.

Any game, the poor kids tried was for some reason or another, not permitted. Either the father, mother or older sister would stop the game. There was strict supervision and the kids believed they were watched closely so as to make them suffer.

To circumvent this, the kids would attain permission from parents to go to some friend's house where supervision was more lax. To obtain permission was not an easy task. One parent may allow the kid to go and if the other said no, no prevailed. If both parents permitted, the child was ready to get their benediction which was a blessing ritual where the child or children knelt before

126

the parents. They would make the sign of the cross and then they were given a litany of advises–all of them started with "Don't". This was not too bad for it was like a must one had to go through and was expected. It was aggravating as hell, because one already had one foot at the friends' house and the litany was only half over.

Permission has been granted, blessings bestowed, litany finished, but wait, Grandma is visiting and now it is her turn to do the blessing. What could hold anyone longer than her blessings? Waiting for hell to freeze over that is what! But it had to be done. The kids had promised to be back on time for lunch. By the time all pre-requirements were completed, the kids probably had and hour to play. Well, an hour is better than being under surveillance of their hawk eyed parents.

At last, the kids are underway to their friends. There is a Mary, the older sister, who knows all the rules of the Lenten season. The kids start playing hop-scotch. The first kid throws his glass. Right there and then, Mary condemns the player. He has just hit Jesus with his piece of glass. He is going to die and for sure, he'll never see Jesus. They start a new game. This time, they play catch ball. The first kid throws the ball, he too, is condemned. He just hit Jesus on the head with the ball. They try soft ball since that doesn't hurt. Mary knows better. The first homer or first strike, the child has hit Jesus with the stick used as a bat. The batter is reprimanded so harshly that he needs to go to the outhouse. He does not make it as he wets his pants as well as the grass. There goes another candidate to hell.

One smart aleck suggests they play run–sheep–run. But before Mary can think of what infraction will be committed by playing this game, it is time to go home.

No one is permitted to eat anything until the blessings before meal is said. The kids are hungry and one kid sneaks a bunuelo (Indian fried bread) while mother is busy and can't watch so many kids.

Every one is sitting around the table and the father offers grace. The food is passed around. Everyone serves a small portion. So goes the rest of the meal. To the children, the temptation of serving themselves a good plateful is much but the respect is more. They fend temptation. This is a feather on their hat, although it is not done with all their will.

After supper, all members go to a home made altar where there is a statue of some saint. The rosary is recited and now comes the offering of the fast.

God knows that some of these fasts are not on the up and up. The offering is made for what ever its worth. The parents are real proud of their children.

The Lenten season, 40 days of it, has a way to drag itself by. On Fridays and Wednesdays, it is the same ritual followed every day except that on those days, the family would go to church to pray the stations. To a small child, this is torture, specially if he has ants on his pants. It wasn't so bad, for many did survive to tell their troubles.

Palm Sunday arrived. Services were so long, that some kids slept while the gospel was read. If parents asked them what the gospel was all about, it was easy for them to answer correctly because the gospel was the same one read year after year. After mass came the procession. By now, the kids had it. There was nothing they could do but what was ordered.

Holy week followed. Lord have mercy! Holy week was a week of nothing but Wednesdays and Fridays. The Way Of The Cross were what the fourteen stations were called. This exercise was held on Fridays. Every day it was to church we go. Everything that meant some fun was a no-no.

Holy Saturday was the day that everyone took his little jar to get the yearly supply of holy water. Many were the uses for the few drops of holy water. If some one got sick, if it was raining, thundering, snowing or any emergency it came handy. Needless to say. The palms brought home on Palm Sunday were used to burn whenever the weather was too unsettled.

Easter Sunday, after mass was like liberation day. It was a day of obligation and everyone seven years or older had the duty to go to communion which was expected at least once a year It was unusual to wait for a year because, if not the parents, priest or nuns would see that each Sunday you received holy communion. Christ has risen and our souls are clean as God wants them but for many not for long.

The reader may believe that this was a rough life. It was, but somehow there was room for a lot of wholesome fun. The kids knew no better so their life seemed as a good one.

This author like his fellow peers went through this ordeal for many years.

— **This picture shows an altar in a private home which was used during a procession which was a custom. The procession lead through town with several stops at different stations.**

A CHRISTMAS IN THE 1930'S

Dear reader, let me share the adventure of a Christmas during the 1930's. So that you may get the most enjoyment of this story, you need to pretend you are a pre-teenager and try to see it through such a pre-teenager's eyes.

What you are about to read is the truth as far as the author is concern. These incidents, scenes, and persons existed and played the parts described.

It is a cold, snowy day and there are about five inches of snow on the ground. The wood stove is going full blast thanks to all the wood I had carried in the day before.

Mother has been in her kitchen since yesterday, baking cookies, empanaditas de carne(meat turnovers), bread, pies, cakes, and posole .

The day before, she had made tamales, cooked beans and atole (a blue corn meal brew).

Dad has been working at the office and today, December 23th, they had their Christmas party at the office.(at the court house). On the way home, he and his friend Mr. Arturo Romero stopped at the Milnor Rudolph's bar and mother sent me to see why the delay of dad not coming home. He was supposed to be home two hours ago. Both, my dad and Mr. Romero are very lenient with their money and this being a holiday that comes only once a year, they felt like giving their friends their Christmas present in the form of drinks. The bar, as usual, was crowded but everyone got his present. The bar tender had a good reason for being happy for he was playing his register as if it were a pianola. The other customers reciprocated and one drink led to another and the hours ticked away.

The crowd was in cloud nine and as I went in to give them my message, they offered me a drink. I declined and besides the bar tender didn't approve of kids at the bar.

My dad was driving a 1932 Chevrolet Sedan(the family car). He was in no condition to drive. Mr. Romero was in a worse condition so I was the only alternative to drive them home. I had learned how to manipulate a car since I was 6 years old but never had driven this car. They didn't trust my driving and we could have walked home but to carry two grown ups would be impossible. They insisted in giving the folks one more round before they would retire. Luckily, before the order was filled, Mrs. Romero came after her husband and I was glad she had come. Now, she could drive. With her, there were no arguments or no "espera me poquito" (wait a minute).

At home, mother was tired of cooking as well as of waiting. She got on my case for staying so long. I explained the delay and so we sat down for a hefty meal. The meal of hot chili and beans with white gravy sobered my dad. After the meal, the pile of dishes needed to be washed, dried and put away. To me, this was no big deal for I have six sisters to do the work.

Early in the morning, everyone is up. The Christmas Tree was decorated since the 15th of the month. There are no presents in sight for at midnight, Santa Clause will bring them.

My mother didn't think I had done a good job of washing my hands so she got a brush and scrubbed them as if they were a dirty rug. That really hurt, my hands had no time to heal. Playing marbles tends to mess up the hands that feel water once in awhile. My dad had given me a haircut even though, I didn't need one. At least I thought I didn't need one just like I thought the hand scrubbing was unnecessary. My mother had admonished me about staying clean during the holiday. Knowing the consequences, I would be a fool to get dirty. This was a real hardship on my part.

The Sisters of Loretto who were our teachers at school would, as a custom, give all the kids a bag of goodies. This was the day. All school children went for their bag of goodies and for religious instructions.

In the evening, my friends come to ask my folks for permission for me to go with them to ask for los Oremos. This was a custom that was similar to our present day Halloween treats.

My mother knew me better than my dad and she, reluctantly, allowed me to go. Dad had no problem, he gave me permission with the understanding that I would behave.

The first few houses we stopped went smoothly. We got our goodies and are sent on our way. There were eight of us. The way we approached each house was the same. We all called in unison,"Oremos, Oremos, Angelitos del Cielo semos si no nos dan oremos, puertas y ventanas quebreramos" (We pray, we pray, we are angels from Heaven if you do not give us what we pray for, we will break down doors and windows)

Next we stop at Mr. Ortega's house. We have known him as a good, easy going person. We recited the oremos. Mr. Ortega opened the door and we entered. The door is shut and Mr. Ortega says "In this house we earn what we get. First of all we will pray and all of you must behave. One more thing, I don't like the idea of being intimidated by anyone. You will break my door and windows if I don't give you treats. I say you must earn you treats".

"Now let us pray. Kneel down. Pray that the Lord forgives us. Maybe two rosaries will be just about right for the treats I will hand to you", he continued.

All of us sweated a cold sweat since we feel that kneeling for such a long time is more punishment than praying. There is no alternative, we are locked in and there is no way out except kneeling and praying.

"God", we think, " If this does not clear our way to Heaven nothing will." Had we known what was about to happen, I would have told my mom not to permit me to go out in such a cold and blistery night.

No sooner had the last rosary been said when from the woodwork it seemed, came three abuelos (boogymen) fully armed with horse whips.

What followed was pitiful. Penitentes probably cherished a whipping but to us it was cruel punishment. My dad had used a whip many a time on me, but it did not smart as much.

The abuelos chanted "Bailen la paloma de huron du du alse la pata, welque el atole y veraste tu" (Roughly translated it says "Dance the pigeon's dance, lift your leg. spill the brew and you will see") This whipping was to atone for your past sins. To most. it was well deserved.

After the whipping, groaning and shouting is over. Mrs. Ortega puts an orange and some candy in our bags. We are relieved when the door was opened. Everyone tried to get out at the same time. The abuelos appeared again and the house was cleared before they could crack their whips.

Back at home. everyone is getting ready for midnight Mass (La Misa del Gallo) All my sisters and I went with mom to church. My dad joined us later. much later. As we approach the St Gertrude's Catholic Church. we can hear beautiful music. The choir is in the loft. Mr. Segura played the violin and two others played the guitar and Miss Maes played the organ. Music seems as that of the Angels from Heaven. The Choir sang "Oh Little Town of Bethlehem". It will be a long while before the mass begins. It is a long wait but the music is so beautiful and we didn't mind waiting.

Little kids sat way out on the front pews. The sisters sat behind. The pews are not comfortable specially for little kids. They sit and their feet dangle about a foot from the floor. Kids got tired and started swinging their legs hitting the pews and making a racket. Sister Malachy knows. by experience who the culprit was. She went over and pulled him by his sideburns. That is all it takes. From then everyone behaved.

Once the mass is over. Next comes the adoration of the Child Christ and the little boys to the left of the church line up to go adore him. They are followed by the girls who seat on the opposite side. It takes six sisters to take care of the boys side while it takes only one on the girls side. The fact is that there were twice as many girls than boys but the logic the sisters used was not conventional. I must say it was practical and it worked for them.

The adults followed the girls. The kids would be waiting for their parents at the back of the church.

Dad and mom, with my sisters came and we are on our way home.
We had walked to church but now we drive back with dad. It is a good thing too. because we are all anxious to get home and open our presents. When we left. there were no presents under the tree. We were confident that Santa Clause would come.

We got home and there under the tree are all our presents. A little red wagon for me. Just what I needed. Well. I had to chop wood and carry it in. and now I had some help. There were other presents but this one is the one I cherished more. I thought that I would cherish it for the rest of my life but it didn't last too long. I overloaded it so that I would have more time to play and so it failed before long. By next Christmas. I was ready for another one.

After enjoying all our gifts. we were sent to sleep. No rosary that night. We said our own prayers and went to bed.

When a child gets a gift he had been praying for. for a long time. how can he sleep? During the course of that night. excuse me. that early morning. I got up many times to admire and to push my wagon around the room. There was no way I would sleep late that morning.

Top picture was taken on Christmas Eve 1933. It shows the St. Gertrudes's Catholic Church's altar and the Christmas decorations.

Bottom picture is the site of the same church   On its right background is the Sister's of Loretto Convent which also served as the High School and housed the home for the Sisters during the 1920's until 1948.

A VISIT TO AN ALL NIGHT VELORIO

A velorio was a wake to honor a saint so as to pay a favor received. It also was a wake with the corpse of a dear departed present, which took place from evening through out the night until the following morning.

The people of the village were very strong believers and very faithful to their religion which was the Roman Catholic Church.

The people were very hard workers and worked from sun up to sunset. They had very little entertainment since there were no movies, television and very few radios. These velorios offered an excellent excuse to visit with the neighbors. It was a must to attend these doings in the mind of most people.

The time is in the late 1930 s. The place is the Mora Valley, to be exact, the hamlet known as El Alto Del Talco.

It was customary to praise and bid Saints for favors and needs. They had a favorite saint for each need. If a person lost or misplaced something, they would come to the statue of Saint Anthony. (The statue is an icon and not an item to worship as some unbelievers would criticize). Prayers were not sufficient so they would promise to spend a night in his honor.

The church was the most popular meeting place to have their wakes but it was more convenient to have it in a private home. The velorio meant that at midnight, a voracious meal would be served. Most of the hamlets had their own chapel with their favorite saint. The El Alto Del Talco Chapel was in honor of Santiago.(St. James).

This story is an experience seen by a teenager. The eyes of a teenager at that time were not very good at observing and many good and interesting things are omitted because of this flaw.

Dona Mercedes was a very devout Catholic woman, just like most of the neighboring women. The women visited more often than the men. They were very friendly and would offer to do things together. They had their quilting parties. They would help cook whenever the men were thrashing their oats, wheat or whatever.

It seemed that Dona Mercedes made a promise to some saint for a favor she had received and was now ready to pay up. She asked all the neighbors to come accompany her. Every member of each family was there.

The house was a long, narrow one. Most houses, if not all, were built with three rooms, namely, the kitchen, el saguan (Parlor) and the bed room. It made no difference if there were five, ten or fifteen members in that family. Dona Mercedes's house was no exception.

As was noted above, there were no wash room facilities besides a big pitcher and a big bowl used to wash ones hands and face. This was in the saguan (parlor). There was a big bucket full of water and a ladle which was used by everyone who needed a drink of water.

For toilet purposes, one had to run down hill to the outhouse which was near the well. Furniture was limited to the essentials and most seating accommodations were wooden boxes. There were some benches borrowed from the chapel. The chapel was in the center of the hamlet and was not far from Dona Mercedes' house.

All the neighbors attended and the house was full. Some were kneeling outside the door and out in the patio. Most of these were men who would, at times, move away from the crowd to talk business or to tell jokes.

The Penitentes took over. They prayed the rosary, sang alabados (solemn hymns) and prayed some more. When they got tired, a lady or a man from the congregation would continue. Many were the beads that were worn out in these velorios. All night long, they prayed and sang. The praying was the time when everyone was on his/her knees. The floors or ground were anything but soft. The kids were well disciplined and took it like good citizens, without complaining ha. At midnight, the long awaited meal was served. During the meal, if a neighbor liked a neighbor girl then this was the time for him to motion with his eyes whenever he had the attention of his subject of love to meet him outside. While her parents were eating, they would hold hands and talk. This was the only time during the wake that it was possible to be together. The parents were very jealous and watchful of their children, specially of their teen age daughters. Respect for their elders was a very sacred thing. Even touching their sweethearts was a no-no in front of any adult. Some were more daring and would take their girls to the orchard that was just beyond the house. If the parents called for the girl, she could come around that other side of the house and give the excuse that she was there all the time with friends.

Sedulous as they were, a wake was a refreshing and restful way to spend some time. These farmers and ranchers were made of some kind of stuff that they could stay up all night and go to their farms, animals, gardens or whatever kind of work they would do every day. The only luxury they had was the time off for some doing in church or in town.

Some kids had a great time running and playing with their little friends. That is, those who could escape from their parents' side and were daring enough to pay the consequences later on.

At the end of the velorio, which was after sun up, the last prayer and the offering of the velorio to the saint who was being honored, were recited and the crowd went home.

A DEATH

During the Era (1900–1940), whenever a person died, it was seen as a great loss. In the case of a girl or a woman, it was as a big loss of a good cook, housekeeper and or a mother. In the case of a man or a boy, it was a great loss of a good farmer, hunter or father and in most cases, a lover.

Deaths were common to most families since nine or more members in one family was the situation. Where there is a great number of members in a group, there seems to have a loss more often than when it is a small group. This stands to reason.

Funeral homes, if they existed, were not known in this small village. Most of the deaths occurred at home, on the field or in town.

Whenever anyone died, the first to be notified was the family, who in turn, would call el coronario publico (Coroner). The coronario publico was a team of local persons who were in charge of deciding two things: (1) If the person was dead and (2) determine the cause of death. They served also as witness.

Most deaths happened at home. The dead person would pass away with eyes wide open. If this was the case, someone with quarters in his pocked would close the victim's eyes and they wouldn't stay closed so a quarter was placed in each eye after it remained closed for a few minutes as it was held closed by the hand of whoever had closed it. Once the cadaver was cold, the eyes remained closed and the quarters were retrieved.

Sometimes, a corpse was found in a sitting position. This caused no big problem if it was caught early enough. If the corpse was dead for awhile, they had to crack a few bones so the body laid flat. The body, now, would wait for the coffin or stretcher like contraption which was used before coffins, would be made. There was no knowledge of embalming procedures so the body had to be buried within two days during the summer season. Sometimes it had to be buried before the two days. It was the duty of a father, son, brother, uncle or cousin to either make a coffin or go buy one at the J.M. Sanchez and Sons Mercantile store.

Before coffins became a necessity, the corpse were buried in a ladder like plank and before this time, the body was wrapped in a blanket and covered with dirt. When digging the depth of the grave, a hole was made where the head would be protected from the dirt shoveled from above. It was more out of respect than for protection.

Later some one came with the idea that a wooden box would be more respectful and certainly more sophisticated. Lumber was more available and saw mills existed nearby. Much later, a box on top of the coffin came to being and much later coffins made out of metal were invented. Later The box on top of the coffin was made out of plastic.

Candles were used during the Mass as well as during the wake. The body was laid on a table with candles shining on the corpse.

In most cases, it was assumed that the priest had performed the last sacrament. This was a sure sign that the soul would enter heaven. The wake was held that night. Neighbors from around and all close relatives came to the wake. The communication most effective was the telewoman. By nightfall, all the town knew about the death of so and so even if so and so had been ill for months.

During the wake, prayers were recited, canticos were sung, the Penitente Society prayed the rosary and sang their alabados. All night, it was a repetition of canticos, prayers, crying and praises for the dead one. Some would congregate outside to rest from kneeling and to just talk to their friends.

At midnight, a meal was served. After everyone had indulged in the meal, the prayers, canticos and crying resumed. This continued until it was time to take the body to the church. Here and now was sung La Despedida (The farewell). If anyone around had not shed a tear, this would not fail. By now, the body was in the coffin. There was a procession to the church. There were no flowers around except the ones that had been in the church, although these had nothing to do with the funeral.

Mass followed, all faithful went to receive communion and offered it for the repose of the soul of the recently departed. After mass, the body was blessed with holy water and incense.

The procession led to the burial site. Here, the casket was opened for the last time and last view of the departed. Everyone passed and paid their last honor or respect. Before the body was lowered to its resting place, the priest, again, said his final prayers and used the holy water and incense.

Some one was asked to give the eulogy. This, being a sad occasion, the eulogy was a farewell that made even the unemotional shed tears. Sometimes the person being eulogized was anything but what the eulogy indicated. It was said that when one dies, all the good comes out.

The body was returned to mother earth and with the same shovels that had been used to dig the grave, the earth was returned to its rightful place.

Everyone was invited to participate in a meal. This meal was usually what was left from the one served at the wake. People would stay around until late that night. Others didn't know when to leave so a place was set so they would sleep.

There were instances where a person was living in sin which meant that this person was not married by or within the church or had committed suicide. That person was buried outside the cemetery's fence. Usually all the cemeteries had an adobe, brick or stone walls.

The family was considered in good standing if the annual dues (Premisia) had been paid and the family attended church services regularly. The societies, as well as the persons who said the rosaries, said the eulogy and served in any other way donated their services

In this thesis, the author will discuss the traits of the Hispanic people as he studied and knew them before 1941. Many traits that are used do not fit the Hispanic of today for many changes have occurred since then.

The author asks for your indulgence in reading this section as well as others and to forgive him for the redundancy that may be found in this portion as well as other portions of his works.

First of all, one needs to understand an Hispanics' past. One must realize that, although, Hispanics were not militant, they were fierce fighters when they were threatened. They had been conquered and were under Moorish rule until King Ferdinand and Queen Isabela of Spain drove them out and the Americas were rediscovered under their reign. This is the first time the new Spaniards discovered they didn't need to be sub-servant to anyone.

In the new world, with some exceptions, they treated the Indians with human kindness. They tried to educate them as Christians. They were treated like human beings. Maybe the reason for this was that they wanted to teach the world that all humans should be given respect since the British and the French showed little to the Spaniards, or maybe it was the teaching of their faith. (Do on to others as you wish them do on to you).

In the new world, the conquered became the conquerors. By 1846, when the Americans came to New Mexico, the Hispanics were settled and making their living.

When General Stephen Watts Kearny came to declare the New Mexico Territory as part of the United States, no shots were fired. Many were tired of taking orders from Mexico.

Everything was going on smoothly until Charles A. Warfield attacked Mora. The Hispanics of the Mora Village were so angered that their hatred for Texans was such that up until World War II, they hated Texans with a passion.

There are many instances that the Hispanics went to fight to defend what they believed was their honor. They killed without mercy. They were depicted as macho men, fearless and did not fear death itself. The men kept their wives at home as housekeepers and as mothers of their children. They believed that the woman's place was at home.

According to their songs, they sang about going after the one who had wronged them by playing around with their wives or girlfriends. They would follow them and would kill both of them. They sang about drinking and came home drunk. They remembered and revered their mothers highly. Few songs favored their fathers.

Each believed himself to be king of his home, and in their groups, few were followers. They did not like to obey rules and regulations, except those that were advantageous to their situation. They were very emotional. They loved feverishly and hated with such passion that the object of their hate often paid with their lives.

On the other hand, they were very generous and believed in the old adage "Mi casa es su casa" (My house is your house). They were adamant to the point of stupidity, that they would cut their nose to spite their face.

They were faithful to their church and believed that it was easier for a camel to pass through the eye of a needle than for a rich man to get to Heaven so, consequently, one would find very few Hispanics in business. They made good servants and workers. They hated to take responsibilities so few would become administrators. Then, too, being underdogs so many times, they didn't get many opportunities to show their leadership.

They were faithful to their wives, that is until they succumbed to the beauty of their neighbor. The wives expected this to happen but could do nothing about it, since the husband was the ruler of the house. One thing is for sure, they would never divorce their wife. She was his for the rest of his life. On the other hand, if the wife was caught fooling around with the neighbors or whoever, the unfortunate one would never live to see the day light the following day.

They aspired very highly, but spent their time and money, when they could afford, buying and drinking whiskey or wine. Their songs indicate that this was one of their favorite pass time.

One wonders why Hispanics have a hard time adjusting to Democracy. There are many reasons and to mention a few, let's look back to see how Democracy came to being in the United State.

The founders of our Democracy were known in Spain as "Los Encyclopedistas", (The learned ones) meaning they were highly educated. They were business men, Protestant, Middle class. They believed in worldly possessions. None of these characteristics fit the Hispanic of that time. They were smart and knowledgeable on many things, although government was not one of them.

What is meant here is that in Spain, there were no dark ages and as far as literature is concerned, they excelled in it. Don Quoxite is an example.

The church taught them to be modest, faithful and strong. But they believed that God told them that He would help those who helped themselves and this they did even though at the expense of the neighbors. They did not call it stealing.

The church also taught them that penance was a virtue so once they went to confession and confessed their sins, the chapter was closed and a new one would follow. Back to the old grinder and their old habits was the result.

There was a madrigal which contains, among other verses, this one:"Penitente pecador por que te andas azotando? Porque me robe una vaca y ahora la ando desquitando." (Sinner Penitent, why are you lashing yourself? Because I stole a cow and now I am making amends).

They were full of love and charity and would share the last tidbit with the object of their sympathy, even though, it meant that they might go hungry tomorrow. If one were to visit these people, the host would feed him with the best in the house and would offer him a place to sleep with out charging for their services.

These people were very modest. They would give the shirt off their back and maybe the following day they would be sorry, but what they said or did, they meant and their word was law. Most of them were poor and they believed in being poor. As long as their natural needs were satisfied, they were happy.

Before World War II, most of the girls dreamt of marrying an Anglo so that their off-spring would not have to suffer the biases they underwent as young Hispanics. An Anglo name assured safety and a good job. Many are these Anglophiles who are still in our midst.

Boys had the choice of changing their names and many did. This was security to find good paying job. Because most of the Hispanics were light complected, all they needed was and Anglo name. Many were successful in finding easy jobs. They passed as Anglo until they spoke up. Their accent was a sure give away. Later on, many attended school in the big cities and they became a citizen of the main stream. Many, as mentioned before, were obstinate, and try to make it as macho Hispanics.

Women and girls were taught to be seen and not heard as were all the children. Their beauty was their selling point and most of them were tawdry. Red was a favorite color for their dresses. They barred no holds when it came to fixing their faces with make-up and lipstick. Their hair was long and beautiful.

As was reported before, their place was at home, but they attended Mass Sunday and went to the dances every Saturday. The girl or woman who had no natural beauty knew how to dress to look elegant. So it is safe to say that there were no Hispanic females classified as ugly.

The boys and men, like their counterpart, Indians, were brave and they never admitted they were beaten. Defeat was a no no for them. This is probably why they made the best soldiers during the two World Wars.

They loved passionately and even if the child was not theirs, they would adopt and treated him as their own. Many were illegitimate but non were abandoned. There was no such word as homeless much less people who did not own a home.

Obstinate or headstrong describes the Hispanics of that time. Proof to that is why did they not lose their culture when the Anglo society insisted on one language, one people. Why do we have tortillas, fijoles, chili etc.? Many are the Hispanic words that have become every day words.

They were proud persons and even if they were humiliated, they kept calm and proud. To those who didn't understand them, they were two faced.

Logic was different from the Anglos' logic. In some cases, logic was revenge. Why revenge when the church taught them differently? This teaching was not to their advantage in many cases.

Discipline was strictly imposed and sometime, if not most of the time, was very harsh. Yet this brutal discipline kept many from going astray.

In politics, they were very astute. The leaders did not like to lose. They knew that as long as they had the people divided and in ignorance, they had it made! Winning was the name of that game and to win, they would do whatever was necessary. They believed that to the victor belonged the spoil and they would cheat, kill or alter election results. Many ploys were utilized. When paper ballots were used, the politicians had it made. For every election there would be different devices used.

Many People would vote for one or two candidates for different offices and would leave blank the others. A crooked judge of the election, when counting the results, would take the ballot and vote or fill all the empty spots. Some who were more shrewd would buy the officers of the opposite party and during the counting they knew who was going to win even before the polls closed.

There were instances where the total ballots cast legally were buried and a new set of ballots were cast by the election officials. Party affiliation was as sacred as their religion. If one was a Democrat and there was a good, honest Republican running against a dog in the Democratic side (No offense to the dog.), the Democrat would vote for the dog. Same thing would happen if the reverse was true. Both parties had their shrewd leaders. Each tried to outsmart the other.

High tempered is another adjective that would describe the pre World War Hispanic. They could be very calm one minute and liable to kill the next. If anyone attacked their politics or religion, they were ready to die defending their honor. They would not bat an eye when they paid someone to vote for their favorite candidate. They would have some one to help the paid person so that the proof was that he earned the money paid to him. Even if the person who sold his vote was literate, He would ask the judge or clerk of the polls to help him mark his ballot. Others had set the table close to a window where a spy would be watching.

The paper ballots were numbered. One number was on one corner and was folded and blacked out. The other was in another corner and was perforated so that the voter would tear it off and take it with him. Most of the voters went believing that was the only evidence of their ballot. Later on after ballots were counted, it was a matter of checking the ballots against the poll book and the politician knew how each one he checked had voted. (How is that for a secret ballot?) When the ballots were burned, everyone was asked to witness that the ballots were destroyed.

The reader may wonder how could people be so naive. The answer is easy. People had been indoctrinated to have faith in their elders with no questions asked. Besides, they had been paid and they cared less who won.

As farmers and ranchers, they were conscientious, sedulous, helpful and had the perseverance of a mule. They would plant and if the year was bad, they never gave up. They replanted and the following year, they would plant again. They were self-sustaining.

In their love affairs, they were surreptitious. Most of the time, they and the object of their love affair, if illegal, were the only ones who knew about that affair. If the lady had a child and was married, the husband was led to believe he was the responsible one. Many times, the husband had to swallow his pride for the neighbor's wife may be delivering his child.

Another example of Hispanic pride which was very obvious was when welfare (called relief now called Welfare) was being offered, the Hispanics would rather go hungry than accept it. They would work in the W.P.A. for their money but they would not take hand outs. Later on things changed and they felt that relief was not a privilege but a right they were entitled to.

Hispanics, like fire, were good servants but poor masters. Maybe the word to describe them is harsh. They would abuse their authority. Grandfather would ask his young grandchildren to bring him a light for his pipe. There were few matches at the time. The child was expected to bring a live coal in his hands. There were no gloves at the time. The children better behave all the time because if they didn't and the parents heard about his misbehavior, they would get a trip to the wood shed. The woodshed trip was not an enjoyable party.

Some readers may not agree with the characteristics that have been presented here. One needs to understand that all kinds of people make up this world. There were many who did not fit some of these characteristics. The vast majority would fit into most of these categories.

For the sake of argument, let the author present you some comparisons between the Anglo and the Hispanic of that time.

1. The Anglos were business men—The Hispanic was an emotional being and cared little for business.

2. The Anglo believed in God but did not fear Him—The Hispanic feared Him and his religion and God were foremost.

3. The Anglo would trade his wife if the price was right.—The Hispanic was married until death would part them. Sometimes they saw to it that she died before leaving them.

4. The Anglo would rent his house or charge for meals.—The Hispanic believed his casa was your casa.

5. The Anglo believed in education.—The Hispanic believed in living happy which meant that the learning was taking place at the church and the disciplining was the parents duty. If their children learned to pray that was enough.

6. The Anglo felt death in the family was to be expected. —The Hispanic saw it as a big loss and maybe a punishment by God.

7. An Anglo's Wake was prayers and songs and back to business. —For Hispanic it meant mourning for a year or so. He would cry and would not forget memories.

8. An Anglo was never satisfied with the status quo.— Hispanic was satisfied as long as there was bread and drink in his table.

9. An Anglo was biased and acted as if he was a better person. —Hispanic was humble and treated everyone as his equal.

10. An Anglo would sell or trade his shirt off his back. —The Hispanic would give it away without any strings attached.

11. An Anglo would buy whatever he needed.—An Hispanic would help himself to whatever he needed and was available.

12. An Anglo was reared by stories and legends. –An Hispanic was taught by proverbs (dichos) prayers and parables.

13. An Anglo would marry the girl of his choice– An Hispanic would be paired by his and her parents. Sometimes the groom met his bride just before they were to be married, other times the girl was betrothed when only a baby.

14. An Anglo would go out into the world to search his luck. –Hispanics stayed at home and inherited their parents land. The land was divided into as many pieces as there were children.

15. An Anglo, if insulted, would grin and bear it.– An Hispanic never forgot and sought revenge.

16. An Anglo believed in good fences which meant good neighbors.– An Hispanic believed that the land was loaned by God and if anyone had a need to use it, he should use it without the need of opening gates.

17. An Anglo believed he made his own luck. An Hispanic believed that God gave his luck.

18. An Anglo was disciplined to obey the laws. An Hispanic obeyed his elders and the laws that were to his advantage.

19. An Anglo had the responsibility of guiding his country. An Hispanic had the responsibility of bringing up his family with strict discipline.

20. An Anglo believed in one or two children to each couple. An Hispanic did not believe in birth control. There were no limits as to how many children they conceived. The more children they had the more help at home.

21. An Anglo depended on his business to feed the family. An Hispanic depended on God and his own sweat to feed his.

22. An Anglo was a social drinker. In his eyes, an Hispanic was a wino.

23. An Anglo's wife was his partner. To an Hispanic, she was his object of love and the mother of his children as well as his house keeper.

24. An Anglo was a nomad and moved quite often. An Hispanic liked to grow deep roots and fell in love with his piece of land.

25. The opposite sex, to an Anglo was more of a need than an object to love, cherish and hold for life. To an Hispanic it was an object of love, obedience and a property for life. An Hispanic's jealousy was very strong.

26. An Anglo thought in a positive way. The Hispanic in a negative way. When asking such questions as "Do you want to go?" He said, "No quieres ir?" (You don't want to go?) or to ask, "Do you love me?" he asks "No me Quieres?

27. An Anglo's loyalty to his political party was more a convenience than anything else. To an Hispanic, his party and his religion were sacred and there was no way that he would change.

28. An Anglo would pull or push his friend up the ladder of success. An Hispanic would pull or push the less fortunate but if his neighbor was getting up there, he would pull him down to his size.

29. An Anglo loved progress and desired good roads and improvements in his life. An Hispanic was satisfied with what was good for grandpa was good for him.

30. An Anglo would go to the store and if he had any change coming, even if it was a cent, he wanted it in cash. An Hispanic would take and orange, a candy, or an apple instead of his change.

One last comparison for whatever it is worth: An Anglo lays a fart. The Hispanic throws it. Oh! Yes, the Anglo gets on the wire to make a phone call. The Hispanic is on the wire when he no longer can take another sip of an intoxicant.

Besides the church and the court house, the general mercantile store was where the people met. Here, the general store was the Morris and Back store owned by the Morris family.

LAS CAVANUELAS

Las Cavanuelas, as believed by our forefathers, were a way to forecast the weather for the whole year.

January, being the first month of the year and having thirty one days, was used as a guide as to what kind of weather each month would bring during that year.

The way this calender worked is that each day of January would decide the weather for its represented month. For instance, the first day of the year as well as the twenty fourth day, represented the weather for the month of January. The second and the twenty third day represented the weather for February and so on.

I need to explain that the calendar is worked on the base of 12.
For you who are not acquainted with bases, our daily number system is in the base of 10. I suppose this because we, normally, have ten fingers and each digit represents a finger. The metric system is designed in this base also. Computers are based on the base of 2 or the plus and minus base.

Now, back to our cavanuelas. First, these forefathers would take each day from one thru twelve to represent the weather for each month starting as number 1 representing the month of January, 2 would represent the month of February, 3 the month of March and so on. When they came to the 13th, they would start backwards where the 13th would represent December, the 14th would represent the month of November, the 15th the month of October and so on. The 24th would represent January again.

From the 25th to the 30th, the day was divided into two parts. The morning of the 25th represented January, the afternoon of that same day would represent February and so on until the 30th of the month which represented November in the Morning and December in the afternoon.

The last day of January (31st) was divided into hours. From 1:00 A.M. to 1:59 A.M. represented January. From 2:00 A.M. to 2:59 A.M. February and so on until Noon, from 1:00 P.M. to 1:59 P.M. the months were reversed so this time would represent December then, from 2:00 P.M. to 2:59 P.M. would represent November and so on.

If it rained or snowed on the 7th, 18th ,or on the 31st at 7 A.M. and at 6 P.M. the average would determine if July would be a wet month and so on for the rest of the months.

When or who started this observation is not to my knowledge. All I know is that my great grandfather taught my grandfather who in turn taught my father and who in turn taught me.

Many people believe this to be a true forecast. I am skeptical, mostly, because I have never been able to document this information throughout the years.

Many times the forecast comes true but I cannot prove if it is a coincidence or if this is a true indication. If anyone of my readers is interested and would like to do a scientific study in this subject, be my guest but do a thorough study. not like mine. Complete it and then let the world know about your findings.

Bust of luck in your undertakings.

Example of the Cavanuelas of 1991

Sun	Mon	Tue	Wed	Thu	Fri	Sat
		1	2	3	4	5
		January	February	March	April	May
6	7	8	9	10	11	12
June	July	August	September	October	November	December
13	14	15	16	17	18	19
Dec	Nov	Oct	Sept.	Aug	July	June
20	21	22	23	24	25	26
May	April	March	Feb.	January	AM-PM	AM-PM
A-M	A-M	A-M	A-M	31		

A.M.	P.M.
1 Jan	1 December
2 Feb	2 November
3 March	3 October
4 April	4 September
5 May	5 August
6 June	6 July
7 July	7 June
8 August	8 May
9 September	9 April
10 October	10 March
11November	11 February
12 December	12 January

Big snow storm of March 1919 This was the C.U. Strong home which had a lumber roof. The only roofs that survived that storm were the few tin roofed homes.

MAJOR LAND OWNERS IN MORA COUNTY IN 1994

Name	Acres
Union Land and Grazing Company (Kipp)	97,382.00
State Land	72,480.00
Ojo Feliz Ranch (Yates)	44,267.00
Mora Ranch	40,432.00
Thompson Ranch	30,880.25
Salmon Ranch	30,187.69
Red River Ranch (McClure)	28,004.02
Cherry Valley Ranch (Marsh)	26,746.53
Federal Land	25,753.00
Moore Ranch	22,998.00
Raska Ranch	16,665.70
U.U. Land Company (R. Blair)	16,570.00
Eureka Ranch (Ornell)	16,330.00
Burger Ranch	12,715.61
Cornell Ranch	10,924.67
E. Wiggins Ranch	10,218.30
Dreyer	9,898.00
Kiowa Cattle Feeders	8,646.00
S & S Ranch Company	7,190.86
Equity Investments Corps. (Daniels)	6,838.00
M. Moismann	6,787.74
Christmas Ranches (Bradford)	6,286.00
J.Jones	6,285.58
Brown	6,204.98
Canon Bonita Ranch (McClure)	5,579.00
D. Jones	5,453.95
Bar 3s Properties Ltd.	5,166.83
H-H-Turf Farms	5,000.00
Fernandez-Montoya	5,000.00
C. Wiggins	4,927.00
Doolittle Ranch	4,893.52
Thal Ranch	4,830.00
Mora Inc.	4,800.00
Philips	4,338.00
Nolan Inc. of Kansas	4,359.00
Albuquerque Lumber Company	4,101.00
Hooser	4,042.68
Total:	623,383.43

When combined these 37 ranches account for 50% of all land located within the boundaries of Mora County.

Some of this information was obtained from the County Assessor's office.

OTHER ODDS AND ENDS ABOUT MORA

Metals produced in the county since 1889
Gold, Silver, Lead, Copper and Mica.

The most common was mica during the second World War and was mined in the hills of El Alto del Talco.

Copper was mined in the El Coyote during the late 1940's and early 1950's.

Gold, silver and lead were mined before the 1940's.   To my knowledge, these metals were mined elsewhere than in Mora proper.

ORGANIZATIONS. CLUBS. SOCIETIES ETC. IN MORA
AT ONE TIME OR ANOTHER

Women's Extension Club
American Legion Post 6 WW I
Amreican Legion Post 114 WW II
American Legion Auxiliary Post 114 reinstated three times.
Veterans of Foreign Wars
Veterans of Foreign Wars Auxiliary
Boys Scouts
Cub Scouts
Girls Scouts
4-H Club
Future Farmers of America
Future Home Makers of America
Helping Hands Inc.
Knights of Columbus
Union Catholica
Legion Of Mary.
Las Guadalupanas
Las Gorras Blancas
Las Gorras Negras
La Gavilla de Silva
Mora San Miguel Electric Cooperative
Mora Water and Sewer Association
La Jicarita Telephone Cooperative
La Jicarita Enterprise
La Agua Negra Telephone Karavas Electric Co.
Catholic Veterans Association
T.V. Power Boosters
Mora T.V. Cable.
St. Gertrudes Credit Union
Lions Club
Ceran St. Vrain Library
David Cargo Library
Mora Democrat Newspaper
Ideas of Mora (1888) Newspaper
Mosquito (1891)Newspaper
Mora Pioneer Newspaper
Mora Star (1981) Newspaper
Eco Del Norte (1907) Newspaper
El Sol de Mora 1930's Newspaper
El Mensajero 1910-1925 Newspaper
La Prensa published by El Sol de Mora up to 1935

AFTER THOUGHTS

It is this author's wish that the readers do not misunderstand him in the writings he has presented.

He wishes to explain that this is not a book written as a conventional book but instead as a group of reports he would like to share as to his knowledge with the readers about what he has learned and accumulated during his lifetime.

You may criticize whatever you want and believe what you care to believe but the idea is to give you what the author has experienced in the light of his wisdom, if it may be called that.

Since 1946, he made up his mind that he would take record of the happenings and all his observations in different views and to share all the information with his children and all the people who may be interested in what he had to say. Notice must be taken as to the fact that he had many more interests to do than to take notice of all the happenings so many actions were missed.

Many are the people who aided him in reviewing different parts of his works, helped in other ways or contributed to the facts and information included in this work. Instead of bibliographies and mentioning each individual's source and parts, and being and unorthodox person, he decided that instead of calling his work his memoirs, he calls it the Lo de Mora .

He would like to remind you that life in this earth is not a bowl of cherries, many hardships are suffered by each of us. The easy way is not the best way most of the times. If it were so, we all would stay at home, travel, or do any thing that we enjoyed all the time. Some one has to pay the fiddler for nothing is free. Unfortunately, too many people want to be served in a silver platter. Maybe too many are served in this manner and then we wonder why people who have to bust their butts to make a living hate the prosperous Americans.

Freedom with out responsibilities has caused too many citizens to become apathetic and forget they are not the only ones who have rights. They expect to be respected but in turn, they do not respect not even themselves.

The worst part was when they kicked God out of the schools and now out of the public offices and other public places.

The last straw is trying to kick Him out of the country. The pledge of allegiance is and example of how they go about doing their thing. Another way is to disarm the individuals. The second amendment to our constitution allows to at least own a gun for our own protection and too many want to get rid of this amendment.

Haven't we learn what Hitler did in Germany?

What about Iraq? Do we wait to get their atomic bomb to be dropped in our midst before we act? It may be to late to build or rebuild the destruction that may occur. Appeasement has never worked because the enemy sees it as a weakness in our part. So think about it.

Back in the good ole' U.S.A., let's talk about politics. No longer do the elected elite do the duty they were elected to do. That is to protect our country. They go represent themselves or the ones who pull the strings for them.

The biggest problem is that we elect officers and then don't back them up. We try to run the office ourselves and do not let the elected official do their duty and when things go wrong we tend to criticize and blame him or her.

We claim that we have secret ballots. The only time we are really equal is inside the voting booth. Your vote is secret until you pull the lever or push the button "Vote".

In the years of the paper ballot, they had a way to check on you. This method was explained in a previous theme.

Now a days, electronics in the form of computers and the internet has brought new science as to how to find out how anyone votes. It seems to me that the voting machines are connected to the internet and what is there to keep whoever is in charge to receive the information and report to whom ever is interested in that information? There is more than one way to skin a cat. If the election does not satisfy them they will recount until they either find a way to prove they won or they give up.

Honesty has a new connotation today. It does not mean the truth. Instead they call it politically right. God only knows to what extreme we will go.

No matter what method is used to record the voting of what people do, politicians will find a way to check and find out what they want to know. The more educated we get the worst it gets. THIS IS FREE AMERICA TODAY!

As a last item in these works, I will conclude with a partial list of this county's people who died and when they died. Just like death is the last experience we will have in this earth. Here, in death, we are truly equal with no questions asked.

So with these thoughts in mind, I conclude these reports.

May God Bless and Help you Always.

NECROLOGY

A list of names of people who resided in the vicinity is offered. This 1930 to 1947 list was taken from my Dad's journal. From then on information is from my own notes. Some dates of death or burial are not included because of lack of information. This Necrology list is far from being complete.

NAME	BORN	DIED	BURIED
George Henry Buck	6/15/1836	Fri 9/7/06	
Jesus Maria Mascarenas		Wed 12/24/1930	
Rosalia Alcon		Sat 12/27/30	
Jesusita A. Montoya	10/5/1855	Wed 1/14/31	
Mrs. Boney Manchego		Thu 1/26/31	
Seferina G. Alcon	1865	Fri 6/27/31	
Lola Montoya		Sun 6/28/31	
Juan Juarros		Tue 9/22/31	
Wife of Teodoro Fernandez		Sun 9/29/31	
Daughter of Feliberto Casias		Tue 10/13/31	
Josifita Duran		Mon 12/28/31	
Gilbert Duran (accident)		Sat 1/16/32	
Rafael Duran		Tue 1/26/32	
Onofre Le Febre		Sat 2/27/32	
Luz Mascarenas		Mon 3/28/32	
David Cruz (accident)		Tue 6/7/32	
Isidora Manchego		Sat 10/1/32	
Patricio Pacheco		Thu 11/3/32	
Porfirio Duran		Tue 12/6/32	
Teles Arguello		Tue 12/27/32	
Eugenio Romero		Sun 1/12/33	
Sister Doloritas			4/6/33
Benito Pacheco (killed by lightening		Sun 7/16/33	
Gov Arthur Salegman		Mon 9/25/33	
Mrs. Sam Sosa			
Adelina Sosa & Luis Sosa (accident)		Thu 10/26/33	
Father Mitchel		Thu 10/12/33	
E. H Bierbaum		Wed 4/11/34	
Montes Butler		Fri 4/13/34	
Belle Strong		Wed 4/18/34	
Jose De la Luz Maestas		Buried with live skunk	4/8/34
Tom Williams (Boiler Explosion)		Mon 4/17/34	
Ben Martinez (Electrocuted)		10/15/34	
Senator Cutting (Airplane crash)		5/6/34	
Samuel Rimbert		Mon 2/3/36	
Luis Montoya		2/4/36	
Antonina Zamora		1941	

Name	Born	Died	Buried / Notes
Isabel Mora	Born	Died	Buried Sat 3/17/45
President Franklin Delano Roosevelt		Thu 4/45	
Thomas Ortega		Mon 4/16/45	
Frank Rimbert		Mon 5/7/45	
Demetrio Medina		Wed 9/5/45	
Jose Inez Sanchez		Wed 9/12/45	
Frank Martinez		Mon 9/17/45	
Vitalia Paiz		Tue 10/23/45	
Pat Quintana		Wed 10/24/45	
Leonides Leyba (Murdered by his father in law Sat 11/3/45			
Manuel Martinez died alone		Fri 11/16/45	
Mrs. George Martinez			buried Thu 1/3/46
Mercedes Manzaneres		Sat 2/23/46	
Eleseo Gonzales		Wed 4/10/46	
Elijio Sisneros		Thu 6/20/46	
Juan Antonio Segura		Thu 6/20/46	
Julia K. Strong		Tue 7/2/46	
Nathan Weil		Sat 7/20/46	
Ben Caricaburro killed by lightening		Wed 8/7/46	
Porfirio Alcon		Sun 8/18/46	
Jose Amalio Bernal		Sun 9/1/46	
Pablo Martinez			Tuesday 10/1/46
Gomecinda S. Maanchego			Sunday 2/2/47
Dometila M. Montoya			Sunday 2/9/47
George W. Armijo		Sun 2/16/47	
Agapito Abeyta		Fri 7/25/47	
Leonore Maes			Wed 8/6/47
Manuel Herrera			Mon 8/11/47
Boney Abeyta			Wed 10/8/47
Carlota V. Montoya	1886	1949	
Manuel Alcon De Buck	1860	1951	
Juan D. Herrera Born	1884	4/1951	
Ezequiel Montoya	1880	1953	
Isabelita Herrera Born	1890	9/1957	
Jose Emilio Martinez		5/23/60 at age of 56	
Antonio Herrera Born	1911	1962	
Juan Margarito Romo Maes	2/20/30	1963	
Benito Lujan Sr.	1895	10/28/63	
Isabel Romero Gandert		2/18/66 at age of 70	
Adelina Alcon Juarros B	4/13/89	12/20/69	
Fidel Valdez	4/23/1897	12/24/67 at age of 71	
Gregorio Cordova		7/30/68 at age of 67	
Manuel Tafoya	11/7/13	9/23/68 at age of 54	
Moises Valdez	4/7/14	9/23/69 at age of 55	

	Born	Died	Buried
Abenicio Alcon	4/18/87	12/15/70	
Benjamin Alcon De Buck	1/17/1886	12/25/71 at age of 85	
Aurora Alcon LeDoux	10/4/14	3/31/78	
Jose Manuel Romo	5/28/1893	7/4/80	
Manuel C. Romo	5/9/25	5/20/81	
Glen R. Martinez	1958	2/24/84	
Rosaura M. Alcon	10/5/1888	2/24/84	
Martina B. Sanchez		12/88	
Benerita Alcon McNeff	2/13/22	8/20/89	
Alfonso Luis Abeyta		1989	
Antonia Romero	7/4/04	3/20/90	
Sara Polaco	4/16/10	3/27/90	
Elfido Sandoval	1900	4/10/90	
Paul Pacheco Jr.	6/26/69	5/26/90	
Altagracia Lucero	8/17/1892	11/21/90	
Mary M. Pacheco	1912	5/20/91	
Benjamin Mondragon		1/1/92	
Elijio Lujan		1/14/92	1/17/92
Miguel Benavidez 1907		3/3/92	3/6/92
Levi Madrid		3/13/92	3/17/92
Felix Garcia		3/31/92	4/2/92
Louis Lucero		5/4/92	5/7/92
Angelina Archuleta		5/4/92	
Jesse Valdez		5/4/92	
Evelyn Archuleta		5/4/92	
Benjamin Bustos		5/5/92	5/8/92
Manuel John Esquibel		5/22/92	
Leonore M. Valdez		5/25/92	
Pablo Gonzales		6/3/92	6/10/92
Carlota Salazar		6/3/92	6/8/92
Eloisa Maes		6/8/92	6/11/92
Donaciano Sanchez		6/10/92	6/12/92
Alcario Gallegos Mother		6/10/92	
Alfonoso Roper			6/19/92
Amalia Medina		6/92	
Jake Silva		7/14/92	7/17/92
Juan B. Vigil		11/6/92	11/9/92
Moises Pacheco 97 yrs. old		12/26/92	
Anastacia Duran		12/92	
Elias "Buckskin' Martinez		1/18/93	1/21/93
Francisquita Sandoval		2/26/93	2/8/93
John Torres			2/6/93
Tiny Sanchez		2/6/93	

	Born	Died	Buried
Patricio Moya		2/7/93	2/10/93
Cantiflas		3/20/93	
Albert N. Valdez		3/27/93	3/29/93
O. B. Gonzales	1919	3/29/93	4/1/93
Acianita Chavez		4/21/93	4/24/93
Michelle Maes		6/12/93	6/16/93
Samuel Martinez Jr.		6/26/93	6/29/93
Abran Chavez	1915	7/17/93	
Desederio Maes	9/1/17	7/14/93	
Andrea Esperanza Weber	4/17/20	8/15/93	
Robert Romero			10/5/93
Clara M. Rudolph	3/24/1939	10/14/93	
John Sorg			10/27/93
Max Fort	10/12/20	10/24/93	10/28/93
Juan L. Garcia	1919		11/22/93
George Rubel Montoya	1929		11/27/93
Robert A. Romero	1943	11/3/93	11/5/93
Ricardo Juarros	10/11/12	12/29/93	
Marcella B. Caranta	1908	1994	
Ranom T. Barela	1931	1994	
Emelina J. Cole	6/22/22	1/6/94	
Apolonio Martinez		2/7/94	2/10/94
Nettie Lucero Aragon		2/18/94	2/28/94
Maclovia N. Martinez	8/14/6	2/28/94	3/2/94
George Martinez		3/94	
Joseph Maes		3/94	
Manuel Lujan		3/3/94	
Juan Medina		3/4/94	
Maggie Olivas		3/9/94	3/12/94
Dora Rivera			3/16/94
Beatrice Alcon			3/18/94
Maria Zenaida Gonzales			3/23/94
Father Walter Cassidy		5/11/94	5/18/94
Jackie Kennedy Onnasis			5/23/94
Ronald Sam Martinez	7/22/70	6/12/94	6/17/94
Donaciano Quintana	4/8/07	6/14/94	6/17/94
Clay Trammel	5/15/20	8/29/94	8/31/94
Felipe Trujillo		9/15/94	9/24/94
Paul Gonzales		9/15/94	9/24/94
Jose Pino			11/5/94
Annie Mondragon		11/31/94	
Tranquilino J. Chavez		11/94	
Benito Lujan Jr.	7/1/29	1/18/95	

	Born	Died	Buried
Alice Rudolph Martinez	7/14/19	3/13/95	
Don Bernal	5/14/08	6/2/95	
Aurora B. Gonzales	5/10/11	10/29/95	
Lucia Trujillo		1995	
Roy Regensberg	1914	1995	
Escolastica Romero	1905	1995	
Trinidad Medina	1911	1995	
Manuel E. Padilla	1912	1995	
Juliette Vansicklen	1920	1995	
Kevin Espinoza		Dec 1995	
Martina Sanchez		Dec 1995	
Anastacia Duran		Dec 1995	
Joe C. Trujillo	7/16/16	2/28/96	3/4/96
Fidel Gauna	5/21/16	6/9/96	
Gabriel Bustos	1/27/24	8/24/96	8/27/96
Cipriano Trujillo	9/3/18	11/12/96	11/18/96
David D. Romero Sr.	5/29/55	11/29/96	
David D. Romero Jr.	10/2/78	11/30/96	
Robert D. Ortega	11/15/38	12/24/96	12/27/96
Helen R. Herrera		12/ /96	
Billy Ortega		12/31/96	1/3/97
Annie Lucero		1/14/97	1/18/97
Eugenio Martinez		1/20/97	
Urbano Trujillo		1/24/97	1/28/97
William "Bill"Gauna	10/30/30	2/11/97	2/13/97
Lincoln Regensberg	9/8/10	4/25/97	4/28/97
Julia Espinoza	9/11/19	7/10/97	7/14/97
Aurora Herrera		7/10/97	7/12/97
Emma Fuggiti	4/19/18	7/12/97	
Sam A. Romero	8/12/24	7/27/97	
Max A. Valdez	8/29/25	8/28/97	8/30/97
Victorino Mora		9/4/97	
Peggy Cassidy		9/24/97	9/27/97
Emilia M. Trujillo	12/21/42	10/7/97	10/10/97
James J. Cassidy	2/29/16	12/28/97	
Levi Cruz		1/7/98	
Bill LeDoux	1/17/13	1/15/98	1/20/98
Jose D. Olguin's Mother		3/26/98	3/30/98
Glave Blatman		3/27/98	
Rafael Archuleta		4/28/98	
James Leger			5/27/98
Victor Garcia's Baby		5/28/98	
Pete K. Beck	1907	6/10/98	

	Born	Died	Buried
Rosendo Romero		6/14/98	
Arnaldo Vigil		6/15/98	6/18/98
Ben Romero			6/25/98
Sandro Abeyta		6/28/98	
Reynaldo Martinez		7/31/98	
Nicomedes Romero	2/20/15	7/31/98	7/6/98
J. Frank Pelon Mtz.	6/13/05	7/28/98	
Joseph P. Trambley	6/6/24	9/13/98	
Juluis C. Garcia	9/17/66	9/14/98	
Lily Jaramillo		9/15/98	
Magdalena Q. Varela	3/14/23	9/18/98	9/22/98
Procopia Alcon		10/22/98	
Margie Trujillo	4/3/13	10/29/98	10/31/98
Andrellita T. Bustos	8/4/03	11/4/98	
Adela Ophelia Medina	11/29/02	11/21/98	11/24/98
Perfecto Duran	11/17/22	12/3/98	12/7/98
Maria R. Tafoya	8/23/09	12/5/98	
Rocke Romero		12/17/98	
Alejandro Abeyta		1998	
Archie "Bunker" De Herrera	11/21/61	3/7/99	
Tomasita L. Alcon	10/3/1899	3/25/99	3/30/99
Eugene Mondragon	5/25/63	6/4/99	6/7/99
Peter D. Sanchez	10/25/61	6/5/99	
Patricio Serna	3/17/28	9/18/99	9/21/99
Rafael E. Martinez	1/13/08	9/19/99	

NEW MILLENNIUM

	Born	Died	Buried
Leandro Leyba		1/15/00	
Pat Romero	11/26/17	1/17/00	1/21/00
Juan B. Duran	3/3/21	1/18/00	1/22/00
Fermin Pacheco	4/27/16	1/27/00	1/31/00
Antonia A. Martinez	10/7/1898	2/8/00	2/11/00
Mary Ida Gandert	11/9/39	3/2/00	3/4/00
Julian Gonzales		3/12/00	
Demetrio Medina		4/11/00	4/15/00
Lawrence Rudolph	2/15/11	4/16/00	
Albina Hurtado		4/17/00	4/24/00
Jose D. Olguin	9/6/20	5/3/00	5/5/00
Adelita Maestas		5/5/00	5/12/00
Mary Alice Marrujo		5/21/00	5/25/00
Eloy Ludi			5/22/00
Frances Pino Lucero	5/6/31		6/23/00
Feloniz Sandoval Armijo		7/4/00	

	Born	Died	Buried
Elite Archuleta		7/4/00	
J. Demostenes Chacon		7/4/00	
Esequiel Romero	7/4/20	8/14/00	8/17/00
Valentine Maestas	2/14/48		9/4/00
Robert Sandoval		9/17/00	9/25/00
Fabian Olivas		10/23/00	
Moises Maestas		10/24/00	
Phillip Paul Hernandez	2/29/68	11/19/00	
Florida D. Salazar	5/23/25	11/23/00	
Ernest E. Martinez	4/2/27	12/19/00	12/23/00
Bernardo Maes		12/19/00	
Benancio Pino		12/21/00	12/23/00
Carolina Romero		12/12/00	
Carolina Garcia			
Annie Maes Martinez			
Maargarita Rael			
Cora Ruiz			
Teresina Hurtado			
Jose Ologio Maestas		1/20/01	1/22/01
Emilia Trujillo	5/19/25	1/29/01	
Robert P. Vigil	2/15/48	2/13/01	2/16/01
Robert Vigil	2/14/01	2/16/01	
Benny "Butch"Espinoza	12/31/33	3/2/01	3/10/01
Priscilla A. Duran		3/10/01	
Filadelfio Martinez			
Roberto Garcia			
Danelle Garcia			
Eugene Vigil			
Alicia Duran			3/10/01
Ofelia Cordova			
Damacio Jaramillo			
Aurora Romero			
Fidela L.Vigil	10/14/07		4/12/01
Lorraine Medina		4/18/01	
Jose F. Branch			4/17/01
Lorraine Medina			
Sidney Regensberg	2/18/38	4/24/01	4/27/01
Arturo Martinez	3/11/11	5/4/01	
Charley "Rooster" Trujillo	1/5/48	5/8/01	
Feleciano Martinez			
Mayo Armijo		6/25/01	
Filadelfio Vigil			
Phillip C.U. Sanchez	3/27/21	6/27/01	7/2/01

	Born	Died	Buried
Filadelfio (Phil) Santistevan			
Santiago Jaramillo			
James Gallegos			
Telesfor Lucero			
Mary Lovato Duran	6/3/21	7/19/01	
Betty Maes 70 yrs old		8/3/01	
Adelia M. Trujillo	2/20/08	8/18/01	8/24/01
Costancia Trujillo	2/17/06	8/26/01	9/1/01
Raymond Valdez			
Harry Nolan	8/3/24		
Vidilia Sandovaal	8/16/13	9/2/01	
Angel Grajada			
Dora Valdez Smathers			
Octaviano Toby Martinez	8/26/28	9/19/01	
Juan Eusebio Chacon	9/1/10	9/27/01	
Lorraine Vigil		10/1/01	
Feliciano Herrera	11/2/21	10/11/01	
Inocencio Cordova			
Alex Gene Sisneros			
Herman Arturo Romero	8/12/45	10/13/01	
Samuel Basilio Garcia	6/17/08	10/16/01	
Rudy Garcia	4/4/58	10/19/01	
Ida Trujillo 87 yrs.		10/23/01	
Elizabeth(Liz)Gonzales Maes	8/13/62	10/27/01	
Jose Leroy Garcia	9/3/26	11/5/01	
Manuel N Velasquez	3/22/16	11/17/01 Saturday	11/20/01
Simonita			
Enrique Henry Aragon	6/1/08	11/26/01	
Samuel Muniz	7/8/1889	12/2/01	
Matt J. Sandoval	8/1/28	12/12/01	
Ricardo Romo Jr.	12/30/01		
Frances M. Olivas		1/30/02	2/4/02
Christopher Vasquez	3/9/87	2/18/02	2/23/02
Elmer Wiggins	1/31/22	2/22/02	
Abenicio Leal	8/29/25	2/24/02	2/28/02
William Romero	6/22/38	3/10/02	3/14/02 Thu.
Albert L. Cassidy	2/2/20	3/11/02	3/15/02 Vigil Fri.
Jose "Willie" Lucero	2/7/1920	3/13/02	3/15/02 Fri.
Marie R. Romero	5/29/20	3/15/02	3/21/02 Thu.
Guillermo Martinez		3/17/02 Sun.	
Rose C. A. Regensberg	4/24/39	3/17/02	3/19/02
Agnes B. Lopez	9/11/22	3/27/02	4/1/02
Alicia Lujan		3/28/02	4/2/02

	Born	Died	Buried
Leroy Olivas			4/3/02
Mark Luis Abeyta	1/30/69	4/8/02	
Pancho Maes	3/7/36	Cremated	4/8/02
Selmer Hoveland	1/29/21	4/11/02	
Frank McNeff		4/10/02	4/16/02
Viola A. Bustos	8/28/17	4/18/02	4/23/02
George Sandoval (King Fish)		5/08/02	5/13/02
Flosha R. Sanchez	12/18/55	5/12/02	5/16/02
Christopher D. Vigil	12/25/82	5/20/02	
Jose Vicente Abeyta	11/29/19	5/21/02	5/25/02
Pedro Abeyta	10/14/1914	5/25/02	5/28/02
Aurora Valdez Netzloff	12/17/04	6/8/02	6/12/02
Mary Rita Rivera Romero	7/16/28	7/7/02	
Claudio Vasquez	5/14/21	7/7/02	7/12/02
Jay Vigil		7/7/02	
Filomena Esquibel	8/1/11	8/10/02	
Romanita T. Maestas	6/17/18	9/19/02	9/23/02
Samuel Maestas	4/4/11	10/2/02	10/8/02
Carl Williams	2/15/27	10/20/02	10/25/02
Placido Pando 93 yrs.		11/6/02	11/9/02
Teodorita Martinez		11/30/02	12/2/02
Fran Hanks		11/30/02	12/7/02 Memorial
Doloritas Velasquez 89 yrs. /14/13		12/28/02	12/31/02
Amadeo Jesus Padilla	11/13/14	1/17/03	1/21/03
Tafoya			1/21/03
William Andres Gandert	11/25/20	1/27/03	1/29/03
Lorraine (Lulu) Vigil 41 yrs.		2/1/03	2/6/03
Joseph R. Melendez 41 yrs.		2/3/03	2/7/03
Maria Lilly Beck	7/15/15	2/9/03	2/13/03
Maryleane F. Sandoval	6/7/78	2/10/03	2/15/03
Maclovia Padilla	9/5/15	2/18/03	2/22/03
Pablo Romo 79 yrs.		2/22.03	2/26/03
Lionor Maestas	9/21/34	3/12/03	3/18/03
Frances V. Archuleta	9/20/10	3/31/03	4/3/03
Felix (Chano) Gauna	7/13/32	4/6/03	4/11/03 Memorial
Ermelina Romero	3/25,1903	4/23/03	4/26/03
Senaida Valdez	6/4/09	5/18/03	5/22/03
Carmen Cassidy	12/27/20	5/18/03	5/21/03 Wed.
Senaida Valdez	6/4/09	5/18/03	5/22/03 Thu.
Lawrence (Big One) Martinez	5/28/48	5/25/03	5/30/03 Fri.
Manuelita V. Romero	5/30/11	6/18/03	
Tonita H. Martinez	6/8/32	6/6/03	6/8/03
Frances V. Vigil	6/19/30	6/20/03	6/21/03

	Born	Died	Buried
Dian Howard Pando	8/25/59	7/10/03 cremated	
Louis Lucero	9/14/17	7/10/03	7/12/03 at La Cueva
Miquelita Martinez	8/29/07	7/10/03	7/14/03
Melvin Vigil	9/16/26	7/14/03	7/17/03
Jose G. Abeyta 79 yrs.	7/15/03		7/16/03
Mary Pauline Chandler	11/13/18	8/8/03	8/14/03
Joseph J. Tinker Maes 34 yrs.		8/9/03	8/13/03
Francesquita Martinez	1/12/06	8/12/03	8/16.03
Adeline Alcon Fuggiti	10/21/23	8/16/03	8/20/03 Chicago
David Bonney	3/26/66	8/16/03	8/20/03
Jose Manuel Olivas. 89 yrs.		8/17/03	8/22/03
Concepcion Flores Trujillo	8/12/05	8/18/03	8/23/03
Pedro I. Martinez	10/22/14	8/22/03	8/26/03
Frank Margarito Valdez	6/1/38	8/21/03	8/29/03
J. Domingo Montoya	1/30/12	8/24/03	8/29/03
Isabel C. Duran	1/19/20	9/2/03	9/5/03
Georgia C. Mares	2/22/23	9/2/03	
Floripa Montoya Rubin	1/15/22	10/3/03	10/10/03 at Wagon Mound
James Lawrence Aragon	8/20/43	10/3/03	
Erlinda Montano	12/22/14	10/5/03	10/9/03
Nestor Maes	1/6/23	10/13/03	Mora
Maria Dolores Mtz.	4/6/27	12/4/03	12/8/03 El Alto
Mary Juarros	10/28/09	12/14/03	12/14/03 Wagon Mound
Enriquez Henry Garcia	12/12/32	1/10/04	1/15/04 Ledoux
Genoveva L. Romero	6/22/11	1/11/04	1/15.04 Holman
Manuel S. Cordova	1/1/32	1/13/04	1/17/04 Holman
Elvira S. Pacheco	12/5/23	1/16/04	1/19/04 Mora
Agnes V. Martinez		1/22/04	r.1/23 1/24/04 Las Aguitas
Gregorio Marrujo Jr.	9/17/37	2/1/04	2/4/04 Carmen
Laudente Montoya		2/17/04	2/18/04 Albuquerque
Victor Sandoval		2/17/04	
Miquelita H. Pacheco	11/20/08	2/21/04	
Dolores V. Medina	5/27/12	2/6/04	Cremated Memorial 2/16/04
Maria E. Cruz Ojo Feliz 91 yrs.		3/1/04	3/5/04 Ojo Feliz
Maria Celani Medina	2/13/19	3/3/04	3/6/04
Boney Williams	12/22/31	3/7/04	r.3/10/04– 3/11/04
Damian Pacheco	3/26/26	3/16/04	r.3/18/04– 3/19/04
Ronnie D. Gandert	7/20/60	3/18/04	r.3/21/04 3/22/04
Bertha Alcon			Colorado
Willie Trujillo		r.4/23/04	
Leroy Chacon		3/22/04	4/30/03 at Holman
Alice Alcon Gardunio	4/14/23	5/1/04	r. 4/5/04 4/6/04 Las Vegas
Nestora O. Abeyta	7/21/18	5/7/04	r. 5/11/04 5/12/04

	Born	Died	Buried
Cleotilde Herrera	4/11/18	5/9/04 r.5/12/04	5/13/04
Juliana M. Molinar	2/6/28	5/30/04 r.6/2/04	6/3/04
Ronald Regan 40th President	2/6/11	6/5/04	
Carpito Torres	1/26/31	12/10/04 r. 12/13/04	12/14/04
Florentino Fresquez		12/26/04	12/28/04
Joe Mascarenas	4/22/24	12/27/04	12/30/04
Bessie Abeyta	1/21/22	1/12/05 r. 1/14/05	1/15/05
Albertito Romero	4/18/10	1/16/05	
Elias Martinez	8/31/26	1/17/05 r. 1/18/05	1/19/05
Juanita Valdez	11/8/34	1/16/05 r. 1/19/05	1/20/05
Andres Herrera		2/3/05	
Rennie Casados	12/27/17	2/17.05 r. 2/24/05	2/25/05
Magdalena Ortega	8/10/10	3/1/05 r. 3/19/05	
Adelaida Lucero	2/24/13		3/26/05
Lucas Valdez	1/15/13	3/9/05 r. 3/11/05	3/12/05
Carolina M. Olivas		3/15.05 r. 3/18/05	3/19/05
Dulcinea Cordova	4/17/12	3/28/05	
Sandra R. Romero	5/10/59	5/7/05 r. 5/10/05	
Cleo R. Garcia		5/13/05 r. 5/16/05	5/17/05
Justin Gabriel Alcon	4/23/74	5/21/05 r. 5/23/05	5/24/06
Lila A. Maes	9/03/28	5/31/05 r. 6/2/05	6/3/05